Military Occupations in the Age of Self-Determination

MILITARY OCCUPATIONS IN THE AGE OF SELF-DETERMINATION

The History Neocons Neglected

James Gannon

PRAEGER SECURITY INTERNATIONAL
Westport, Connecticut · London

Library of Congress Cataloging-in-Publication Data

Gannon, James.
    Military occupations in the age of self-determination: The history neocons neglected /
    James Gannon.
        p. cm.
    Includes bibliographical references and index.
    ISBN 978–0–313–35382–6 (alk. paper)
1. Military history, Modern—20th century. 2. Military history, Modern—21st century. 3. National
liberation movements—History—20th century. 4. National liberation movements—History—21st
century. 5. Anti-imperialist movements—History—20th century. 6. Anti-imperialist movements—
History—21st century. 7. Military occupation—History—20th century. 8. Military occupation—
History—21st century. I. Title.
D431.G26   2008
355.02'8—dc22   2008008986

British Library Cataloguing in Publication Data is available.

Library of Congress Catalog Card Number: 2008008986
ISBN-13: 978–0–313–35382–6

First published in 2008

Praeger Security International, 88 Post Road West, Westport, CT 06881
An imprint of Greenwood Publishing Group, Inc.
www.praeger.com

Printed in the United States of America

The paper used in this book complies with the
Permanent Paper Standard issued by the National
Information Standards Organization (Z39.48–1984).

10 9 8 7 6 5 4 3 2 1

To my grandchildren—Aaron, Sophie, Jocelyn, and Caitlin—in the hope that they will not have to live through other unnecessary wars.

CONTENTS

PREFACE

In June 2003, I wrote an article for my local newspaper, the Rockland County (New York) Journal News, condemning the American attack on Iraq as preemptive, elective, aggressive, and without justification. I compared it to Israel's ill considered invasion of southern Lebanon in 1982 when Israel drove the Palestine Liberation Organization out of Lebanon, and then stayed behind as an occupying army. It withdrew eighteen years later considerably worse off for the experience, having suffered more than four thousand troops killed and wounded, mostly from Hezbollah suicide attacks and roadside bombs. I predicted that America might well suffer the same fate in Iraq, and eventually pull out in defeat. Nearly five years after the invasion, the United States still occupied Iraq looking for a graceful exit.

I tell this story to show that I am not piling on President Bush at a time when the occupation of Iraq has gone bad—the gains of the surge, notwithstanding—and he is losing the support of the American people. When I wrote the 2003 article, the administration was flying high. Bush had declared victory and belittled the insurgents who had begun to take American lives. "Bring 'em on," he had said of the insurgents and explained that America had sufficient troops to handle them. There is no doubt that the American military is powerful enough to maintain its occupation for many years to come—if the American people will allow it to accept the steady toll of casualties and the waste of American treasure. But the pattern of recent history shows that the stream of killed and wounded inevitably sets a powerful dynamic in motion. Bereaved survivors on the home front begin to ask questions, and before you know it, a national debate is in full swing over whether the occupation is worth the sacrifice.

What has not usually been part of the debate is the historical evidence of the post–World War II era—what I call the age of national self-determination—that when a great power like the United States inserts an occupying army in a smaller nation like

Iraq, or Israel in southern Lebanon, or the Soviet Union in Afghanistan, or the United States in Vietnam, the great power almost always loses when a credible insurgency rises up to challenge it. Even in the dying days of colonialism, great imperial nations like Britain and France lost their colonies to local insurgencies, or if they did not lose militarily, they lost politically by boldly facing the inevitable and granting the colonies their freedom.

It defies our common mindset! The most powerful armies fail to subdue undisciplined, ragtag fighters who wage a different kind of war, darting in and out of the shadows, laying ambushes, setting traps, exploding roadside bombs, and in more recent times blowing themselves up in crowded places, leaving the occupiers to fight wars in garrison mode without front lines. The occupying soldiers do not know when the next attack will come, or from where.

Enough of these insurgencies have occurred in the past six decades to call into question the judgment of any leader of a great nation who chooses to waste the power of a first-rate army by entering into a war of occupation and stalemate. Thus, to conclude that conquest is a losing proposition in the modern era is not an emotional plea against war; it is a statement of fact derived from the events of history. This empirical method based on hard evidence, I believe, trumps the ethereal polemics of neoconservatives who argue for American imperial expansion and preemptive war. I leave it to the jury of readers to determine if I have made my case that the invasion of Iraq was a strategic error of historic proportions. In fact, nearly five years of insurgency in Iraq have tempered the bombast of the Bush Administration, which has put more emphasis on diplomacy to resolve problems with North Korea and Iran.

The ebb and flow of the Iraq insurgency have raised hopes, dashed them, and raised them again—a declaration of sovereignty followed by suicide bombs, an exhilarating election only to revisit the horror of slaughtered innocents. In 2006, Sunni insurgents bombed a sacred Shia mosque and blew off its dome. Shia militants went on a rampage of ethnic cleansing, killing Sunnis in droves and driving the survivors out of Baghdad's mixed neighborhoods. In 2007, America reinforced its occupation army, pulled units out of their walled fortresses and billeted them in the troubled areas of the city to reassure the populace, and then, with former Sunni Iraqi insurgents at their side, attacked and neutralized some Islamist strongholds. It helped that the leading Shia militia, the Mahdi army, called a moratorium on violence. The American initiative, christened the "surge," reduced the bloodbath, but did not end it. Occupation troops and innocent Iraqis died at a lower rate. How long it will last, nobody knows. If the historical pattern holds up, the final result will be American withdrawal, one way or another.

This book is meant as a contribution to the national debate over the decision to attack Iraq. The oft-imputed shadowy reasons for going to war—such as the strategic importance of oil or the commitment to Israel—and the mistakes frequently cited in the prosecution of the invasion and occupation are irrelevant to the argument presented here that the occupation in and of itself critically drained the American military of its advantages in firepower and mobility. The Bush Administration is left with only bad choices in a hole it dug for itself, and seems stone-deaf to any suggestion of a failed policy. My hope is that future leaders will weigh more heavily than did Bush the consequences of squandering a powerful army in the military occupation of a small nation that should be allowed, in any case, to control its own political destiny. We no longer live in the age of colonialism. American power is limited. The rest of the world is not ours to dominate.

I wish to thank my editor, Manohari Thayuman, of BeaconPMG for her careful editing of the manuscript under contract with the Greenwood Publishing Group, of which Praeger Security International is a part. Several people have read and made valuable comments about one or more chapters in the book. With apologies to anyone I may have left out, I give particular thanks to Sheila Lamb, Michael Nest, Nancy and Edward Applebee, Paul Crawford, and Charles Coates. Responsibility for any errors of fact or judgment is entirely mine.

INTRODUCTION:
THE PERILS OF OCCUPATION

Those who cannot remember the past are condemned to repeat it.
—George Santayana (1905)

When the Democrats took control of Congress in January 2007, they set out to reverse the course of the Iraq war, believing it to be their mandate from the American people, who gave them a majority in both houses the previous November. But while the Democrats wanted the troops out, President Bush as commander in chief of the armed forces ordered reinforcements—commonly referred to as the "surge"—to head off defeat and, he said, to shore up America's strategic position in the "war on terror." Outgoing UN Secretary General Kofi Annan took note of this high-level split in American resolve and concluded that America was trapped in Iraq. "It cannot stay and it cannot leave," he said.[1]

Getting out of the trap was the pressing issue of the moment, but the larger historical issue, all but drowned out in the din of political combat in Washington, is how we got in. Observers agree that multiple mistakes have been made in pursuit of the war, including the lack of security that permitted Iraqi looting, too few American troops, inadequate armor, prisoner abuse, the slaughter of Iraqi civilians, disbanding the Iraqi army, barring all Baathist from government jobs, giving contracts for security and reconstruction to American companies instead of putting Iraqis to work rebuilding their own country, and the original pullback from Fallujah that temporarily left a safe haven for insurgents, to name only a few. But the mistake that mattered most was the original decision to invade when Saddam Hussein was successfully contained. All else followed. Even if the surge of 2007 were to succeed in reducing or even eliminating the violence, will it have been worth the cost in American blood and treasure or the awful trauma inflicted on the Iraqi people?

While it may be too late for the politicians and too early for the academics to dwell on the decision to invade Iraq, it remains a hot issue on the back burner relevant to future policymaking. Those listening carefully could hear opponents of the war speaking out against that fateful decision. Senate Democratic Majority Leader Harry Reid gave a blunt assessment in February 2007. He saw it as "the worst foreign policy mistake" in American history, worse than Vietnam.[2] Former Vice President Al Gore had used almost identical language two months earlier. He called Iraq "the worst strategic mistake in the entire history of the United States."[3] Earlier in 2006, former President Jimmy Carter labeled it, "one of the most troublesome and important errors ever made in the international policy of the United States."[4] William Odom, former national security advisor to President Reagan, retired Army general, Vietnam War veteran, and now a Yale professor and a Hudson Institute fellow, was an early critic of the war. He is quoted repeatedly as saying that fighting in Iraq "was never in the interest of the United States," and only serves the interests of Iran, Osama bin Laden, and other Islamists.[5] Anthony Zinni, a retired Marine general and former commander of the Central Command that includes Iraq, criticized the war even before it started, putting it near the bottom of foreign policy priorities for the region.[6] The conservative firebrand and former presidential aspirant Patrick J. Buchanan suggested in a book published in 2004 that the invasion "may yet prove [to be] a textbook example of the imperial overstretch" that has brought down empires of the past.[7] Another early critic was a little-known military historian; Jeffrey Record wrote in December 2003 that Bush had committed "a strategic error of the first order" by failing to distinguish between the threat from Iraq, which posed no imminent danger to America, and that from al Qaeda, which carried out the 9/11 attacks on America. Bush compounded the error, said Professor Record, by establishing illusive goals like eradicating terrorism, imposing democracy in Iraq, and suppressing the proliferation of nuclear, biological, and chemical weapons.[8]

These strongly worded condemnations of Bush policy—really only a tiny sample— square with the realities of history. The decision to invade Iraq ignored the facts since 1945, the year the United Nations established the right of national self-determination in its charter, that great powers occupying small nations usually (not always) lose when confronted with a credible insurgency. Since then, Britain, France, the United States, the Soviet Union, and Israel have all lost insurgencies in countries they tried to control with powerful armies. The point is important not simply to prove that Bush's pre-emptive invasion of Iraq was a mistake. That is done and cannot be reversed. It matters because it exposes the danger of pursuing the neoconservative formula for an interventionist foreign policy backed up by an all-powerful military, which has proved to be not all that powerful. The case for avoiding military occupations simply makes more sense. Why provoke long-term insurgencies that favor the insurgents? Why start a war we are likely to lose when our survival is not at stake? Why waste the lives of our brave young men and women in endless static conflict?

Beyond the immediate suffering and destruction, losing even a small war can have unintended long-term consequences. Britain and France lost their empires. The United States spent a generation coming to grips with its defeat in Vietnam. The Soviet retreat from Afghanistan was the beginning of the end of the Soviet empire. The Israeli loss in Lebanon gave Palestinian militants the idea that suicide terrorism would lead to victory over Zionism, and they used it with horrific results in the al-Aqsa intifada from 2000 to 2003. (The Israeli retaliation was equally horrific.) In the rush to war in Iraq, Bush and his neoconservative allies ignored the facts or failed to read the history of recent insurgencies. Bush later argued that America should "stay the course" in Iraq because losing would be disastrous when for that very reason he should never have started the war. The full consequences of his historic mistake remain to be seen.

To demonstrate that occupations like the one in Iraq are inherently dangerous for the occupiers, the experiences of five great powers since 1945 are examined in the following pages: Britain in Palestine leading to the birth of Israel, France in Algeria, the United States in Vietnam, Israel in Lebanon, and the Soviet Union in Afghanistan. These five confrontations ended in victory for the insurgents (as did the French struggle in Vietnam). Colonial Britain, on the other hand, managed to defeat insurgencies in Malaya and Kenya in the 1950s. The Malaya campaign, which prevented a communist takeover, gained from ceding power to the Malayans. Kenya witnessed the slaughter of poorly armed Kikuyu tribesmen and the cruel torture and death of Kikuyu prisoners, but London overturned the British victory for the sheer brutality of the put-down. Britain won these wars, but lost the two colonies. Other colonies, it gave up with less violence. That leaves the West Bank of Palestine where a great-power occupation, that of Israel, has lasted four decades. (No attempt is made to be all-inclusive. Disputes over Russia in Chechnya and China in Tibet are treated lightly or not at all. The post–World War II occupations of Germany, Japan, and Korea belong in a different category altogether.)

While no two wars are identical, the confrontations generally fitted a pattern favorable to rebels of fighting in the shadows against superior armies, a form of warfare variously called "irregular," "unconventional," or "asymmetrical." Ethnic and sectarian differences often complicated their struggles. The occupation armies did not lose in the conventional sense; they simply did not win in any real sense; and the conflicts dragged on until the political winds blew them down. The Iraq war has followed a similar pattern with discrete twists.

Iraq was a faith-based, as opposed to a fact-based war, because all the "facts" alleged to justify it—WMD (weapons of mass destruction) and Iraqi connections to al Qaeda and the 9/11 attacks—have proved wrong, and we were left with a faith in democracy in a part of the world where tribal values prevail. Iraq was an unintelligent war supported by faulty intelligence skewed to fit the administration's preconceived ideas. Like all wars, it has left death and destruction in its wake.

The Bush Administration made regime change part of its case. Undeniably, Saddam was a cruel dictator and conducted a reckless foreign policy that threatened his neighbors. He even murdered his own subjects. His agents tried to assassinate the first President Bush. His idol was another cruel dictator, Joseph Stalin, infinitely more dangerous in his time than Saddam in his. But during all the years of the Cold War, in Stalin's tenure and beyond, no American president chose to invade the Soviet Union, even during the dangerous Cuban missile crisis in 1962 when President John F. Kennedy stared down Chairman Nikita Khrushchev under a nuclear cloud. It was one thing to stand up to the Soviet menace, quite another to strong-arm Iraq. Why did ten Cold War presidents draw back from attacking the greater peril, while George W. Bush charged with a full-throated war cry into the lesser threat? Only one plausible explanation presents itself: the "schoolyard bully" syndrome. Bush and his advisors, thinking like colonial masters of yore, considered Iraq a pushover for the world's greatest military power.

They were dangerously mistaken. The Iraq war has required a huge investment from America. Our role in the destruction of Iraq and the slaughter of innocents is probably immoral, but that is not the point here, unless national self-preservation has a moral dimension. Iraq is sucking the life blood from our veins, wasting our resources, and ruining our credibility. We are less secure for having triggered an irregular war that is beyond our power to win militarily. With al Qaeda and other Islamists having joined the fight against us after the invasion, the stakes are higher in Iraq because the Islamic radicals are the real enemy.

The initial American-led thrust into Iraq in 2003 was a triumph of modern arms. It took the American and British forces only three weeks to crush the third-rate Iraqi army and topple the rogue regime of Saddam. Then the war regressed into a clone of recent great-power losers. Baath Party loyalists from the Sunni minority who formerly dominated the Iraqi government and professional soldiers from the disbanded Iraqi army went underground to mount an insurgency against the conquerors. Radical Islamists eagerly infiltrated into Iraq to fight against America. The situation devolved into a static occupation favorable to insurgents. No longer in blitzkrieg mode, the Americans and their partners hunkered down in garrison duty, ceding the initiative to shadow warriors who planted roadside explosives, unleashed suicide bombers, and sabotaged infrastructure. The world's only superpower found itself caught in a trap of its own making, fighting the kind of irregular warfare against a weaker foe that great-power occupiers have usually lost since the end of World War II.

America knew firsthand about this phenomenon from its experience in Vietnam, 1965–72, where its superior military force won most of the battles and lost the war to a determined and patient enemy. The Gulf War of 1991 was a different story altogether. After an American-led coalition took only a hundred hours of ground combat to drive the Iraqi army out of Kuwait, the administration of President George H. W. Bush proudly proclaimed that America had exorcised the ghost of

Vietnam. That overstated the case. America and its coalition allies had merely won a conventional war for which they were marvelously trained and equipped. But the first Bush Administration wisely decided not to push on to Baghdad. The national security advisor, Brent Scowcroft, saw the danger. "At a minimum, we'd be an occupier in a hostile land," Scowcroft later told Jeffrey Goldberg of the *New Yorker*. "Our forces would be sniped at by guerrillas, and, once we were there, how would we get out?... [W]hat do you do with Iraq once you own it?"[9]

Scowcroft recognized the fundamental difference between the two types of conflict: one a conventional war in which outcomes can be measured by armies destroyed in great battles and territories won or lost, and the other an irregular war without front lines in which there are no great battles and the belligerents inhabit the same territory. The three-week drive to Baghdad in 2003 was a conventional war similar to the 1991 Gulf War. But the aftermath was more like Vietnam, a war of attrition without front lines with the two sides trading casualties.

These results, from Vietnam to post-invasion Iraq, were not accidental. History offers examples of small powers inviting sudden disaster by directly challenging superior armies as Iraq did in the Gulf War in 1991, and large occupying powers risking slow death when they confront strong-willed insurgents in their homeland ready to fight and die for freedom. In unconventional wars, the insurgents use hit-and-run tactics to bleed the occupying army one painful cut at a time, and usually do not discriminate between military and civilian targets. In such circumstances, there need not be a decisive engagement, or a clear-cut winner and loser. Small military victories for the insurgents get magnified into large political defeats for the occupiers. Body bags and flag-draped coffins bring the harvests of war home to the occupying power without any apparent gain on the battlefield.

This gives rise to a paradox of irregular warfare cogently expressed by Henry Kissinger in the context of the Vietnam War, "The conventional army loses if it does not win. The guerrilla wins if he does not lose."[10] In Iraq we call the rebels "insurgents," and they win if they do not lose. (Through 2007, they had not lost.) When the occupiers, far from home, grow weary of bleeding, they will look to their self-interest and leave.[11]

Something then Secretary of Defense Donald Rumsfeld and his generals said repeatedly in the summer 2005—and something they did not say—goes to the heart of this book. These were Rumsfeld's words during a television interview on June 26:

> [The U.S. is] not going to win against the insurgency. The Iraqi people are going to win against the insurgency. That insurgency could go on for any number of years. Insurgencies tend to go on five, six, eight, ten, twelve years.[12]

That could be interpreted in different ways. Maybe he was just blowing smoke. Maybe he was preparing with Delphic prescience to put the blame on the Iraqis for a future American failure. Or, perhaps he was reassuring the American public of ultimate victory. In other words, be patient, America. Our side is going to win, one way or another. Rumsfeld himself said he was recognizing the political nature of the insurgency. In any case, it became the administration's mantra. President Bush repeated it after the death of Abu Musab al-Zarqawi more than three years after the invasion, and a year after that, in June 2007, General David Petraeus, the new commander in Iraq, made a similar claim. But history contradicts them. The assumption of inevitable victory in this kind of warfare manifests a triumph of faith over experience, or it is an exercise in self-deception. Counterinsurgencies usually take nine or ten years, General Petraeus said[13]—and the insurgents usually win, he did not say.

Since the end of World War II—and this is what Rumsfeld, Bush, Petraeus, and the others left out—long-term insurgencies against powerful occupying powers in which guerrilla and terrorist tactics are employed have more often ended in victory for the insurgents, a condition that from the start has dictated poor odds for an American military victory in Iraq. Rumsfeld said the Iraqis, not the Americans would defeat the insurgency. That is his wish, obviously, but the fulfillment remains to be seen. Governments set up by foreign occupiers are often short-lived, as in the American withdrawal from South Vietnam, the Soviet retreat from Afghanistan, and the Israeli debacle in Lebanon.

The winning struggles of Lilliputian nations have enriched the post–World War II period, decades marked by the end of colonialism, the Cold War from start to finish, and the rise of militant Islam. It began with the signing on June 26, 1945 of the UN Charter, which contains the declaration of the right of national self-determination.[14] The great power/small power confrontations summarized in this book broadly illustrate the ultimate futility of great-power occupations. In all these insurgencies, the rebels used guerrilla and terrorist tactics, which decisively affected the outcome.

The most striking truth about this lineup of fallen stars is the remorseless humbling of the giants. Britons once boasted that "the sun never sets on the British empire," and eventually it did, and not always peacefully. Gone, too, are the empires of France and other colonial pretenders. America and the Soviet Union emerged from World War II as the dominant world powers, facing one another through ideological blinders, their fingers nervously cradling the triggers of the most lethal WMD known to mankind. They both lost insurgency wars, American in Vietnam, the Soviet Union in Afghanistan. Israel, the superpower of the Middle East after the 1967 Six-Day War, stumbled in Lebanon. To this day (late in 2007) one great-power intervention defies the odds: Israel in the West Bank of Palestine. A review of these insurgencies provides an unconventional perspective on the Iraq adventure.

Of the five historical insurgencies covered, not one of the liberated countries has ever invaded its former occupier. Wars occurred when the weaker people became fed up with their subordinate status, whether in the era of colonialism or in the new age of great-power military intervention in the internal affairs of small nations. America in Iraq is a classic intervention, but the invasion, intended to fight terrorism, has inflamed it instead. Or as Buchanan succinctly put it in a television debate with the Israeli, Natan Sharansky, on NBC's *Meet the Press,* "Interventionism is the cause of terror. It is not a cure for terror."[15]

Terrorism, one potent weapon of insurgents, needs some context. Like war, it is murder by another name. Societies usually sanction war, but condemn terrorism. Yet insurgency is a form of warfare, and terrorism seems to be an inevitable fellow traveler of insurgency. Who can deliver us from conundrums we would rather not face? The term "terrorism" is so sensitive that scholars have detected more than a hundred definitions.[16] Even dictionaries cannot agree. The Oxford English dictionary defines it as "government by intimidation," as in the Jacobin Reign of Terror during the French Revolution, or more generally, "a policy intended to strike with terror those against whom it is adopted."[17] The American Heritage College dictionary turns the Oxford definition on its head, describing it as an antigovernment instrument: "The unlawful use or threatened use of force or violence to intimidate or coerce societies or governments, often for ideological or political reasons."[18] Webster's dictionary defines it as "the systematic use of terror as a means of coercion."[19] The late actor, Sir Peter Ustinov, is credited with summing it up, tongue-in-cheek, in terms of class warfare: "Terrorism is the war of the poor; war is the terrorism of the rich."[20]

President Bush, like the leaders of powerful nations who preceded him, frequently misuses the term to demonize his enemies. History is replete with this kind of name-calling and mud-slinging. Native Americans fought for their lands against white invaders and colonizers, and we called them savages for killing and scalping settlers. Kikuyu tribesmen hacked a few white families to death in 1950s Kenya, and the British colonists denigrated them with the derisive term, Mau Mau. The whites and black loyalists slaughtered more Kikuyu by at least one order of magnitude. Now Arabs and other Muslims fight for their lands against Western intruders, and we call them terrorists for staging suicide attacks against occupiers.

One complication is that the very same act can be terrorism or not, based on how it is employed. For example, during the second intifada, Hamas used suicide bombing against Israeli civilians, while Hezbollah had employed it to drive the Israeli army out of Lebanon. The first example is terrorism; the second, self-defense. Terrorism can be used in the struggle for power or in the suppression of that struggle. Saddam was a hit man for the Baath Party before he became dictator of Iraq. He used terrorism both as a rebel to gain power and as a cruel sovereign to maintain it. Hitler, Stalin, Idi Amin, and Pol Pot were notable terrorist-dictators of the twentieth century.

Obviously, the practice of terrorism preceded its first modern articulation in the French Reign of Terror. Political violence has always existed as a tool in human society's ubiquitous struggle for power. In the first century AD, Jerusalem's Zealots committed terrorist acts when they assassinated Jews who collaborated with the Roman occupiers. And when the Romans laid siege to Jerusalem in AD 70, starving inhabitants watched in horror at the sight of Roman soldiers crucifying Jews caught venturing out of the city in search of food.[21] When Antioch was under siege in 1098, the Arab writer Amin Maalouf informs us, the Christian crusaders catapulted the heads of soldiers from a defeated Arab relief force over the walls of the city, a terrifying signal to the people of Antioch that their neighbors would not save them.[22] The Mongol conqueror, Tamerlane, also knew something about terrorism as a concept, even when the word did not exist. While capturing a city, he would typically slaughter its inhabitants, and outside conquered cities of central Asia in the fourteenth century, he would build pyramids out of the skulls of his thousands of victims to keep survivors in line.[23]

It seems that the definition of terrorism is up for grabs. The reader is free to define it for himself/herself. Here, it is defined simply as the willful killing of innocent noncombatants for a political purpose.

In the 1940s, Menachem Begin called his Irgun Zvai Leumi followers "soldiers" fighting in a Zionist army for Jewish statehood against the British occupiers of Palestine. Insofar as it relates to the issue of self-determination, Begin had it right. Occupied people are justified in attacking a foreign army occupying their homeland, although at the time the Palestinian land for which the Irgun fought was not internationally recognized as the Jewish homeland. Never mind that Begin's "soldiers" did not wear uniforms. Neither did some American guerrilla fighters opposing the British army in the American Revolutionary War. The principle has also worked against the Jewish people. During the Israeli occupation of Lebanon, 1982–2000, Lebanese suicide bombers from Hezbollah blew up Israeli military headquarters in Tyre and on different occasions, plowed into Israeli military columns to detonate their bombs. Israeli leaders called them "terrorists," but if one follows the Begin line of reasoning to its logical conclusion, labeling the Lebanese Hezbollah "terrorists" was unjust. They were "soldiers," too, insofar as they were fighting against the Israeli military occupiers of Lebanon. Similarly, if the native-born insurgents in Iraq were to confine their attacks on the occupation troops, they would also be "soldiers" under the Begin principle. (Many, in fact, were soldiers before the occupation authority disbanded the Iraqi army.) Significantly, when the State Department issues its annual report on terrorism it omits attacks on American occupation troops.[24]

As for the insurgents, they could not care less about such nice distinctions. They do what they think they must to win their freedom.

Once a great power has intervened, there are few, if any good choices. For as long as the occupation goes on, the casualties continue to add up. The great power is left with one other option: get out. Occupying armies have taken extreme measures by fighting terrorism with terrorism. They possess the military where-with-all to do that, while at the same time they reduce themselves to the level of the terrorists by killing and maiming innocents, destroying homes, and alienating the general population. War breaks the bonds of civility that keep mankind's darker nature in check, stirring civilized men to commit barbarous acts. An often-repeated phrase that cynically summed up the Vietnam War, "We will save Vietnam by destroying it," applies to combating some other insurgencies.

For example, the British in Palestine destroyed the family homes of Jewish "terrorists," a practice later emulated by the Israeli army in the West Bank and Gaza. In 2004 American Marines "liberated" Fallujah by making that city of 300,000 people temporarily uninhabitable.

The French tortured and summarily executed Algerian captives, conducted invasive sweeps of urban neighborhoods, and resettled a million or so peasants from their rural villages to barbed wire encampments to isolate them from guerrilla fighters. Peasants lived in these encampments for months and years under appalling conditions. The Americans pursued a similar policy of resettlement in Vietnam, attacked and burned villages thought to harbor Vietcong, turned a blind eye to the torture of prisoners, and assassinated Vietcong leaders. In Iraq, the Americans tortured and humiliated prisoners.

The Israelis in Lebanon tried a different method of separating the alleged terrorists from the general population. They bombarded villages in southern Lebanon to create a stampede of Shiite peasants fleeing north away from the terrorist hunting fields. The Soviet Union pursued a scorched-earth policy in Afghanistan that created six million refugees. Such practices often had the effect of driving the people not already hostile to the occupiers into the arms of the insurgents.

This journey into recent history begins with President Bush's great strategic blunder, the preemptive war on Iraq, by delving into the underlying neoconservative motives for war, and the campaign to sell the war with half-baked intelligence (chapter 1). Then, to set the context for the insurgency that followed, it reviews some lessons the neoconservatives did not heed: the Jewish insurgency in Palestine against the British Mandate (chapter 2) and the Algerian war of liberation (chapter 3). Before leaving the colonial era, chapter 4 briefly covers British military successes against insurgencies in Malaya and Kenya, and then the narrative moves on to the American intervention in South Vietnam (chapter 5). A different style of irregular warfare that features the suicide bomb is then brought into focus. Chapter 6, which sketches Hezbollah's fight against Israel in Lebanon, is highlighted by the first suicide bomb in the Arab/Israeli conflict. Chapter 7 deals with the Israeli occupation of the West Bank and Gaza and the two intifadas that arose from it. Chapter 8 covers the mujahidin war against the Soviet Union in Afghanistan. With the context firmly established, chapter 9 returns to the Iraq insurgency that has cost America so dearly in blood and treasure. A brief Afterword sums up the argument for avoiding occupations that breed small wars, and urges the least of the bad options now available to us, the soonest possible orderly withdrawal from Iraq.

CHAPTER 1

IRAQ: THE HEIGHT OF FOLLY

A phenomenon noticeable throughout history regardless of place or period is the pursuit by governments of policies contrary to their own interests.
—Barbara W. Tuchman (1984)

If one were to update the late Barbara W. Tuchman's wry history of folly that ended with the Vietnam War, the American-led intervention in Iraq must certainly be included. For the second time in three generations, America met her definition of the term by acting contrary to its own interests despite timely advice against the invasion and the availability of an alternative course of action.[1] Beyond the moral objection to the wanton creation of killing fields, the cost in blood and treasure and the damage to America's image around the world were far out of proportion to any U.S. gain that might have been derived from the rapid advance on Baghdad. The Bush Administration pegged its justification for the war to erroneous assumptions that Iraq possessed WMD and was linked to al Qaeda and the antithetical idea that democracy, government by the people through elected representatives, can be imposed at the point of a gun. These assumptions have been thoroughly discredited.

While Saddam Hussein had in the past embarked on weapons programs for nuclear, chemical, and biological warfare, and had even gassed Iranian troops and Iraqi Kurds, the United States had no credible evidence that the programs still existed. In fact, UN inspection teams and American air and missile raids all but eliminated them in the 1990s. Still, because the Iraqi dictator was so untrustworthy, Western intelligence agencies believed that he was trying to reconstitute them. The Bush Administration did everything it could to reinforce that belief, even ignored the results of UN inspections in late 2002 and early 2003 that had found no evidence of WMD up to the time that America cut them off and went to war, only to find from its own inspections after the invasion that Iraq possessed none of these exotic weapons at the time of America's counterproductive invasion.

And while the world, especially the Middle East, has seen strange alliances in which incompatibles embrace, the secular Saddam and the Islamist Osama bin Laden were emphatically not political bedfellows. Iraqi intelligence had been in touch with al Qaeda, but that was as far as it went. They did not cooperate on WMD and Iraq was not complicit in the 9/11 attacks. Before the invasion of Iraq, with daily overflights in northern and southern zones and the regimen of UN inspections, Saddam was not an imminent threat to any other country, especially the United States.

A major fallout of the Iraq invasion was the diversion of forces from the war against America's deadliest enemy, al Qaeda, or more broadly, Islamic extremists. Eventually, American troops did wind up fighting the Islamists in Iraq—not because the Americans went looking for them, but because they went looking for the Americans. The adverse experiences of great powers against nationalist insurgents elsewhere in the twentieth century, including America in Vietnam, plus the tendency of Islamist zealots to leech onto other peoples' insurgencies, as in Bosnia and Chechnya, should have given the Bush team pause. If not, there were other red flags.

Vice President Dick Cheney eloquently stated the case against invading Iraq—in 1991, when he was secretary of defense for the first Bush President, George H. W. Bush. The Gulf War had just ended in a smashing victory for the U.S.-led coalition. The elder Bush decided to stay within the UN mandate simply to drive the Iraqi forces out of Kuwait, and disregarded calls from the radical right wing in America to take out Saddam. Cheney spoke these words in defense of his then president:

> If we were going to remove Saddam Hussein, we would have to go all the way to Baghdad. Once...we'd gotten rid of Saddam Hussein and his government, then we'd have had to put another government in its place. What kind of government? How long would we have had to stay in Baghdad to keep that government in place? What would happen to that government once U.S. forces withdrew? How many casualties should the United States accept in that effort to try to create clarity and stability in a situation that is inherently unstable?...It's my view...that it would have been a mistake for us to get *bogged down* in the *quagmire* inside Iraq.[2] (Emphasis added.)

Alas, twelve years later as the most powerful vice president in American history, not only did Cheney strongly favor going to Baghdad, he seems to have pressured the CIA to accept dubious intelligence to justify the invasion. If in 2003 he had only heeded his own counsel of 1991, America might not have got itself into such a mess.

The Bush team did not even need to read history to catch the danger signs. They had only to pay close attention to an avalanche of friendly advice from inside their own Republican Party. Senator Chuck Hagel, the maverick from Iowa, and former Secretary of State Lawrence Eagleburger, two moderate Republican voices, the archconservatives Patrick J. Buchanan, who had helped spoil the first President Bush's bid for reelection in 1992 for raising taxes, and Jack Kemp, former vice presidential candidate on the 1996 Bob Dole ticket, spoke out against an invasion of Iraq. Brent Scowcroft, the national security advisor to Bush's father and one of the architects of the Gulf War, warned in an op-ed article in the *Wall Street Journal* that an attack on Saddam would be a needless diversion from the war on terror.[3] What most surprised the White House was opposition from the staunch Texas conservative, Dick Armey, the House majority leader, who said that an unprovoked war with Iraq "would not be consistent with what we have been as a nation."[4]

Prior to that, on August 5, 2002, Secretary of State Colin Powell, the distinguished career soldier and former chairman of the Joint Chiefs of Staff, privately expressed to President Bush some homespun words of wisdom. He briefed the president about the negative consequences of the war: the possible destabilization of friendly regimes, the diversion of energy and resources from the war against al Qaeda, and the impact on oil supplies and prices. Then, as reported by journalist Bob Woodward, he laid down the "Pottery Barn" principle: You break it; you own it. "You are going to be the proud owner of twenty-five million people," Powell told the president. "You will own all their hopes, aspirations, and problems. You'll own it all."[5]

Powell's was a military voice. He had worked his way up the ranks to the top as chairman of the Joint Chiefs under Defense Secretary Cheney during the Gulf War a decade earlier. Other important military figures shared Powell's doubts, but most of them did not speak out. Marine Lieutenant General Gregory Newbold, director of operations on the Joint Staff, actually resigned from the military rather than contribute to a mission he did not support, but he did not speak publicly about his views. He gave the standard excuse for his resignation, family considerations, and described himself in his Pentagon job as "a round peg" in a square hole.[6] One prominent senior officer, retired Marine General Anthony Zinni, finally did express public disapproval of the war. He told a meeting of the Middle East Institute in early October 2002 that ousting Saddam should have a low priority. Zinni, a former commander of Central Command, had drawn up a contingency plan in 1999 for an Iraq invasion, which the Bush Administration shredded in 2002.[7]

By the time Zinni spilled his gut feelings, his was a faint echo in the wilderness. The administration plunged ahead, airily confident of its mission, cooking intelligence to taste, promoting war as if selling soap, calling it a last resort while drawing up the battle plan, and misleading Congress and the American people about the justification for its actions. A final warning against committing folly reached the White House in the form of a professional intelligence analysis that came out of the CIA in January 2003, two months before the invasion. The National Intelligence Council, a government think tank that advises the director of central intelligence, quietly warned the administration that an American occupation of Iraq could set off an insurgency by Saddam loyalists and Islamic terrorists and intensify anti-American hostility in the Muslim world[8]—precisely what happened.

The Neoconservatives

The invasion of Iraq grew out of big ideas about America's post–Cold War destiny that emanated from an elite coterie of right-wing intellectuals with hawkish views on foreign policy. These far-out thinkers are often loosely called "neoconservatives," a label that reflects a liberal bent on social issues and toughness on defense, but applies, strictly speaking, to only a few of those in the war party who started their political careers as Democrats. The hard liners saw the fall of the Soviet empire as an opportunity for the United States, the only remaining superpower, to use its singular strength as a springboard for remaking the world in America's image. In 1996, the movement's two leading theoreticians, William Kristol, publisher of the *Weekly Standard,* a Rupert Murdoch-bankrolled magazine, and Robert Kagan, a senior associate at the Carnegie Endowment for International Peace, challenged America to adopt a policy of "benevolent global hegemony" as "the only reliable defense against a breakdown of peace and international order." To achieve it, they proposed "a neo-Reaganite foreign policy of military supremacy and moral confidence." Their formula went beyond merely supporting U.S. friends or gently pressuring less-than-friendly nations. They prescribed harsher policies toward so-called rogue states that were "ultimately intended to bring about a change in regime."[9] It was not a far philosophical leap from there to justifying the invasion of Iraq.

In 1997 Kristol and Kagan founded a think tank called the PNAC (Project for the New American Century), which urged America to grasp the mantle of world leadership "to ensure our security and our greatness" in the twenty-first century. Twenty-five conservative partisans signed PNAC's statement of principles, among them three prominent war hawks with broad foreign policy experience in previous Republican administrations—Cheney, Donald Rumsfeld, and Paul Wolfowitz.[10] For these and others, the "neo" in neoconservative is not apt. They are established Republicans and always have been, hard liners on defense and comfortable with the PNAC agenda. Wolfowitz, whose views were shaped by the Holocaust, stands out for his intellectual contribution to the movement.

The following January, after Saddam had stopped cooperating with UN weapons inspectors (the program was restored in 2002), Kristol and Kagan shot off a letter to President Clinton urging him to declare a policy of removing Saddam from power, by military action if necessary. Rumsfeld and Wolfowitz signed it, along with other prominent neo-Reaganite campers that included Richard Perle, mocked by his critics as the "Prince of Darkness" for his mordancy toward the Soviet Union while an assistant secretary of defense in the Reagan Administration; John Bolton, future ambassador to the United Nations, and Zalmay Khalilzad, future ambassador to American-occupied Iraq and the United Nations.

With Bush's election in 2000, a substantial number of conservative ideologues laid their eager hands on the levers of power, and brought their expansive ideas with them. Bush was a shrewd Texas politician whose born-again Christianity played well in the American heartland, but he had a glaring hole in his resume: no familiarity with foreign affairs. Cheney, however, possessed all the experience that the new president lacked, going back to the Nixon Administration. Under Gerald Ford he became the youngest White House chief of staff in U.S. history. After a decade in Congress, he served as secretary of defense in the administration of the first Bush, which made him a key player in the planning and successful execution of the Gulf War. In 1993, he swirled through the revolving door of the military-industrial complex to work for Halliburton, an oil services corporation that owned KBR, a defense contractor. In the new Bush Administration, Cheney was politically the most powerful of the neo-Reaganites and closest to the neophyte president whom he overshadowed.

Rumsfeld came aboard in 2001 as Bush's secretary of defense with the goal of upgrading missile defense and the armed forces. He followed a career path similar to Cheney's: seven years in Congress, a hitch in the Nixon Cabinet where he groomed Cheney, the White House chief of staff and secretary of defense in the Ford Administration. Then he departed government for the private sector. Rumsfeld, a highly skilled political infighter, wanted to gather the intelligence bureaucracy under his control, an obsession that might have put him at odds with CIA Chief George Tenet, except that Tenet did his best to please Rumsfeld and accommodate the neoconservative agenda.[11]

Wolfowitz became the Pentagon's number-two man in the new Bush regime, his third tour of duty in the Defense Department. He had also served as ambassador to Indonesia during the Reagan years. Unlike Cheney and Rumsfeld who headed large corporations, Wolfowitz opted for academia when out of government. From 1993 to 2000, he was dean of the School of Advanced International Studies at the Johns Hopkins University. As one who had contributed to the theoretical foundation for a neo-Reaganite foreign policy, his interest in attacking Iraq was huge.

During the administration of the first President Bush in 1992, the year after the Gulf War, Wolfowitz, then the undersecretary of defense for planning, had supervised the drafting of a biennial policy declaration called "Defense Planning Guidance." He assigned the job to I. Lewis "Scooter" Libby, another prominent neoconservative. Libby asked Khalilzad to write a report, which contained aggressive ideas for acting unilaterally and suppressing any new rival to American military supremacy. In the Middle East and southwest Asia, it projected America as the predominant power in the region with the goal of preserving "U.S. and Western access to the region's oil."[12] The draft was never officially approved because someone in the Pentagon leaked it to the *New York Times*.[13] When it threatened to become an election-year issue, the White House ordered it rewritten to stress collective military action for resolving disputes through international organizations like the United Nations. Libby revised it to soften the language, but subtly left in the neo-Reaganite issues that Khalilzad had planted.[14]

The Defense Planning Guidance of 1992 became the prototype for a neo-Reaganite 2000 Bush campaign paper, "Rebuilding America's Defense," which urged that the U.S. block the rise of any new great-power competitor. America's powerful military force would be unchained to "fight and decisively win major theater wars." The United States would also maintain its nuclear superiority, upgrade its armed forces, reposition them to permanent bases in the far reaches of the world, such as the Middle East, central and southeast Asia, and southeast Europe, and deploy the navy to "reflect East Asian concerns" (viz. China). The nation's main military mission was put in language with Orwellian overtones to "secure and expand zones of democratic peace."[15] During the buildup to the Iraq invasion, these thoughts were recycled as American policy.

Wolfowitz said he never saw the 1992 Khalilzad draft, but there is no doubt that he agreed with the ideas expressed in it. Yet at the end of the Gulf War, Wolfowitz raised no objection when the first President Bush decided against going on to Baghdad. By the late 1990s, he was second-guessing that decision and criticizing the Clinton Administration for an ineffective policy to contain Saddam. In a 1997 article in the *Weekly Standard* coauthored by Khalilzad, he called for Saddam's removal by military force to "[liberate] Iraq from tyranny."[16] (Khalilzad's hindsight was better than his foresight. In March 2006, three years after the invasion as the American situation in Iraq spiraled downward Khalilzad told the *Los Angeles Times* that by toppling Saddam the United States had opened a "Pandora's box" of ethnic and sectarian tensions.[17])

Some neoconservatives were joined at the hip, philosophically, with Israel's right-wing Likud Party. Two former CIA analysts, Kathleen and Bill Christison, charged them with "dual loyalties," unable to "distinguish U.S. interests from Israeli interests."[18] Perle, for example, led a team in 1996 in the preparation of a policy paper for newly elected Israeli Prime Minister Binyamin Netanyahu entitled, "A Clean Break: A New Strategy for Securing the Realm," sponsored by the IASPS (Institute for Advanced Strategic and Political Studies), a Jerusalem think tank with an office in Washington. The paper advised Netanyahu to seek strategic regional alliances with Turkey and Jordan to counter the hostility from states like Syria and Iraq. One of its recommendations was ". . . removing Saddam Hussein from power in Iraq" to foil Syria's regional ambitions, and as an important Israeli strategic objective in its own right. Eight names were listed on the document. Perle's was at the top, with the rest in alphabetical order, notable among them Douglas Feith and David Wurmser.[19] The Jewish *Forward* reported that Wurmser, who worked for IASPS at the time, was the principal author.[20] Wurmser went on to write a book, *Tyranny's Ally,* which expanded on the "Clean Break" theme. Netanyahu filed the report away, but in 2001 the neoconservatives proposed regime change in Iraq to the new American President, George W. Bush, who ran with the idea after 9/11. In the new Bush Administration, Perle, a major player in the neoconservative movement, became chairman of the Defense Policy Board, an advisory group to the Defense Department. That gave him access to defense secrets while he pursued his business ventures. He later resigned as chairman under a cloud of conflict-of-interest accusations, but remained a member of the board. Rumsfeld had originally offered him Wolfowitz's old number-three position, undersecretary of defense for policy, but Perle turned it down and recommended his protégé, Feith, who took the job.

Feith is an outspoken supporter of Israel's right-wing Likud Party, the Jewish settler movement in Palestine, and other Zionist causes. His father, Dalck Feith, once belonged to Betar, the Zionist youth movement in Poland prior to World War II, which contributed fighters to the Jewish underground in Palestine. Dalck Feith lost his family in the Holocaust—his parents, three brothers, and four sisters. Douglas graduated *magna cum laude* from both Harvard and Georgetown law school and won high accolades from his boss, Rumsfeld, as a "brilliant" government official.[21] Yet, he failed to impress some career military officers. General Tommy Franks, who drew up the Iraq battle plan, described Feith as a "theorist whose ideas were often impractical" and who had gained a reputation around the Pentagon as "the dumbest fucking guy on the planet."[22] Jay Garner, a retired lieutenant general chosen as the first administrator in occupied Iraq, found Feith, in the words of author George Packer, to be "overbearing and mentally scattered."[23] Clearly, Feith was not on their wavelength, and they were not on his. This disconnect cannot possibly be attributed to his IQ. While outstanding as a conceptualizer, even his admirers admit that he was a poor manager. He fussed over grammatical errors in memos from his underlings while important substantive decisions awaited his approval.[24]

No list of war enablers in the Bush Administration is complete without Libby's name. He first met Wolfowitz as an undergraduate at Yale—Libby a bright young student, Wolfowitz the cerebral political science professor. Libby graduated *summa cum laude*, and went on to Columbia Law School and a law practice in Philadelphia. His government career began in 1981 when Wolfowitz invited him to Washington for work in the State Department. Since then he has alternated between high-level government jobs and private law practice. His hard-line views on defense came through in his work on the Defense Planning Guidance and other neoconservative documents. In 2001, he became Vice President Cheney's chief of staff and one of the most influential advisors in the Bush White House.[25]

Banging the Drums of War

Once inside the new Bush Administration in 2001, Wolfowitz, strongly influenced by the writings of Laurie Mylroie, was the highest-ranking early advocate of military action to topple Saddam. Mylroie, who prior to Saddam's conquest of Kuwait tried to broker a peace agreement between Iraq and Israel, authored a book first published in 2000, *Study of Revenge: Saddam Hussein's Unfinished War Against America,* that argued contrary to the evidence uncovered by the CIA and other professional intelligence shops that Saddam was behind the first bombing of the World Trade Center in 1993.[26] In February 2001, at the administration's very first NSC (National Security Council) meeting ten days after the inauguration, and more than eight months before the 9/11 attacks, Iraq dominated the conversation. "From the very beginning," then Treasury Secretary Paul H. O'Neill told CBS News correspondent Leslie Stahl, "there was a conviction, that Saddam Hussein was a bad person and that he needed to go.... The president [was] saying 'Go find me a way to do this.'"[27] Wolfowitz was the outspoken agitator at that meeting, and after 9/11 he was first to advise a full-scale assault on Iraq, an idea that Richard Clarke, the counterterrorism chief attached to the NSC, placed on the screwball level of invading Mexico after the 1941 Japanese attack on Pearl Harbor.[28]

But al Qaeda's attack raised the pressure on President Bush to do something about Iraq. The next day, September 12, 2001, the president spoke privately with Clarke and members of his staff in the White House conference room. "See if Saddam did this," he instructed. "See if he's linked in any way...." As Clarke tells it in his book written after he left government service, he was "taken aback, incredulous." One of his staffers concluded, "Wolfowitz got to him." They had already looked into it several times and found no linkage, but they looked again, and again found no linkage. "A memorandum to that effect was sent up to the President," Clarke said, "but there was never any indication that it reached him."[29] The indication, on the contrary, was that the neoconservatives had not given up on the idea, because shortly thereafter, former CIA Director James Woolsey was dispatched to London with a team of Defense and Justice Department officials to seek evidence that Iraq was behind the 9/11 attacks. They went with the blessing of Wolfowitz and Feith.[30] There is no indication that they found what they were looking for, and the president had not yet set a course for war on Iraq. On November 21, however, Bush asked Rumsfeld to update the Iraq war plan, "And get Tommy Franks looking at what it would take to protect America by removing Saddam Hussein if we have to."[31] So preparations for war began, even though Bush would say that no final decision had been made until the invasion was near at hand.

Bush eventually subscribed to the Wolfowitz argument that al Qaeda could not have visited this horror on America without state sponsorship, and that the sponsor was Iraq. Having settled on this conclusion, the neoconservatives set out on a quest for evidence to support it. Packer put it this way in *The Assassins' Gate:* The war hawks "were working deductively, not inductively: The premise was true; the facts would be found to confirm it." They started with "the higher insights of political philosophy rather than evidence from the fallen world of social science."[32] There was also an acceptance among several who came to work for Bush of a need for secrecy and deception as a way to do government business. At least, that was the practice they followed and a hallmark of the Bush Administration.

Back in the Pentagon after the post–9/11 meeting in the White House, Wolfowitz conferred with Feith about building a case for invasion. They viewed the intelligence bureaucracy, including the CIA and the Pentagon's own DIA (Defense Intelligence Agency), as major obstacles because they cast doubt on Iraqi links to al Qaeda and the 9/11 attacks. Neoconservatives had long held the CIA in contempt, and after 9/11 attacks Perle scorned the agency's analysis of Iraq as "not worth the paper it's written on."[33] (The neoconservative analysis turned out to be worth even less.)

With Rumsfeld's approval and without fanfare, Wolfowitz and Feith created an in-house intelligence operation to bypass the agencies on matters relating to Iraqi involvement in WMD and terrorism. Feith's fellow-Likudnik, Wurmser, the principal author of the Israel strategy paper, "Clean Break," was brought in to head what became known as the Counter Terrorism Evaluation Group, or the Wurmser–Maloof project, or simply the "B Team." Wurmser and F. Michael Maloof, from Perle's bullpen of neoconservatives, used powerful computers to reanalyze documents that had already been through the mill at the CIA, DIA, the NSA (National Security Agency), and other agencies to see if any overlooked or rejected nuggets could be mined to fit their preconceived ideas. They also welcomed information from Iraqi defectors considered unreliable, if not outright liars, by the intelligence professionals. One source of informers was the INC (Iraqi National Congress), a group headed by Perle's friend Ahmad Chalabi and supported by the Pentagon to the tune of about $4 million a year until funding was cutoff in 2004.[34] The intelligence thus derived went unvetted by skeptical professional operatives. Years later, the Pentagon's inspector general did a study of Feith's operation and determined, not only that his conclusions were "at variance with the consensus of the intelligence community" and therefore "inappropriate," but also that it "did not provide the most accurate analysis of intelligence to senior decision-makers."[35] Long after the invasion, Vice President Cheney continued to justify it based on Feith's discredited assertion of a "mature" and "symbiotic" prewar relationship between Iraq and al Qaeda.[36]

The administration's justification for invading Iraq had three major components: a linkage between Saddam's regime and al Qaeda that would make Iraq complicit in the 9/11 attacks, an Iraqi buildup of WMD that would threaten America's security, and the need for regime change in Iraq that blossomed into a rationale for spreading democracy in the Middle East. The first two came together in false information that Iraq was training al Qaeda in the use of WMD. The Pentagon's backroom neoconservative intelligence apparatus set out to fortify these assumptions.

An early boost for linkage came with a supposed meeting in Prague in April 2001 between Mohamed Atta, the lead pilot in the World Trade Center attack, and an Iraqi intelligence official, Ahmad Khalil Ibrahim Samir al-Ani. On September 12, after Atta's picture appeared on Czech television, a Czech intelligence agent investigating a related case told his superior officer that he recognized Atta as the unknown Arab who had met Ani on April 9. The information was relayed to the CIA through secure channels, and less than a week later an unnamed source leaked it to the Associated Press. Efforts to verify the report have been inconclusive. The FBI learned that Atta checked out of a Virginia Beach hotel on April 4, and agents picked up his trail again on April 11 in Florida. The intervening week was a blank, except that Atta's cell phone was used four times in Florida, not necessarily by Atta. There was no record that he left the country. If Atta went to Prague, he traveled under an assumed name with a fake passport, which he was not known to do. The other possibility is mistaken identity, although Czech intelligence has reckoned a 70 percent probability that its agent correctly identified Atta. But Czech government sources said Ani was out of town at the time of the supposed meeting. The Iraqi agent Ani has denied that the meeting took place, as have Khalid Sheikh Mohammed and

Ramzi Binalshibh, two key al Qaeda figures involved in the 9/11 attacks who later fell into American hands. The 9/11 Commission concluded long after the Iraq invasion that "The available evidence does not support the original Czech report of an Atta–Ani meeting."[37] In the meantime, the alleged meeting in Prague became a hot political issue in America, and a loose hook on which to hang a war.

Shakier still was information extracted from a senior Islamist detainee, Ibn al-Shaykh al-Libi, who told his American captors that Iraq had provided al Qaeda with chemical and biological weapons training, the kind of scary information that excited the Wurmser–Maloof team. But the DIA warned that Libi might be "intentionally misleading the debriefers" by describing scenarios "that he knows will retain their interest." The CIA, on the other hand, found Libi's testimony "credible," but hedged its assessment, pointing out that he was not in a position to know whether such training had taken place. This idea of Iraqis training Islamist terrorists was part of the administration's larger effort to assert a close relationship between Iraq and al Qaeda. But again, the DIA dismissed it with this admonition, "Saddam's regime is intensely secular and is wary of Islamic revolutionary movements. Moreover, Baghdad is unlikely to provide assistance to a group it cannot control." When administration officials spoke later about close Iraqi-al Qaeda relations and Iraqis training al Qaeda in chemical and biological warfare, they left out the caveats, which were declassified three-and-a-half years later after Libi had recanted his allegation.[38]

The American intelligence community also split over the issue of UAVs (unmanned aerial vehicles). That they existed, everyone agreed, but for what purpose was in dispute. The convenient explanation adopted by the neoconservative war cabinet was to deliver chemical or biological payloads, possibly on the United States. The broad assessment of the intelligence agencies came down to the delivery of biological agents. That conclusion was qualified with the word "probably" and, more importantly, with the objection raised by the NASIC (National Air and Space Intelligence Center), the intelligence arm of the Air Force and the agency that knew more about UAVs than all the others. NASIC determined that the primary role of the Iraqi drones would be reconnaissance.[39] The public would hear from the Bush Administration about the threat of Iraqi UAVs dispersing chemical or biological poisons on the United States but nothing about NASIC's informed dissent until after the invasion.

Iraq's alleged nuclear threat loomed large in the calculations of the neoconservatives. When shipments of aluminum tubes on their way to Iraq were intercepted, the Wurmser–Maloof team jumped to the conclusion that Iraq was trying to reconstitute its nuclear weapons program. Indeed, that was one possibility. Depending on their measurements, the cylinders could be used in uranium enrichment or the manufacture of short-range missiles. Not surprisingly, Iraq explained them in the latter context. But Wurmser and Maloof chose to believe the alternative. Feith carried that news to the war cabinet. Meanwhile, experts in the Department of Energy determined that the tubes' diameters were too small and the aluminum too hard for use in nuclear enrichment, and were designed instead for missiles, as Iraq had claimed. The State Department's INR (Bureau of Intelligence and Research) accepted the DOE's expertise and concluded that the evidence did not measure up to the nuclear weapons theory. Despite this division within the ranks, administration officials trumpeted only an Iraqi nuclear buildup for public consumption.

The "yellowcake" incident offered yet another example of selective intelligence disclosures. In October 2001, little more than a month after the attack on America, the CIA reported that Niger planned to sell several tons of uranium oxide (yellowcake) to Iraq. It credited an unnamed foreign government source, and cautioned that it had no corroboration from other sources. It also noted that Iraq possessed no known facilities for processing the material. Both Iraq and Niger denied the report. The following February, the same source pinpointed the date of the agreement, July 5–6, 2000, and said Niger would send Iraq five hundred tons of yellowcake a year. The CIA was slow to accept the intelligence, and after Cheney asked for clarification, it sent former diplomat Joseph Wilson to Niger. Wilson returned with very little new information, but did provide the CIA with credible corroboration that an Iraqi delegation visited Niger in 1999. That helped bring the CIA around. It now believed the yellowcake story (although Wilson did not). Most of the other interested agencies fell in line—with one notable exception. The State Department dissented because it thought the transaction would be too difficult to conceal and because a French consortium controlled the Niger uranium industry. It concluded, further, that claims of Iraqi pursuit of natural uranium in other parts of Africa, namely Somalia and the Democratic Republic of Congo, were "highly dubious." The yellowcake documents were soon proved to be forgeries.[40]

Eventually, the CIA came into possession of information about the Iraqi nuclear program that went beyond "dubious," hard intelligence that, in fact, the program had been dead for more than a decade. The story is told in the *New York Times* reporter James Risen's book, *State of War.* The Iraqis were working toward a nuclear bomb and were, perhaps, three years away when the Gulf War arrived. In early 1991 an American pilot was on a bombing mission near Baghdad and had two bombs left over after hitting his primary target. Before turning home, he asked where he might unload them and was directed to a complex of buildings about twenty miles north of the city. It was just an afterthought, a promising target, without solid knowledge that it was the site of a uranium-enrichment facility. Damage assessment from surveillance photos after the strike showed unusual activity that made the Americans suspicious that the facility was more important than they imagined. So they ordered another strike, this time a B-52 carpet bombing that completely destroyed it— and ended the Iraqi nuclear program. But America's human intelligence in Iraq was so bad that the CIA never learned about it until the late summer of 2002 when it tapped amateurs for a dangerous spy mission. It recruited about thirty Iraqi-Americans related to Iraqi scientists to visit Iraq so they could pump their relatives for information about the status of the nuclear program. The agency even supplied the recruits with specific questions designed to give a detailed reading of the program's progress. When all the recruits came back with the answer that the nuclear program was dead (including one whose brother had worked on it), the CIA did not believe it. The report was filed away, not shared with the Pentagon or the State Department or the White House.[41]

It seems unlikely that the neoconservative policymakers would have believed it either, even if they had been made aware of it, because they cherry-picked the intelligence. When doubts arose about such things like the aluminum tubes and the Niger yellowcake, they invariably chose to publicly express the version that bolstered the case for war and not mention the contrary indications. Ultimately, these proved to be missteps that caused embarrassment to the administration, but none more so than the "Curveball" saga.

Curveball was a young Iraqi chemical engineer, Rafid Ahmed Alwan, who sought political asylum in Germany in 1999. Hoping to improve his chances of obtaining a visa, he told German authorities that he once led a team that equipped vans for the manufacture of biological agents, and claimed to know where the Iraqi regime might be hiding the vehicles. The BND (Federal Intelligence Service) was so interested it put debriefers on the case for months on end, but would not allow American agents to interview him. It was an awkward situation. Curveball described to the Germans in Arabic things he allegedly witnessed in Iraq; the Germans relayed their second-hand information in German to an American DIA agent assigned to the BND, who passed on his now-thirdhand information in English to American intelligence in Washington. Something got lost in translation and retelling. But worse than that, it turned out that Curveball was lying in the first place. (Knight Ridder Newspapers reported that Curveball was the brother of a top Chalabi lieutenant.[42]) Nobody bothered to check things out in Iraq. But the more the German agents questioned him, the more they found cracks in his story, and they began to think he was mentally unbalanced. These doubts were transmitted to Washington, and the American intelligence community became divided over Curveball's reliability. But after September 2001, with pressure from the war party in power, Curveball's information loomed larger in the CIA's assessments of Iraq's bioweapons capabilities.

The stage was set for perhaps the greatest self-inflicted intelligence failure in the history of the nation.

In public the administration promoted the concept of preemptive war. In a speech on June 1 to the 2002 graduating class at West Point, Bush depicted the war on terror as "a conflict between good and evil" and advised the graduates to be ready for "preemptive action." The idea was formalized in September with the release of a lengthy document called the "National Security Strategy for the United States of America," in which the president placed "preemptive" over "preventive" and "proactive" over "reactive." "We cannot let our enemies strike first," said Bush. Neoconservatives praised him for his "moral clarity."

Most of the world did not realize it then, but the inner circles in Washington and London knew that Bush intended to strike first. Richard Dearlove, then chief of MI6, reported as much to Prime Minister Tony Blair in July 2002, eight months before the invasion. He had been to Washington for consultations with his counterparts in U.S. intelligence. "Bush wanted to remove Saddam through military action, justified by the conjunction of terrorism and WMD," according to notes of Dearlove's briefing to Blair about his Washington meetings. "But the intelligence and facts were being fixed around the policy."[43]

Dearlove's confidential report to Blair did not become public until 2005, but in the summer of 2002 antiwar pressure was already building, some of it from the president's own party, as indicated above. The administration was especially shocked at the opposition from rock-solid Republicans, and responded by quietly creating the WHIG (White House Iraq [or Information] Group), to rally the support of the American people around the invasion. Among its members were the president's security advisor, Condoleezza Rice, political machinators Karl Rove and Libby, and wordsmiths Karen Hughes and Mary Matalin. They plotted a media blitz to sell the war, starting on Sunday September 8 with an article in the *New York Times* reported by Michael Gordon and Judith Miller that Iraq was trying to purchase specially designed aluminum tubes for use in centrifuges to enrich uranium for nuclear bombs.[44] In follow-up Sunday television appearances, both Cheney[45] and Rice[46] mentioned the aluminum tubes as evidence that Iraq was reconstituting its nuclear program. Rice articulated the famous line created by the White House speechwriter Michael Gerson, "We don't want the smoking gun to be a nuclear cloud." There was no reference either in print or on television to contrary opinion about the tubes. Powell went on still another talk show to claim, "[T]here is no doubt in our mind that [Saddam] has chemical weapons stocks."[47] That day, WHIG played the media with consummate skill.

In another *sub rosa* move, a significant change was underway at the Pentagon. Gone were Wurmser and Maloof—Wurmser to the State Department on the staff of Undersecretary John Bolton, and Maloof out of government, his security clearance revoked for an association with a businessman under investigation for gunrunning to Liberia. In their place Rumsfeld created the OSP (Office of Special Plans), which did essentially the same work on a larger scale. The OSP was placed under Feith's jurisdiction in the office of his deputy, William J. Luti, who came over from Cheney's office. To head it, they brought in Abram N. Shulsky, another Perle referral who had roomed with Wolfowitz during their college days at Cornell and Chicago. The OSP became part of an existing unit, the Near East and South Asia section, and effectively ate it up. Shulsky removed veteran experts who did not agree with the neoconservative agenda by transferring them elsewhere in the department or pushing them into retirement.[48] Then he and Luti and a much larger staff, but still the B Team, got on with the job of reshaping the facts in the presidential pipeline, based in no small measure on reports from anti-Hussein exile groups. Some called it "Feith-based intelligence," a word play on Bush's faith-based initiative for funding religious programs. The OSP would create talking points about Iraq's alleged WMD and connection to al Qaeda that found their way into the speeches and public comments of administration officials and their Republican supporters on Capitol Hill.

In February 2007, Defense Department Inspector General Thomas Gimble released a report on the intelligence process in Feith's office, and concluded in testimony before the Senate Armed Services Committee that the Feith assessment given to senior administration officials about Iraqi ties to al Qaeda differed substantially from that of the intelligence community. Among the raw intelligence data that Feith took at face value was the reported meeting in Prague between 9/11 terrorist Atta and Iraqi agent Ani. Feith briefed the CIA, and the CIA disagreed with half of his findings, including the Prague meeting. Later Feith briefed Libby and deputy national security advisor Stephen J. Hadley at the White House, and in the absence of anybody from the CIA, he ignored the CIA's objections. He also inserted a dig at government intelligence that he had not made at the CIA briefing, asserting "fundamental problems with the way the intelligence community was assessing the information." That might have ignited CIA Director Tenet to a defense of his agency, but the seasoned bureaucratic turf fighter did not learn of the White House briefing until two years later.[49]

Vice President Cheney was fully engaged in the effort.[50] The *Washington Post* reported several months later that he and Libby made multiple visits to the CIA in the months leading up to war. Not satisfied with the daily intelligence briefings, Libby kept his lines open to Luti, Wurmser, and other well placed colleagues in the vast intelligence bureaucracy to get the latest neoconservative slant. Thus armed, the vice president's visits to the CIA made it possible for him to challenge the analysts who actually wrote the daily briefings, and not just the debriefers who came to his office. Some analysts, said the *Post,* felt that they were being pressured. It quoted a senior CIA official as saying the visits by Cheney and Libby "sent signals, intended or otherwise, that a certain output was desired from here."[51] At the Pentagon, Rumsfeld acknowledged that he would press the CIA staffer who briefed him: "What I could do is say, 'Gee, what about this, or what about that? Has somebody thought of this?'"[52] Wolfowitz and Feith ("browbeaters," they were called) waded in contemptuously on the intelligence professionals at the Pentagon, as to a lesser extent did Tenet at the CIA.[53] Tenet, a holdover from the Clinton Administration, proved to be a compliant timeserver in the Bush Administration, and humbly fell on his sword by resigning when the dismal prewar intelligence failure became public knowledge.

With the war clouds gathering, Democratic Senator Bob Graham of Florida, then chairman of the Senate Select Committee on Intelligence learned from Tenet on September 5 that the White House had not ordered a NIE (National Intelligence Estimate) to underpin the case for invasion. Democrats on the committee demanded that one be prepared in time for Congress to vote on a resolution authorizing the use of force in Iraq a little more than a month later. The NIE reflects the consensus of the entire intelligence community. Tenet grudgingly produced it, ninety-three pages long and classified, unavailable to the public and most members of Congress.

As Graham described it more than three years later in a *Washington Post* op-ed piece, it strongly asserted an Iraqi WMD buildup, but it also contained the dissenting opinions. Tenet acknowledged under questioning in a closed committee hearing that certain dubious information had not been independently verified.[54] On October 4, the CIA released an entirely separate document from the NIE, a 28-page White Paper on the Iraqi threat that had been under preparation since May, which the committee later condemned in a 521-page post-invasion report for watering down dissent and eliminating qualifiers that left judgments to appear as facts, and for exaggerating Iraq's ability to attack the United States.[55] Having seen the NIE, Graham asked that an unclassified version be made public, and Tenet responded with an unclassified letter that was little more forthcoming than the White Paper about disagreements within the intelligence community. Knowing the whole story, Graham voted against the resolution, but he was under oath not to reveal classified information. So most members of Congress voted on what they knew from the laundered unclassified documents.

The CIA's clever bamboozlement of Congress was part of the administration's wider campaign to bang the drums of war with selective intelligence. In the month leading up to the war-resolution vote, five top administration officials—Bush, Cheney, Rumsfeld, Powell, and Rice made numerous misleading statements about Iraqi WMD and al Qaeda connections in public appearances.[56] On September 8, for example, Cheney asserted that "[Saddam] now is trying through his illicit procurement network to acquire the equipment he needs (...specifically aluminum tubes) to be able to enrich uranium to make bombs."[57] Bush also mentioned the tubes in a speech on September 12 before the UN General Assembly: "Iraq has made several attempts to buy high-strength aluminum tubes used to enrich uranium for a nuclear weapon,"[58] ignoring their possible use in conventional artillery. In testimony before the House Armed Services Committee on September 18, Rumsfeld stated, "[Saddam] has at this moment stockpiles of chemical and biological weapons."[59] On October 2, the president said, somewhat vaguely, "On its present course, the Iraqi regime is a threat of unique urgency....It has developed weapons of mass death."[60]

By October 7, President Bush was ready for prime time. In a speech to the nation from Cincinnati, carried by the broadcast networks and cable news channels, the president implicitly connected Iraq to 9/11 without saying it in so many words. He called Saddam "a homicidal dictator who is addicted to weapons of mass destruction," claimed that Iraq possessed "massive stockpiles" of biological weapons, "thousands of tons" of chemical agents, ballistic missiles, and unmanned drones that could deliver chemical or biological payloads to the United States, and mentioned mobile weapons facilities that made detection difficult. All these points were either exaggerated, disputed within the American intelligence community, or flat untrue. But his *coup de theatre* concerned the greatest by far of all WMD, the nuclear bomb, and again, he overplayed the threat. He offered the problematic aluminum tubes as proof positive that Iraq was trying to reconstitute its nuclear program. If Iraq could produce, buy, or steal enriched uranium of a size a little larger than a softball, he solemnly intoned, it could have a nuclear bomb in less than a year, and be in position to threaten the Middle East or the United States, or make nuclear technology available to terrorists. "Facing clear evidence of peril," he declared with the recycled image from his speechwriter, "we cannot wait for the final proof—the smoking gun—that could come in the form of a mushroom cloud."[61]

The speech amounted to an imposing edifice of foreboding, built on a foundation of deductive reasoning, cemented by cherry-picked intelligence. Some day it would crumble, but on October 10 and 11 the Congress, dazzled by its jaundiced view of the superstructure, voted overwhelmingly—77-23 in the Senate; 296-133 in the House—to authorize the use of force if Saddam continued to defy UN resolutions imposing arms limitations. After release of the Senate Select Committee report on prewar intelligence in July 2004, Chairman Pat Roberts, a Republican White House loyalist, said that if Congress had known in October 2002 what the committee learned from its investigation, "I doubt if the votes [for war authorization] would have been there."[62]

But in the fall of 2002, most of the world was persuaded that Iraq possessed WMD, although the Iraqi government continued to deny it. In November, the UN Security Council voted to send weapons inspectors to Iraq. Bush promised the "severest consequences" if Iraq failed to comply, while the administration pressed on with its campaign of vilification against a regime that the world already knew to be villainous. In the two months leading up to war, the administration's five leading officials made more misleading statements about Iraqi WMD, according to Democratic watchdogs in Congress.[63] These included Bush's often-quoted sixteen inaccurate words in his State of the Union message, "The British government has learned that Saddam Hussein recently sought significant quantities of uranium from Africa," followed by nineteen other erroneous words, "Our intelligence sources tell us that he [Saddam] has attempted to purchase high-strength aluminum tubes suitable for nuclear weapons production."[64]

Bush delivered the State of Union on January 28. Powell would make the administration's unvarnished case for war to the United Nations eight days later. He was an ironic choice to carry the ball for the neoconservatives. He had crossed swords more than once with Cheney and Rumsfeld in foreign policy debates within the administration. In particular, he had persuaded the president to take the case against Iraq to the UN Security Council, and then won a unanimous vote to send weapons inspectors to Iraq. But by mid-January, Powell had lost his argument with Cheney and Rumsfeld. Bush was firmly resolved to go to war, and he called Powell in for a private meeting to convey his decision. "Are you with me on this?" the president asked. "I think I have to do this [invade Iraq]. I want you with me." "Yes, sir," said the career soldier who knew a command when he heard one, "I will support you. I'm with you, Mr. President."[65]

The CIA had prepared the original version of Powell's February 5 speech to the United Nations even before it was decided that Powell should deliver it. It was first drawn up as a public response to Iraq's declaration in December that it had no

WMD. When the State Department's intelligence bureau, the INR, saw that CIA document, it objected to thirty-eight specific questionable claims contained in it. During several days that Powell spent at the CIA in often-heated discussions with the agency's authors and their neoconservative backers, twenty-eight of the claims were either removed or altered,[66] including the assertion that Iraq was seeking uranium ore in Africa and the disputed meeting in Prague between Atta and Ani. But there was enough left over to turn Powell's earnest UN speech into a classic blunder.

One of the subjects Powell broached in his speech was the production of biological agents—mobile germ factories—on vans and rail cars to avoid detection. His first source was the defector, "Curveball," the Iraqi chemical engineer living in exile in Germany and linked to Chalabi's INC. The organized Iraqi defectors had pitched Curveball to American intelligence, with all the tortured baseball metaphors that the image elicits. When Powell took the Curveball offering, he thought he hit a home run, as he forcefully brought the point home. The mobile factories, he told the UN delegates, "can produce enough dry biological agents to kill thousands upon thousands of people." He went on from there to talk of Iraq's alleged chemical stocks that he estimated at 100–500 tons, enough "to cause mass casualties" in an area five to twenty-five times the size of Manhattan. He insisted that the aluminum tubes could be modified for uranium enrichment and that UAVs could be used to spray toxins on the United States, but on both items he acknowledged differences of opinion within the intelligence community. He also spoke of the "sinister nexus" between Iraq and al Qaeda, referring to an unnamed informant who claimed that Iraq offered chemical and biological weapons training to two al Qaeda fighters.[67]

It was thigh-slapping time in the vice president's office and high fives all around for neoconservatives in and out of government. Their nemesis, Powell, had made their case from the world's pulpit. And indeed, five-and-a-half weeks later, after warning UN weapons inspectors to clear out, American and British boots began trampling on Iraqi soil. Three weeks after that, U.S. troops were in Baghdad, and the conventional phase of the war was over. Bush, now the owner of Iraq in Powell's charming phrase, prepared to fix the shattered glass. But he must have forgotten the advice of the National Intelligence Council about the danger of setting off an insurgency of disempowered Sunnis joined by radical Islamists. That unconventional war came to pass and posed a serious challenge to American resolve.

Then the administration's glossy case for war crumbled to dust. The experts who had challenged the accepted stories on the Iraq–al Qaeda connection, aluminum tubes, African uranium, and UAVs were vindicated. Curveball's mobile lab story had been a wild pitch. Ibn al-Shaykh al-Libi, the al Qaeda captive, recanted his account of Iraqis training Islamist fighters in WMD. American weapons inspectors scoured the Iraqi countryside and found no WMD: no chemical or biological stores and no sign of a nuclear program. They discovered, in fact, that what was left of Saddam's WMD program was destroyed in 1998 when the United States rained 415 cruise missiles and more than 600 bombs on Iraq over a four-day period in an operation called "Desert Fox," launched in response to Saddam's ouster of UN weapons inspectors. The targets included chemical weapons plants and storage depots, missile sites, and command and control facilities.[68] The onslaught left Saddam in a wretched state of weakness. Yet, he refused to let the world know that he was no longer a threat to his neighbors.

This was not an intelligence failure like Pearl Harbor or 9/11 where the guards were arguably asleep at the gate, but a more proactive fiasco, as if amateur sleuths tried to do the work of professional detectives. In their gullible acceptance of false information, Bush's neoconservative dabblers bear comparison to Nazi loyalists who took over the German intelligence agency, the Abwehr, late in World War II after its professional leaders were purged for plotting against Hitler. Because Hitler thought the Allies would come ashore at Calais, the British employed visual and audio deception, double agents, and signal intelligence to reinforce his belief, hoping to ease the Allied landing at Normandy in June 1944. The Nazi dilettantes swallowed the bait hook, line, and cipher,[69] just as the neoconservatives fanned on Curveball. There was one major difference: while the Nazis were deceived by their enemies, the neoconservatives were led astray by their friends. But both can lay the blame primarily on their own blind faith. In the case of Iraq, a president's most solemn decision, whether to send the nation's youth to war, turned on the vagaries of ideology.

Many excellent books have been written about the political and military errors of the Iraq occupation, even by commentators who originally supported the war or accepted the dubious proposition that deposing Saddam would seriously damage global terrorism. While these accounts make valuable reading, they obscure the larger issue about the decision to invade, the first major strategic error by a global power in the twenty-first century. The history of great power post–World War II occupations from the British in Palestine to the Israelis in Lebanon offers hard evidence that the intervention so confidently advocated by neoconservatives and other hawks was all but doomed from the start. The bitter Iraq insurgency will be reviewed near the end of the book. Before that, the context for what is shaping up as a probable American failure must be established, beginning with Britain's loss of Palestine.

CHAPTER 2

ZIONISM: VIOLENT RETURN HOME

> Good Lord, the world is vast enough, there are still uninhabited countries where one could settle millions of poor Jews who may perhaps become happy there and one day constitute a nation.... But in the name of God, let Palestine be left in peace.
>
> —Yusuf al-Khalidi (1899)

The Arab–Jewish conflict can be traced at least as far back as Biblical times when Joshua's zealous army waged holy war, annihilating "by the edge of the sword all in the city [of Jericho], both men and women, young and old, oxen, sheep, and donkeys." (Joshua, 6:20–21).[1] Other Canaanite settlements suffered the same fate in Joshua's brutal fulfillment of God's promise of a Jewish homeland. Subsequent gentile conquerors from ancient to modern times swept through the Promised Land, subjugated the Jews, and scattered them to the far corners of the earth. Through the millennia, the Jewish longing for a land of their own has never died, and when in the late nineteenth century, the Jews began their long revanche, their tactics were generally far more subtle than those of the heavy-handed Joshua. Farmers, artisans, clergy, and scholars entered into a decades-long migration, bought land where they could, built communities, and tried to get along with their new Arab neighbors.

But Arabs viewed them as intruders and resisted them. Violence could not be avoided—Arabs against Jews, Jews against Arabs, and Jews against the British Mandate after World War II. In that context, Jewish terrorists—operating, it must be said, outside the mainstream of Zionism—made a substantial contribution to the birth of Israel. They are not to be identified with the suicide bombers and perverse decapitators of the modern Islamist struggle. None of that happened in the

Jewish uprising. Yet, the Irgun (Irgun Zvai Leumi, or National Military Organization) murdered Arab women and children in the late 1930s in countering Arab reaction to the rising Jewish tide, and, along with the LHI (Lohamey Heruth Israel, or Fighters for the Freedom of Israel, or Stern Gang), killed more innocents a decade later as they waged an insurgency against the ruling British in Palestine who stood in the way of Jewish statehood. One can argue that Jewish statehood was inevitable with or without terrorism, but there is no denying the historical fact that Jewish extremists, condemned by mainstream Zionists, helped make it happen. This chapter traces the triumph of Zionism over the Arabs and the British Mandate, and the contribution thereto of the Jewish insurgency.

Zionism and Arab Nationalism

The British took Palestine away from Turkey during World War I. That was the easy part. In the three decades of British rule, things went from bad to intolerable. The famous Balfour Declaration of 1917 set the standard for diplomatic double talk. British Foreign Minister Lord Alfred Balfour voiced official support for "the establishment in Palestine of a national home for the Jewish people" without prejudice to "the civil and religious rights of existing non-Jewish communities in Palestine." In 1920, the League of Nations sanctioned the British takeover by designating Palestine a Mandate to prepare the native peoples for self-government. The incompatible, passionately held goals of a Jewish national home and Arab statehood left the British in the middle of a firestorm, unable to please either side.

The seeds of destruction were planted long before the British came. Jews have lived continuously in Palestine since ancient times. For centuries it was their homeland. Even in defeat at the hands of the Assyrians in the eighth century BC, the Babylonians in the sixth century BC, and Romans in the first century AD, and the Diaspora that scattered them far and wide, some Jews remained in Palestine. Until the late nineteenth century, they were mostly Orthodox Jews who strictly observed the Torah and coexisted peacefully with their Arab neighbors in segregated communities. They took no part in politics, content to leave their fate up to God— and to the Ottoman Empire, which governed both Palestinian Arabs and Orthodox Jews during the heyday of imperialism.

European Jews began arriving in the 1880s, bringing a hidden agenda to establish a Jewish state in the ancient Jewish homeland. That put an entirely different cast on the Jews' relationship with the Arabs. At first, the Jews came quietly as settlers and bought land that nobody else wanted for more than it was worth. Only a few held on for dear life through hardship and disease. They drained the swamps and irrigated the barren soil, cultivated the land, and made it bloom. They created agricultural communities, kibbutzim, and kicked out the Arab tenant farmers whose families had worked the soil for centuries. These were homeward-bound Zionists at heart, even before the term was invented.[2] Some European gentiles who held strong anti-Semitic views saw a Jewish homeland outside of Europe as the solution to the

"Jewish problem" within Europe.[3] Hardly any European—Jew or gentile—seemed to care that the land was already occupied. David Ben Gurion, Israel's symbolic George Washington, argues in his memoirs that, in effect, the land was not occupied: "There was nothing here [in Palestine]. It was literally a forgotten corner of the Turkish Empire and of the globe. Nobody wanted it, certainly not the Palestinian Arabs who were placidly vegetating in their poverty under the Turks."[4] It soon became clear, however, that the Arabs did not want the Zionists to have it either. Or to state it less harshly, it is fair to say that the Jewish nationalism that the Zionist brought to Palestine awakened an Arab nationalism in the Palestinians.

The pre-Zionist Jews did not talk openly about their intentions because they did not want to provoke the Palestinian Arabs. But correspondence cited by the Israeli historian Benny Morris leaves no doubt of it from day one. A settler wrote to his brother in 1882, "The ultimate goal . . . is, in time, to take over the land of Israel. . . ." Another promised to "conquer the country, covertly. . . . We will not set up committees [so that the Arabs will not know] what we are after; we shall act like silent spies, we shall buy, buy, buy."[5] Major financing for land purchase and maintenance of settlements came from the wealthy French Zionist, Baron Edmund James de Rothschild.

The British Mandate and Jewish Militancy

Into this poisonous atmosphere, the British colonial masters brazenly stepped. At first the Arabs showed great deference to the new rulers. In reaction to the Balfour Declaration, about a hundred Arab dignitaries addressed a moderately worded petition to His Majesty's government expressing sympathy for Jewish suffering in other countries. But, "there is a wide difference between this sympathy and the acceptance of such a nation . . . ruling over us and disposing of our affairs."[6] Inevitably, tensions led to civil disturbances. Arab rioting broke out in 1920 and 1921, costing about a hundred Jewish and Arab lives. The politically sensitive British, who had been largely unmoved by the elegant protest of the Arab dignitaries, reacted to the violence by paying closer attention to Arab interests.

The Jews organized for their own security. The military arm of the Jewish resistance movement, the Haganah, grew out of the 1920–21 disturbances under the sway of the secular socialist left, led by Ben Gurion. It hewed to a defensive posture vis-à-vis the Arabs: protect the Jewish settlements and the Jewish urban neighborhoods, but do not antagonize the Arabs; Jews and Arabs must learn to live together, side-by-side. Throughout the 1920s, Jewish immigration, while it slowed down at times, never stopped, and gave rise to more expressions of Arab grievance. In 1929, the pot boiled over once again, and the British were unprepared for the ensuing riots. In Hebron, Arab mobs killed sixty-four unarmed and poorly protected Jews and wounded fifty-four over two days. These were Orthodox Jews whose families had lived for centuries in the community. The toll would have been greater if sympathetic Arabs had not given shelter to Jewish neighbors. Fighting flared up in Nablus,

Beisan, Jaffa, and Tel Aviv, and in Safed there was another massacre of vulnerable Jews. The British, with fewer than three hundred police in all of Palestine, rushed troops in from Cairo and Malta, and dispatched additional battalions from far-off Britain. It took a week to quiet things down, and by that time 133 Jews and 116 Arabs had been killed.[7]

When the dust settled and the blood dried in 1929, the Haganah admitted that it had failed in its primary mission. It reorganized on a more conventional military scale with a central command structure, greater discipline, recruitment, and training. But it still adhered to a defensive posture, reflecting the core beliefs of mainstream Zionist leaders—men such as Ben Gurion, Theodor Herzl, and Chaim Weizmann, whom Israeli author Amos Elon refers to as the "ideologists of settlement," men of humanist, liberal, and socialist persuasion who abhorred violence.[8] The more important Jewish reaction to the 1929 riots was the rise of the breakaway group, Irgun consisting of Haganah's most militant members who spurned Ben Gurion's self-restraint and adopted an aggressive strategy of retaliation and conquest.

The soul of the Irgun movement was a formidable intellectual named Vladimir Jabotinsky, a linguist, orator, writer, poet, and restless generator of big ideas. He was born in Odessa and studied in Switzerland and Italy. Zionism was the sort of impossible dream to attract him, but his sense of justice was probably the greater motivator to join the movement after pogroms in Russia in 1902 and 1903. His ideas for Zionism were bigger than most, a Jewish state stretching from the Nile to the Euphrates and the transformation of the poor Jew into an aristocrat. He advocated military training, national service in the homeland, and, to hurry things along, Jewish immigration of forty thousand people a year for twenty-five years—a million Jews to Palestine, a very big number at that time. It hardly needs saying that his grand scheme left no room for Arab aspirations—if, indeed, the Arabs had aspirations other than to keep the Zionists out. In World War I, Jabotinsky was one of two prominent Zionists—the other was Weizmann—to support the Allied side, which included the despised tsarist regime in Russia. In 1921, he founded the Union of Revisionist Zionists and infused it with his own alternative ideas for armed rebellion and the forced resettlement of the Arabs outside the Jewish homeland. In 1923, he created a youth movement in Poland, Betar, which measured by the intensity of its training and indoctrination ranked somewhere between the Boy Scouts and the Hitler Youth. Critics on the left thought of Jabotinsky as a fascist without the anti-Semitism. He definitely opposed the socialist ideology of the Haganah.[9]

Initially, the Irgun numbered about three hundred disenchanted Haganah rebels. It reflected all shades of opinion except the left. The first commander, Avraham Tehomi, quickly reached out to recruit young immigrants who had trained in Jabotinsky's Betar camps in Europe, and he oversaw a buildup of arms, whether by open purchase or smuggling. Recruits were sometimes asked to supply their own weapons. In three years he built the Irgun up to a force of three thousand fighters and established training programs in Jerusalem, Tel Aviv, and Haifa. The Betar held up as a reliable source of Irgun recruits until German troops overran Poland in September 1939.

Tehomi and Jabotinsky, however, disagreed over how to respond to Arab attacks on Jews—with violent reprisals or a go-slow approach. Tehomi finally settled the issue by returning to Haganah, leaving to the Irgun perhaps two thousand dedicated fighters and an unsettled command until David Raziel took over in 1937. Raziel, a strong believer in a military solution, took the Irgun deep underground. He was a devout Jew with a probing intellect and a proclivity for Talmudic scholarship. He planned every operation with meticulous care, and his quiet competence inspired deep loyalty among the troops.[10]

With the Irgun leadership unsettled on April 15, 1936, an Arab gang set up a road-block on a winding country road and shot three Jews, two of whom died. The next day Irgun gunmen killed two Arabs. The fighting accelerated. Arab mobs rioted in Jaffa, and Jewish mobs from nearby Tel Aviv retaliated. Arab leaders overcame their internal rivalries and joined forces around the AHC (Arab Higher Committee) led by the Mufti of Jerusalem, Hajj Amin al-Husseini. The AHC called for Arab strikes against Jewish employers and Arab boycotts of Jewish goods, and resorted to attacking both Jewish and British targets in the cities. Jews no longer felt safe outside their neighbor-hoods. The British hoped the uprising would simply die down. They offered to limit Jewish immigration, but the Arabs would accept nothing less than a total cutoff.

After the fighting had gone on for six months, the British finally brought in twenty thousand troops and declared martial law. Then they started clearing the Arab rebels out of the cities and towns, setting curfews, and sometimes blowing up homes. Arab leaders publicly deplored the violence while they quietly raised funds for the purchase of more arms for the rebels. Money poured in from fascist Italy and Nazi Germany, and volunteer Arab fighters crossed the border from neighboring countries. The Jews remained warily defensive, but they were generally content to let the British bear the brunt of the fighting.

In the fall, the fighting died down as a royal commission headed by Lord William Robert Peel, former secretary of state for India, conducted a blue ribbon investiga-tion. He recommended partition and the transfer of 225,000 Arabs out of the pro-posed Jewish territory. The Arabs flatly rejected it. The Jews were not happy either, but the Jewish Agency, the political umbrella organization that included Haganah, accepted it as a step toward the Jewish state.[11] Fighting reignited after Arab assassins murdered a British official in the Galilee. Hundreds of small Arab bands sprang up outside the cities. Altogether there were several thousand full- and part-time fighters, but they lacked central control. They attacked British, Jewish, and even nonsuppor-tive Arab targets, and killed or wounded hundreds of people. At times they managed to bring some rural areas under their control.

This time the Irgun under Raziel jumped into the fray with unrestrained terror. They not only retaliated, but they also taught the Arabs new tricks in the art of terrorism, or as Israeli historian Morris put it, they inserted a "new dimension" in the conflict. "Now, for the first time," said Morris, "massive bombs were placed in crowded Arab centers, and dozens of people were indiscriminately murdered and maimed.... This 'innovation' soon found Arab imitators...; during coming decades Palestine's (and, later, Israel's) marketplaces, bus stations, movie theaters, and other public buildings became routine targets, lending a particularly brutal flavor to the conflict."[12] The Irgun campaign started in November 1937 with an attack at a bus depot near Jaffa that killed two Arabs and wounded five. Within days several Arabs were killed in attacks around the country. The anti-Arab Irgun terror peaked during the following summer. On July 6, 1938, an Irgun operative disguised as an Arab planted two bombs in large milk cans in the Arab market in Haifa. The explosion killed twenty-one and wounded fifty-two. On July 15, an Irgun bomb killed ten Arabs and wounded twenty-nine on a crowded street in Old Jerusalem. On July 25, at the same market in Haifa an explosives-laden container labeled "sour cucumbers" killed thirty-nine and injured forty-six. On August 26, an explosion in the Jaffa market killed twenty-four Arabs and wounded thirty-nine. The Jewish public refused to believe at first that Jews had planted the bombs. The Haganah condemned the Irgun's slaughter of innocents, while at the same time it became more active on a smaller and less ruthless scale. A pro-Zionist British officer, Capt. Charles Orde Wingate, organized Special Night Squads of Haganah volunteers to attack the Arabs when they least expected it.

Still, in that awful summer of 1938, Arab terrorism went on unabated. Forty-four Jews and twelve police died at Arab hands during a three-week period in July.[13] The Arab revolt finally slowed in the fall of 1938. By that time the British had deployed seventeen battalions, which were cracking down hard on the Arab rebels. Many were captured and imprisoned; some were hanged; families were sometimes held hostage; rebel villages were heavily fined, and hideout houses were destroyed. The rebels helped to defeat their own cause by taking repressive measures against uncooperative Arabs who refused to contribute money or give them haven. The rebellion sank into virtual anarchy with rebel bands sometimes fighting each other. It faded out in 1939 after the Palestinians had suffered more than 5,000 killed, 15,000 wounded, and 5,600 imprisoned in three years of rebellion.[14]

The War Years

The British troubles were only beginning. The Irgun had come to the conclusion that Britain, not the Arabs, was the greater obstacle to Jewish statehood. The British Colonial Secretary Malcolm MacDonald made this abundantly clear in March 1939 by announcing limitations on Jewish immigration and land purchases, declaring there would be no Palestinian state of any kind, Jewish or Arab, for ten years, and making its creation subject to Arab approval. On May 17, the day these terms so discouraging to the Jews were published in the form of a White Paper, the Irgun blew up the Palestine Broadcasting Service, and in succeeding weeks set off a series of bombs around the mandate. All this happened with Raziel in prison. He had been arrested in May at about the time the round of violence started. In August, an Irgun bomb killed two British security officers, after which the police rounded up the rest of the Irgun command, which included the hyper-militant Avraham Stern.

When World War II arrived, the Irgun split over which side to back. Jabotinsky declared for the allies five days after the German invasion of Poland. Raziel followed his lead. But Stern, among others, insisted the Irgun should continue to wage terror in Palestine against Britain. In late October 1939, Raziel was released from prison, while the other Irgun leaders were kept behind bars to wonder why their leader rated such special treatment. Raziel's commitment to the support of Britain against Germany made it impossible for him to pick up the terror campaign where it had left off. The Irgun went comatose. The following June, the rest of the Irgun leaders were released and for a few weeks all the Irgun fighting was done with words inside its own high command. Many of the leaders wanted Raziel replaced by Stern. But Jabotinsky reappointed Raziel with whom he had established a good rapport.[15] Stern and his supporters went their own way. Within a week Jabotinsky died, and the Irgun, without their inspirational leader, or their source of strength from Betar, or even a clear mission in Palestine, was adrift without a rudder. Some members joined the British Army. Others bided their time in Palestine. In the spring of 1941, Raziel was killed on a sabotage mission to Iraq for British Special Operations. Irgun's future looked very bleak, but the Jewish struggle gained momentum from a new source.

Stern was deeply committed to and passionately driven by the dream of a Jewish state, and he believed that guns and bombs were the right tools for success. He had joined the Haganah in the 1920s, and then departed with the Irgun after the 1929 riots because he was impatient with Ben Gurion's cautious leadership. As part of the command structure, Stern was satisfied with the Irgun as long as it actively pursued the Zionist dream. No one ever doubted his talent, but Jabotinsky passed over him for the top command out of fear that he was too reckless. So after the Irgun suspended operations against the British with the onset of war, Stern opted out and took most of the Irgun high command with him. The new group numbered several hundred, but was desperately short of arms and cash, and lacked the outside support. They called themselves Fighters for the Freedom of Israel, or LHI for the Hebrew version, but they would live in lore as the Stern Gang.

In truth, forced to fall back on their own resources, LHI acted as much like a gang of criminals as a cadre of freedom fighters. Effective political activism is never cheap. Their first act under Stern was a successful Arab-bank heist in Tel Aviv, which netted them five thousand pounds. More symbolic of their purpose was a bomb planted at the immigration office in Haifa to protest the deportation of illegal Jewish immigrants. Stern even contemplated far-out alliances against the British, in one case with Arab rebels and, in another, with the Axis powers (before word of the Holocaust began leaking out of Europe), but nothing came of either idea.[16]

Early in 1942 the Stern Gang went beyond the pale. In a robbery on a Jewish bank in Tel Aviv, a gunfight broke out when tellers refused to hand over the money. Two Jewish bank employees were killed. The Jewish public was horrified. What Jewish cause justified the holdup of a Jewish bank and the feckless spilling of Jewish blood? The British police picked up two LHI suspects, against whom two high-ranking police officials (both of them Jewish) were well enough informed to provide damaging testimony. Fully aware of this, the LHI responded with a bomb trap that reflected their intimate knowledge of police routine: they set off what appeared to be a premature explosion at one of their bomb factories, and when the security forces rushed to investigate, the Irgun detonated another bomb that killed the two potential witnesses and seriously wounded two other policemen.

That direct assault on the police lifted any lingering restraints for action against the LHI. Immediately, the "freedom fighters" went on the run, and with very little support from the Jewish community, they had few safe places to hide. In early February, acting on a tip, the police raided the LHI headquarters in Tel Aviv, arrested four LHI leaders, and discovered another bomb factory. Although all four men surrendered, Police Inspector Geoffrey J. Morton opened fire, killing two and seriously wounding the other two. Morton said he feared they might set off a bomb.[17]

Stern was next. There was a thousand-pound price on his head, a considerable sum in those days. His picture was carried in all the newspapers and on wanted posters plastered on walls throughout Palestine. Police patrols looked everywhere for him. He slipped from one place to another until he ran short of trusted friends willing to give him shelter. On February 12, again acting on a tip, police raided Stern's hiding place in Tel Aviv and flushed him out of a closet. Inspector Morton was not there at the time, but Constable J. T. Wilkin ordered another officer to call him. When Morton arrived, everyone cleared out except Stern and one other policeman. Stern lay on the sofa, handcuffed. According to the generally accepted account, Morton jerked him up, pushed him toward the window, and shot him in the head. He crumpled to the floor. Morton shot him again in the chest, and then he turned to the officer and said, "You saw that he tried to escape."[18]

Stern was gone, but the Stern Gang carried on without him. Leaderless for the time being, LHI operatives sought to avenge their leader's death. Morton was enemy number one, but he proved to be an elusive target. They tried to detonate a bomb as his car passed on his way to work, but they missed him. The LHI, however, proved to have a long memory. They succeeded several months later in eliminating Israel Pritzker, a shadowy Irgun double agent believed to have been the police informer who led the British to Stern. Another two years after that in broad daylight on a Jerusalem street, they gunned down Wilkin, who had called in Stern's assassin.

What the LHI needed most after Stern's death was a new leader. But all the potential successors were in jail, and, somehow, had to be sprung. They got out in two clever escapes over several months. One escape took that much time because the prisoners had to dig a tunnel more than seventy meters long right under the collective nose of the guards. Once these men were back in circulation, the LHI decided on a triumvirate at the top. It consisted of Yitzhak Yzertinsky (later Yitzhak Shamir, premier of Israel), Dr. Israel Scheib, and Nathan Friedman-Yellin. These were three very different men leading a small, disparate group, all bound together by their common Zionist goal. Scheib was personally nonviolent; he refused even to carry a pistol. While he believed that it would take force to create the new Jewish state, others would have to do the dirty work.

The restructured LHI more or less picked up where it had left off fighting gun battles with the police, until coming to the realization that simple vengeance would not change history. The leadership decided instead to make a bigger splash by killing a prominent official. They targeted Sir Harold MacMichael, the British High Commissioner for Palestine, whom they considered pro-Arab and who followed a policy of exiling illegal Jewish immigrants. The LHI studied his movements carefully over several months, and tried six different times to assassinate him, but every effort failed. On the last occasion, an assassination team ambushed him as he traveled with his wife and two police officials from Jerusalem to Jaffa. At a point where the road snaked along the side of a cliff, they set off a firebomb ahead of his limousine and raked the car with submachine gun fire. The driver and a police escort were seriously wounded, but MacMichael suffered only a slight hand wound and his wife was untouched. MacMichael soon left Palestine at the end of his tour of duty, and LHI went after an even bigger fish, Lord Moyne (Walter Edward Guiness), the British Minister of State in Cairo and close political ally of Prime Minister Winston Churchill. This time, their luck held out.

Eliahu Hakim, a twenty-year-old Sephardi from a well-to-do family, and Eliahu Bet-Zouri, twenty-three and a sabra, eagerly volunteered to carry out the assassination. In autumn 1944, the two men quietly blended in with the Cairo throngs as they staked out Moyne. After a few weeks studying his patterns of work and movement, they struck on November 6. Moyne was arriving for lunch in the posh Gezira district, across the Nile from his office in downtown Cairo. Bet-Zouri shot the driver, Lance Corporal A. Fuller, in the chest as he got out of the limousine to open the door for Moyne. Hakim jerked open the back door and fired three times point blank at Moyne, who died that night in the hospital. Bet-Zouri and Hakim were caught before they could escape. They remained silent for twenty-four hours to give their LHI comrades in Palestine time to scramble for cover, and then gradually let the world know who they were.[19] After their trial and conviction in January, they were hanged on March 23, 1945, as the Allied armies fanned out over Germany in the closing days of World War II.

The Jewish Insurgency and the British Defeat

British intelligence had estimated in 1942 that Haganah had thirty thousand members, and at least half of them were lightly armed. Irgun had a trained cadre of about a thousand men and several thousand auxiliaries and supporters. The LHI radicals were only a few hundred strong, with limited support in the wider community. During the war, tens of thousands of Palestinian Jews served in the British and Allied armies. The British helped to mobilize an elite Jewish unit known as the Palmah for use as a guerrilla force in case of a German occupation of Palestine. The Palmah, about two thousand strong, remained more or less intact after the war under Haganah control, living and working in scattered towns and kibbutzim two weeks out of the month and devoting the rest of their time to fine tuning their military skills. The Haganah regarded their role as defensive against Arab attacks, but British leaders were wary after the war of the Palmah's use in a possible Jewish revolt against the Mandate, especially if Haganah should ally with Irgun and LHI. The British worries were well founded.

The Irgun had already come back to life with Menachem Begin in command. Well known to the Jewish underground, Begin possessed natural qualities of leadership. He joined his local Betar chapter in Brest-Litovsk in 1929 soon after his sixteenth birthday. He idolized Jabotinsky and became a devoted follower. Yet at the World Betar Conference in 1938, he opposed his leader by urging a more aggressive military strategy to bolster the Irgun struggle in Palestine. Jabotinsky cautioned that immigration should take precedence until Jews had gained sufficient manpower to make a military solution effective. Begin won the argument, and in the end rammed through a compromise resolution with Jabotinsky's support.[20] From that bold, but unrancorous challenge to his idol, Begin gained such stature within the Zionist movement that Jabotinsky soon appointed him Betar leader.

The war destroyed Betar, just as it devastated the Jewish population of Poland. Begin fled Warsaw, but after a year hiding out, Soviet police arrested him. Set free after the German invasion of the Soviet Union, he joined the Polish army-in-exile. His unit was on its way to the Middle East, and when the army reached Palestine, Begin was reunited with his wife and some of his old comrades from the Betar. He soon left the army and took over the Irgun in December 1943. On the following February 1, he issued a Proclamation of Revolt, declaring "war to the end" against the British Administration in Palestine and demanding the transfer of power to a provisional Hebrew government. He invoked the shield of God. "The God of Israel, the Lord of Hosts, will aid us," he proclaimed. "There will be no retreat. Freedom— or death."[21]

Begin was tapped for his political skills. The details of military planning he left to others. His specialty was propaganda. He had a way with words, oral or written. From safe houses where he lived under assumed names, he wrote a newspaper called *Herut* (Freedom), which his followers posted on Palestine's walls. The Irgun also broadcast short, intermittent radio messages from shifting locations, trying to keep one step ahead of British tracking technology. But these propaganda efforts, aimed at gaining public sympathy, were initially unsuccessful. The Jewish population generally did not support either Irgun or LHI, fearing that their tactics would ruin chances for a Jewish state.

To wordsmith Begin, the Irgun was a military organization. He considered his men to be soldiers, not terrorists. While waging war against the British, he meant to spare noncombatants. But whether one describes the Irgun as military or terrorist, its activities inevitably cost innocent lives. Early in the Irgun campaign in a botched attack on police headquarters in Jerusalem, six policemen and two Irgun men were killed shooting it out in a courtyard while a demolition team was lifting explosives to a second-story balcony. Writing in *Herut,* Begin regretted the loss of life, but added, "These victims fell in battle, in planned military attack. Soldiers of Irgun do not shoot from ambushes at accidental opponents. There is morality to their arms, and an aim to their war."[22]

While after the assassination of Lord Moyne, the LHI suspended operations for the duration of the war, the Irgun continued to attack government offices and police stations in defiance of the Jewish Agency and the Haganah. In November 1944, Ben Gurion's patience ran out. He declared "open season" on the Irgun. Haganah and Palmah teams waged a determined anti-Irgun campaign that included capturing and torturing Irgun agents and turning in Irgun suspects to British authorities. The Irgun weathered that assault, somewhat battered, and to his credit, Begin refused to retaliate against the Haganah. The thought of Jews fighting Jews horrified him, and he remained true to that principle for life.[23]

In March 1945 as the war in Europe drew to a close, Ben Gurion suspended the hunt for Irgun activists. War's end changed the dynamics in Palestine. For guilt-ridden Europeans and Americans, the Holocaust transformed the Zionist dream into a moral imperative. Jewish leaders called on Britain's Churchill Government to take steps leading to Jewish statehood and turn responsibility for regulating the immigration of Europe's displaced Jews over to the Jewish Agency. But Churchill was voted out of office, and the Labor Government of Clement Attlee adopted a pro-Arab line. Anti-British feelings stirred even within Haganah. The Irgun and LHI had already resumed their attacks on the Mandate, and the Haganah joined them in an uneasy alliance called the Hebrew Rebellion Movement. Britain's worst fears materialized. Palmah units went into action on guerrilla missions, sabotaging railroads and blowing up two Coast Guard stations and eleven bridges connecting Palestine with neighboring Arab countries.[24]

A month later the Irgun carried out its most spectacular act under Begin's leadership by bombing the King David Hotel, a significant center of British colonial activity. The highest Mandate officials had their offices there, including Lieutenant General Sir Alan Cunningham, the high commissioner, and Sir John Shaw, the chief secretary, or administrative officer. The complex was tightly guarded, surrounded with barbed wire, and protected with nets overhead to prevent terrorists from tossing grenades onto the grounds. The key offices were wired to an alarm system that, when triggered, would set off a loud siren and bring patrol cars to the scene. Yet the King David continued to function as a hotel that attracted an elite clientele from near and far. Bombing it held out a near-certain prospect of civilian casualties.

The Irgun planned the attack with creativity and attention to detail, but ultimately slipped up. Amahai "Giddy" Paglin, who became the Irgun's operations officer in the spring of 1946, noticed that deliveries went routinely through British checkpoints to the hotel's basement kitchen. He calculated that large bombs, properly placed next to weight-bearing pillars, would bring the six-story southwest wing crashing to the ground. At midday on July 22, a delivery truck eased past the sentries and pulled up at the basement entrance. Several men and a woman dressed as Arabs unloaded heavy milk churns and carried them beyond the kitchen to the designated pillars while two other Irgun "Arabs" held the kitchen staff at bay with submachine guns. A British officer noticed something strange going on and walked into the kitchen to investigate. He was shot. Someone called the police control center, and a patrol car was dispatched to the hotel. But the Irgun team took only eight minutes to place the bombs and set the timing devices, and before a general alarm could be sounded, they had hustled back into the truck and driven away in a hail of gunfire. Firecrackers and small explosions were set off in the surrounding area to keep civilians away from the hotel. In the lounge above the kitchen a small mixed group of military and civilian people sipped preluncheon aperitifs and engaged in lively chatter, oblivious to the commotion outside and below.

The huge explosion at exactly 12:37 caused the southwest wing to buckle, and then collapse top-to-bottom, one story falling on the next. A large gray-brown cloud rose several hundred feet into the sky, visible from every neighborhood in the city. Stunned onlookers could hear the cries of the wounded and trapped. Soon they saw dust-covered, blood-spattered figures stumble out of the smoke and rubble. Rescue workers arrived on the scene within fifteen minutes, but managed to save only a few. The final human toll came to ninety-one killed and forty-five injured.[25] Begin said the attack was carried out by "soldiers of the Irgun Zvai Leumi," and blamed the British for the "tragedy" of lost lives because they had ignored warnings called into the hotel switchboard, which the British denied receiving. Begin expressed selective compassion for the dead and wounded. "We mourn the Jewish victims," he said, but "We leave the mourning for the British victims to the British." The most numerous victims, the Arabs, he did not mention at all.[26]

Haganah was acutely embarrassed by the incident. Consistent with their partnership in the Hebrew Resistance Movement, Haganah was kept abreast of the planning. But as the appointed day approached Moshe Sneh, the Haganah commander, asked three times for a postponement, the last time on the morning of the bombing. Begin delayed once, and then went ahead without Haganah's say-so. Ben Gurion, who had ascended to political leadership of the world Zionist movement and had initially given the green light, condemned Irgun as "the enemy of the Jewish people," called an end to their short-lived unified resistance, and halted Haganah's own "guerrilla" operations. The British lashed out half-blind with rage. The Commanding General, Sir Evelyn Barker, forbid his soldiers from having "social intercourse with any Jew" for the purpose of punishing them "in a way the [Jewish] race dislikes as much as any, by striking at their pockets and showing our contempt for them."[27] The anti-Semitic tone of his remark caused an international furor that almost overshadowed the bombing itself. Acting on a tip that the Irgun bombers were holed up in Tel Aviv, British troops cordoned off the city for four days and conducted house-to-house searches. Hundreds of suspects were arrested, but none of them was a major figure. Begin spent the time in a cramped secret hide-away in his own house.

After the spectacular King David incident, the Irgun returned more or less to violence as usual: bombing attacks against British offices, taxi and truck bombings on the streets, shoot-outs with police, raids against the railway system, and raids to gather arms or raise money. Occasionally the Irgun and LHI coordinated their attacks, but most of the time they operated separately. Begin frequently conferred with LHI leaders, even if only to make sure they did not get in each other's way.

The British reacted to the terrorist onslaught by setting curfews, beefing up security, and spreading dragnets. The Mandate authorities brought in heavy military support—a hundred thousand personnel at the height of the crisis—and adopted a siege mentality, closing themselves in behind barbed wire and sandbag barricades, which the Jews contemptuously called "Bevingrads," a play on words that combined British Foreign Secretary Ernest Bevin and the besieged cities in the Soviet Union during World War II. Teddy Kollek, later mayor of Jerusalem, told a British officer, "Congratulations! You have finally succeeded in rounding yourselves up."[28]

At the same time, the British pursued policies that infuriated the resistance organizations. Their treatment of Jewish immigrants was particularly harsh. The luckier ones were merely hassled. Many were denied entry, sent to detention camps in Cyprus, or even returned to Germany with its hateful reminders of the Holocaust. It seemed that the harder the British tried to assert their dominion, the more difficult it became to enforce the Mandate laws. The Irgun and LHI responded an "eye for an eye." The British became so frustrated they sought to teach the Irgun a lesson in the spring of 1947 when a military court sentenced two Irgun prisoners to heavy prison terms and flogging. After the flogging was carried out on one of the prisoners, the Irgun grabbed a British officer and three sergeants, and gave each eighteen lashes in retaliation. The court promptly canceled the second flogging, another blow to the troops' morale, already beaten down by months of confinement to quarters, insults from Jewish residents while on patrol, and in the words of the author A. J. Sherman, "a pervasive sense of political drift and imperial humiliation." Begin rubbed it in with posters assuring the individual British soldiers that Irgun had nothing against them personally, but targeted the British regime that "oppressed the Jews in the homeland."[29]

The confrontation went from ugly to vicious. Among the British captives were one LHI and five Irgun prisoners under death sentences. Begin could not believe the British would actually carry out the sentences, but promised to retaliate in kind if they did. To make his threat credible, the Irgun kidnapped two Britons, a retired army officer and a sitting judge, and promised to hang them if the Mandate went through with the executions. When the British postponed the sentences, the Irgun released the hostages, a gesture they regretted when it turned out that the postponement was only that, and not a commutation. On April 16, 1947, the first four men went to the gallows singing the Zionist anthem, "Hatikvah." The execution of the other two was to take place at dawn six days later, April 22. But shortly before midnight of the 21st, they cheated the hangman by blowing themselves up with a hand grenade that had been smuggled into their cell.

The British hunkered down while the Irgun combed the deserted streets in a frantic search for hostages. The drama that ensued played out as black comedy. After several fruitless days and nights they found an Englishman named M. M. Collins one evening in a Tel Aviv bar. They grabbed him and hustled him out to a nearby orange grove, noose at hand, ready to string him up. They checked his identification and questioned him. Who was he? He was a sales manager for a British manufacturer on a business trip to Cairo, and had decided to stop off in Palestine where he had arrived that very day. Why did he come? He was Jewish with an anglicized name. Astonished, the death squad asked him to prove it. All he could think to say was that he had been circumcised, but so had a lot of goyim. The hangman, impatient to put the noose over his head, suddenly made Collins aware of his innocent peril. The Briton lapsed into incoherence, and then, staring death in the face, he began to recite a Hebrew poem of thanks to God for waking children in the morning, and then the Kaddish, the Hebrew lament for the dead, both of which he had learned as a child in the original Hebrew. Finally convinced, the would-be executioners put the rope away, took Collins back to his hotel, and set him free.[30] He left Palestine the next morning, and must have thanked God for waking him up.

The Irgun turned its attention away from retribution to one of history's great prison escapes, the breakout of thirty Irgun and eleven LHI prisoners from the Acre prison on May 4, 1947. They all made it to the street through a hole that an Irgun team blew from outside in a wall of the prison's kerosene storage room, and then piled into three separate trucks and headed out of the city one truck at a time in different directions. (When Arab prisoners discovered the opening, scores of them also fled into the old Arab city.) British paratroopers shot up the first Irgun truck and wiped out its escaping Jews. The others made their getaway with only one man killed by a stray shot. However, a five-man Irgun blocking squad from outside failed to evacuate in time. They were captured. Two were juveniles under the law, and received fifteen-year prison sentences. The other three were condemned to death.

That set the Irgun off on another death-stakes tit for tat. After a couple of bungled kidnapping tries, an Irgun team finally grabbed two police sergeants off a street in Natanya, took them to a diamond factory, and stuffed them into an underground bunker about ten cubic feet in size with a week's supply of food. The bunker was sealed so tight they needed oxygen bottles to stay alive. The British authorities, having no doubt as to Irgun intentions, searched exhaustively for the missing policemen. At the same time, they stubbornly refused to back down from the court sentence, and hanged the three Irgun prisoners on July 29. After conferring with Begin, Paglin hurried to the Natanya hideaway with a few of his men while police scoured the streets outside looking for the two hostages. The terrorists plucked them from their hole-in-the-ground and hastily strung them up from a rafter without allowing them so much as a final message. Then they took the bodies to an orchard outside of town and after setting booby traps left them dangling from a eucalyptus tree. The incident shocked the world. In Britain the act was universally condemned. The Jewish agency in Geneva expressed "mortification" that some Jews were capable of such "vileness."[31]

A thought other than horror already prevailed in London—withdrawal. The *Economist* demanded partition "in the best interest of the long-suffering British."

It described Palestine as "a drain on their resources, a death-trap for their soldiers, and a source of degradation, both to the men who are sent there and to the growing number of potential anti-Semites at home."[32] Britain had other problems as well. In recession from the devastating effects of World War II, it was a financial basket case, deeply dependent on the United States. Its grip on the empire was slipping. India and Burma would soon be independent. As for Palestine, the American government had adopted a pro-Jewish stance at odds with British policy. The die was cast. Withdrawal was only a matter of time. In fact, the British cabinet had already voted earlier that year to take the problem to the United Nations.

The UN General Assembly responded in its bureaucratic fashion by forming a committee to investigate the problem, the UNSCOP (United Nations Special Committee on Palestine), which consisted of delegates from eleven nations, arrived in Palestine on sentencing day for the Irgun men captured in the Acre prison break, and during a five-week stay the committee was on hand for the sorry episode of their hanging and the Irgun retaliation. The delegates also bore witness to the conditions that prevailed in the Mandate: Jewish terror, British armed patrols, barricades, roadblocks, and barbed wire.

After UNSCOP's departure, Paglin carried out one of his most inventive deeds, rubbing salt in the British wounds. Police headquarters in Haifa, housed in an eight-story building and protected by a high wire fence and stacks of sandbags, represented a difficult challenge for the experienced saboteur—but he jumped at the opportunity. On September 29, 1947, an Irgun team pulled up outside the fence in a large gray truck. Elevated on a scaffold above the truck's bed, two runners sloped down off the right side, with a large barrel bomb locked on the runners. The entire apparatus was hidden under a loose tarpaulin. With the pull of a lever, the barrel bomb slid out from under the tarp, cleared the fence, hit the ground, and rolled to the front wall of the building, where it rested momentarily with wisps of smoke trailing from the fuse. Then it exploded. The blast caused extensive damage to the building, killed ten people, and wounded fifty-four. The next day Paglin mailed photographs and diagrams of the bomb to British authorities and Palestine newspapers.[33]

On August 31, 1947, UNSCOP recommended the partition of Palestine, but left open the question of who would enforce the changeover. The British press, venting the public fatigue over the war's terrible toll, made it clear that Britain wanted nothing more than to get out from under their burden. "If the report has to be implemented by force, it must not rest on British arms," exclaimed *The Evening Standard*.[34] On November 29, the General Assembly accepted the UNSCOP proposal by a vote of 33-13. The plan, which recommended an international status for Jerusalem, gave the Jews about three times as much land as had the Peel report a decade earlier, but its real significance was international recognition of the Jewish right to form a state. Ben Gurion accepted it as a practical first step. Begin denounced it as "a bisection of our homeland," but he could only complain and continue working toward the larger revisionist goal.[35] The Arabs found nothing in it to like. The Arab League called the partition of Palestine illegal. Within days, the British Cabinet set May 15, 1948 as the official date for withdrawal. Until then, British troops would observe strict neutrality. The Arabs immediately became the Jews' enemy number one, and the two sides have been in off-and-on conflict ever since.

Britain had been blind-sided by the ferocity of the Jewish campaign. When it wrested Palestine from Turkey during World War I, it could not have imagined this outcome. Its Irgun and LHI enemies did not even exist until several years later. Palestine was a prize of war, another jewel in the imperial crown that sparkled under a sun that never set. But this jewel was deeply flawed in the form of Jewish and Arab nationalism and mutual animosity. Eventually, the jewel fell off the crown, and, in fact, the moldering crown fell off the imperial head. The British had not recognized when they added Palestine to their empire three decades earlier that the age of colonialism was drawing to a close.

The Mandate ended pathetically on May 14, 1948, with government at a virtual standstill and essential services almost nonexistent. A British official complained in the closing days that "the Government's authority is being flouted right and left by both [Arab and Jewish] sides...."[36] No formal transfer of power took place. The British did not know whom to transfer power to, so they just picked up and left. On the last day, the High Commissioner, General Sir Alan Cunningham, reviewed a small honor guard at Government House in Jerusalem. The military band played "Auld Lang Syne" and "God Save the King." He then flew to Haifa where he reviewed more troops before boarding HMS *Euryalus* for the voyage home. The *Euryalus* remained in Palestine waters until the Mandate ended at midnight. The next day the Jewish state was born.

CHAPTER 3

ALGERIA: SAVAGERY UNCHAINED

The naked truth of de-colonization evokes for us the searing bullets and bloodstained knives, which emanate from it. For if the last shall be first, this will only come to pass after a murderous and decisive struggle between the two protagonists.

—Franz Fanon (1963)

Southern Europeans colonized Algeria in the nineteenth century the way Europeans had colonized North America: they came to stay and they took what they wanted from the natives: the most fertile land. There is no question that they made something out of what they took—for their own purposes. For one thing, they planted vines and created a thriving wine industry when the French vines were dying. They built cities along the coast that looked a lot like the European cities they had left behind. In other words, they brought their own culture and planted their own roots. They considered the land part of France and called it *Algerie francaise.* Native Algerians gained from this European enterprise only on the upper fringe. The brightest and the best of the Algerians learned in the French schools and shared in the French culture. The rest were left behind, many in grinding poverty.

By mid-twentieth century, eight million Algerians were ready to take back their land, but one million Europeans were not willing to give it up. To the Algerians, the Europeans were occupiers, but the colonizers saw themselves as legitimate sons of the Algerian soil. These were the circumstances leading up to a bloody war involving undisciplined Algerians learning on the job against the superior, well-trained French army. It was not an even fight. The Algerians took a terrible beating. They tried to improve the odds by using every available weapon, including terrorism against the Europeans, terrorism against Algerian moderates, guerrilla warfare in the countryside, propaganda in the international sphere, and, not least, the ideas the French taught them about justice and freedom. The war lasted seven-and-a-half years from 1954 to 1962. Casualty figures vary widely, as low as 300,000 deaths and as high as a million. Whatever the cost, the Algerians got their land back.

Algerie Francaise

France's tempestuous love affair with Algeria started with a slap in the face. As French history books tell the story, two North African Jewish traders with a profitable monopoly on Algerian exports to the French army in Italy and Egypt ran up a large debt to their Algerian suppliers. When the Algerians demanded payment, the traders appealed to politically connected friends in Marseilles, the transshipment port, who prevailed upon the French consul to intervene on the traders' behalf with Hussein Dey, the governor of Algiers. At that time, 1827, Algeria was loosely under Turkish rule. When the two met they argued, and Dey ended up swatting the Frenchman in the face with his ostrich-feather fan. In Paris, the tottering regime of Charles X took the trivial incident to be a grievous insult, and in 1830 dispatched a military expedition to Algeria. The tail had wagged the dog.

If French Algeria had a droll beginning, there followed an unequal, harsh, sometimes-brutal colonial relationship. In a matter of weeks, the French captured Algiers, but it took another seventeen years to subdue the interior. A young resistance leader named Abd-el-Kader repeatedly outmaneuvered the French army in the rugged mountains of central and western Algeria. The French responded with a ruthless scorched-earth policy. On one occasion, they trapped five hundred Algerian men, women, and children in a large cave and lit fires at the entrance. The smoke asphyxiated all but ten of them. Abd-el-Kader finally surrendered in 1847 and was exiled to Damascus.[1]

Once the French had dug their boots into Algeria's sands, they remained for 132 years. But only a minority of the settlers came from France. Most were Italian, Spanish, and Maltese. By World War I, about 20 percent of non-Muslims in Algeria were of French origin. But the immigrants willingly became French subjects. By the 1950s, 80 percent of the *colons,* or *pieds noirs* (black feet), as the Europeans came to be called, and 20 percent of the Algerian population lived in the cities, where the urban North Africans outnumbered the urban Europeans two to one (except in Oran where the proportion was reversed), and about a third of them huddled in overcrowded shantytowns in dire poverty. Except for the shantytowns and the old Kasbah in Algiers, the two communities were not segregated as in the old American South, but neither were they truly integrated. At the social level of the lower middle class, some lived side by side in the same neighborhoods, and led separate lives, with little intermarriage or social contact. Neither side understood the other very well, or even tried.[2]

Politically, the *colons* considered Algeria an integral part of France. The highest official was the French governor-general under the Ministry of the Interior. He oversaw the prefects, or chief administrators of Algiers, Oran, and Constantine.

These subdivisions were treated as French departments, entitled to send legislators to the parliament in Paris under a two-tiered system that favored the one million *pieds noirs*. French reformers tried to facilitate Algerian assimilation, but always came up short in the face of unremitting opposition from European colonizers whose social attitudes resembled those of white South Africans under apartheid.

In short, Algeria was a powder keg. It exploded on May 8, 1945, when Algeria got a taste of the revolution to come. Unlike the Europeans, who celebrated the Allies' victory over Germany that day, Muslims took to the streets of Setif in protest against French rule. Setif was a predominantly Muslim town eighty miles west of Constantine. Some in the crowd displayed provocative banners, such as "For the Liberation of the People" or "Long Live Free and Independent Algeria." Others unfurled the green-and-white flag of the early resistance leader, Abd-el-Kader. Local gendarmes intervened to seize the offending banners, but at twenty policemen to eight thousand demonstrators, they were quickly overwhelmed. The rioters fanned out looking for Europeans to murder. They killed more than a hundred, wounded a hundred more, and raped many women including one aged eighty-four in a five-day rampage before troops were brought in to restore order. The many mutilated bodies of the dead testified to the savagery of the attacks: women were found with their breasts slashed and men had their sexual organs cut off and stuffed in their mouths.[3]

Retribution carried out in a blind rage was swift and bloody. The Muslims paid many times over for the uprising. The army combed the villages in a "pacification" campaign that led to hundreds of summary executions. Vigilantes entered the jails, pulled out Muslim prisoners, and lynched them in public. The official death count was more than a thousand. Unofficially, it ranged from 15,000 to 45,000. The senseless waste at Setif was an eye-opener for Algerians. A writer who was sixteen at the time, Kateb Yacine, is reported to have said that he never got over "the shock of that merciless butchery," and, in particular, he was incensed at the "betrayal of the values which the French had given us."[4] Ahmed Ben Bella, a future leader of Algeria and a decorated veteran of fighting with the French army during World War II, expressed the sentiments of many Algerians when he wrote, "The horrors [of the Setif massacre]...succeeded in persuading me of the only path: Algeria for the Algerians."[5]

Nine years later, Ben Bella was one of the nine Algerian "historic chiefs" involved in the birth of the FLN (*Front de Liberation Nationale* or National Liberation Front) at a series of meetings in 1954. He was out of the country, however, for an important secret meeting in Algiers, which focused on organizing the FLN and planning for a war of liberation against the French. For purposes of guerrilla operations, Algeria was divided into six autonomous zones, or Wilayas, and a date was set for the start of operations, November 1, 1954, All Saints Day on the Christian calendar. The plotters collected old firearms where they could find them and established crude bomb factories, one in the Kasbah and another thirty miles outside of Algiers. Still, they were desperately short of arms. One goal of the All Saints uprising was to capture

French weapons. By and large, in separate attacks along the breadth of coastal Algeria, the guerrillas performed amateurishly and accomplished very little at a cost of several men killed, including a leader who had attended the organizational meetings.

The FLN launched its offensive with a proclamation that set out the goals of the struggle. Among its salient points, the FLN pledged to restore "the sovereign, democratic Algerian state within the framework of the principles of Islam," to "liquidate the colonial system," and to internationalize the Algerian problem. While vowing to "continue the fight by every means until we realize our aims," the FLN offered to negotiate a peace settlement based on French recognition of total Algerian sovereignty.[6]

From Algiers to Paris, the French scoffed. Interior Minister Francois Mitterand, whose responsibilities included Algeria, told parliament on November 12, "I will not agree to negotiate with the enemies of the homeland. The only negotiation is war."[7] Premier Pierre Mendes-France had just finished negotiating withdrawal from Indochina following the disastrous French defeat at Dien Bien Phu, but on the Algerian issue, he adamantly refused to give ground. He also spoke to the parliament that day: "The Algerian departments are part of the French Republic....Never will France...yield on this fundamental principle....*Ici, c'est la France!*" (Here, it is France!)[8] It would take six years of brutal, uncompromising war before the French under Charles de Gaulle would finally agree to negotiate a settlement within the framework of Algerian sovereignty laid out by the FLN in 1954.

Due to the ineptitude of the rebels' All Saints offensive, the government underestimated the FLN threat. It concluded that stepped-up police action would meet Algeria's security needs, except in the rugged Aures mountains where elite paratroops from France were dispatched to pursue the guerrillas. A war of attrition left the Algerians in the Aures severely depleted by winter's end, but youthful volunteers quickly made up the losses. In the spring, a replenished FLN renewed the offensive against police and army targets throughout coastal Algeria. They also began to attack Muslim civilians and village officials who cooperated with the French. In the Kabyle mountains just east of Algiers, they ordered Muslims to stop using tobacco or alcohol to deprive *pied noir* farmers of a market for their produce, and enforced their ban by cutting off the nose or the lips of offenders. Villagers thus mutilated and unable to close their mouths were said to display the "Kabyle smile."[9]

The government brought in more troops. From 57,000 on All Saints Day, the French army in Algeria swelled to 100,000 by the following spring. More ominously, the French adopted a policy of "collective responsibility." If, for example, FLN attackers could be traced to a certain village, the entire village was held accountable. Villagers might be required to repair any damage done, or, depending on the gravity of the offense, a village might be destroyed and its inhabitants removed to internment camps to isolate them from the FLN. The stress of war and the fear of death took its toll on the troops who became increasingly brutal in the treatment of prisoners, to the point of summarily shooting them. But the more the French cracked down, the more they alienated the Algerian people.

By late summer 1955, the steady pressure of French counterinsurgency had the FLN reeling. Only in Wilaya 2, in eastern Algeria around Constantine, was the resistance in any condition to mount an offensive, although it was hurting there too. Its leaders, Youssef Zighout and Lokhdar Ben Tobbal, were among the most militant in all the FLN. They deliberately plotted a massacre of *pieds noirs* that would bring the wrath of the Europeans down upon their own people, hoping that way to build more resentment against the French and strengthen the FLN's standing with the Algerians. It was shades of Setif, except that the 1945 outbreak of riot and revenge had been more spontaneous.

Zighout and Ben Tobbal decided to abandon their policy of limiting attacks to military targets and, instead, go after civilians of either sex or any age—collective reprisals for collective repression by the French, is the way Zighout put it.[10] They fixed their sights on Constantine, the port city of Philippeville a short distance to the north, and other locations in the area where Europeans lived and worked among the Algerians. They set the date for August 20.

Some of the worst atrocities occurred in al-Halia, a pyrite-mining town outside Philippeville, where 130 Europeans lived among 2,000 Algerian Muslims. Thirty-seven men, women, and children were brutally murdered. Women were raped and disemboweled or decapitated. Small children had their throats slit, or were banged against walls until their heads caved in. Zighout's ugly command was carried out to the letter in al-Halia. The reprisals were automatic. Captain Paul Aussaresses, a French intelligence officer, reported the summary execution of well over a hundred guerrilla captives.[11]

The reprisals over the wide area of the uprising came through in accord with Zighout's strategy. Soldiers fired indiscriminately into crowds of Algerians, killing the innocent along with the guilty. Vigilantes formed committees and administered their own kind of justice. The French gave an official death toll of 123 Europeans and innocent Algerians killed in the FLN attacks, and 1,273 Algerians killed in the reprisals. The FLN claimed that the number of Algerians killed amounted to as many as 12,000.[12]

Despite the awful toll, the FLN considered Philippeville a net gain. Its most powerful political leader inside Algeria, Ramdane Abane, whom the French had released from prison in the spring of 1955, advocated more terror not only against the French, but also against the rural Algerian masses to instill fear in them and bring them in line with the FLN's goals. That set the tone for the elimination of rival Algerian political organizations, including the Communist Party, and led the FLN into its biggest mistake of the war, a terrorist campaign in Algiers.

The Battle of Algiers

The execution of two FLN fighters on June 19, 1956, triggered the Battle of Algiers. Ahmed Zabane had murdered a gamekeeper, and Abdelkader Ferradj had killed eight people in an ambush, including a woman and a seven-year-old girl. In his capture, Ferradj had been crippled and lost sight in one eye. His walk to the guillotine was depicted in the Gillo Pontecorvo film, *The Battle of Algiers,* as part of the education of Ali la Pointe (Ali Amara), a petty criminal and street hustler, watching the execution in the courtyard from his cell in Barberousse prison.[13] Ali became a key figure in the FLN's campaign of terror. Larbi Ben M'hidi, the Algiers leader and one of the historic chiefs, was enraged by this instance of colonial justice. He ordered reprisals against the *pieds noirs* without harming women, children, and elderly men. Saadi Yacef, the military leader in Algiers (who played himself in the movie), went to work on it immediately. Between June 21 and 24, Yacef's fighters gunned down forty-nine European men.[14]

As usual, the reprisals led to counter-reprisals. On August 10, a bomb set by *pied noir* vigilantes blew up a home in the Kasbah where three of the June terrorists allegedly lived. The blast was so powerful it also destroyed three neighboring homes. It killed seventy people altogether, including women and children. That changed the unwritten rules of the struggle in Algiers: Unlike Zighout in the outback, Ben M'hidi had not previously sanctioned a terrorist act with the intention of harming women and children. He ordered Yacef, who had 1,400 men and women in his paramilitary organization, to prepare for a major offensive.

Yacef struck on September 30, a Sunday, choosing three women—Zohra Drif, Djamila Bouhired, and Samia Lakhdari—to deliver bombs to European hangouts in the center of Algiers to avenge the August 10 Kasbah explosion. To get there, they had to pass checkpoints at the edge of the Kasbah, so they changed from their Muslim clothes and dolled up to look like European women on their way to the beach. Each placed a two- to three-pound bomb in her tote bag and covered it with beach paraphernalia. The bombs were set to go off at one-minute intervals, starting at 6:30 p.m.

On their way out of the Kasbah, the women went through separate checkpoints. Zohra Drif actually exchanged flirtations with a Zouave (an Algerian in the French army), and then headed for the Milk-Bar, a cafe across from French military headquarters. Many of its customers were women and children on their way home from the beach. That gave her pause, until she remembered that women and children were among the seventy people killed in the Kasbah bombing. She calmly ordered a soft drink, pushed the bag under her table, paid the cashier, and left. Samia Lakhdari took her bomb to the Cafeteria, frequented by students, where young men and women were dancing to music from a jukebox. As she left without the beach bag she declined an invitation to dance. The two bombs killed three and injured more than fifty. Djamila Bouhired's bomb, which she placed in the hallway at the Air France downtown office, failed to explode.

Ali la Pointe was converted in prison to the FLN cause. Before placing full trust in him, however, Yacef put him through a dangerous test by providing him with an unloaded gun in a mission to kill a cop. When Ali confronted the intended victim and the gun failed to discharge, he had to run for it. If caught, he would have faced a very long prison term. He was in a rage when he next saw Yacef, but calmed down after the leader explained that it was part of his initiation, and then he accepted a real assignment to assassinate a revered figure among the *colons,* seventy-four-year-old

Amedee Froger, mayor of Boufarik, an Algiers suburb, and president of the Federation of Mayors of Algeria. On December 28, Ali killed Froger outside the latter's home with three shots at point-blank range, and then made his escape. French authorities never solved the murder. An innocent man was executed for the crime; the true story emerged after independence. The next day, as Froger's funeral cortege approached the cemetery, a time bomb exploded near the gravesite. Because the cortege arrived late, no one was hurt, but the *pied noir* crowd went into riot mode, striking out at Muslims wherever they could be found. Four innocent Algerians were killed and fifty injured that day. The FLN lay low until the following day when its hit squads went back to work.

With 1,500 Algiers police unable to cope, 4,600 paratroopers under General Jacques Massu were called upon to pacify the city. The "paras" began moving into position in mid-January 1957. The terms of their deployment left Massu, a tough-minded soldier, in total charge of the city. He was not enamored with the assignment. He told his chief of staff, Colonel Yves Godard, to expect heaps of *emmerdements* (deep shit).[15] Massu took care to spread it around. To seal off the Kasbah he assigned the 3rd Regiment of the Colonial Parachutists, under Colonel Marcel Bigeard, a much-decorated officer who had fought bravely at Dien Bien Phu. He also set up a special secret unit for intelligence and "action implementation." To lead it he chose an old comrade, Lieutenant Colonel Roger Trinquier, and, as Trinquier's deputy, Aussaresses, formerly assigned to Constantine and recently promoted to major. Trinquier handled the intelligence, leaving Aussaresses to take care of the "action implementation," which included torture and summary execution. The *emmerdements* did not get any deeper than that. Aussaresses tried to refuse the assignment, but Massu insisted, and told him after he reported for duty that if the paras failed in Algiers, powerful, determined *pieds noirs* threatened to drive a convoy of full gasoline delivery trucks to a wide avenue at the top of the slope on which the Kasbah rests, park them bumper-to-bumper, open the spigots so that the gasoline would flow down through the Kasbah's narrow passageways, and then ignite it, touching off an enormous conflagration that would kill tens of thousands of Algerians along with the leadership of the FLN.[16]

Armed with the police files, which contained dossiers on about two thousand FLN suspects, Aussaresses used a triage system to sort out the most hardened terrorists, whom he interrogated for further leads. The rest were sent off to the barbed wire encampments—concentration camps—in the countryside. By and large, at this point in the war, the Battle of Algiers was waged at night, and that was when Aussaresses did his dirty work with a squad of twenty or so men. "Only rarely were the prisoners we had questioned during the night still alive the next morning," said Aussaresses, who published a book about the experience four-and-a-half decades later, admitting the torture and summary execution of FLN prisoners in 1957.[17] Torture was not as common as most people supposed at the time. "It was only when a prisoner refused to talk or denied the obvious that torture was used," he explained, and when torture became necessary, he favored "beatings, electric shocks, and, in particular, water torture."[18] Whether or not a prisoner was tortured, he was almost always killed, allegedly to save the creaky justice system from case overload. The interrogations and, when needed, tortures took place at an isolated villa called Tourelles outside of Algiers, and the executions were carried out at remote locations farther removed from the city, never twice in the same spot. The bodies were buried where they fell.[19] Aussaresses had never used torture before, but the experience in Philippeville had hardened his attitude. War can do that to people.

The paratroopers' first crisis was a nationwide eight-day general strike, which the FLN had previously planned to coincide with the opening of a UN session in New York, part of its policy of "internationalizing" Algeria's plight. The starting date was January 28. In Algiers, Massu had orders to break the strike at all costs by any means. The strike began in the capital with near total Muslim compliance: shops were closed; municipal workers and school children stayed home. Before the day was out, the paras hitched store shutters by cable to their armored cars and pulled them off the shop facades. Street urchins helped themselves to exposed goods until the proprietors hurried down to guard their stores. Then soldiers went to the homes of municipal workers and escorted them to their offices. Aussaresses gave first priority to utility workers to assure uninterrupted electricity. The missing workers were back on the job within an hour or so. The next day the troops brought the absent children back to school. By the end of the second day the strike was effectively broken. The United Nations had all but ignored it.

Before and after the strike, Yacef carried on with the bombing campaign. On one raid he sent three women to the fashionable part of town to place their bombs in popular gathering places, including a student bar, a brasserie, and the Cafeteria, the place previously bombed. The three bombs killed five people and injured sixty. Fifteen days later, two teenage girls planted bombs in two crowded stadiums that left ten dead and forty-five injured. But the noose was tightening in the Kasbah, and it was getting harder to mount such operations. A waiter at the brasserie swore that a woman had sat at the table where the bomb went off, and gave an accurate description of Djamila Bouazza, another of Yacef's bomb delivery girls. Soldiers now searched all women leaving the Kasbah. The two girls in the stadium bombings were tracked down and arrested. Then the French picked up two key men in Yacef's network, the bomb courier and the mason who had built the bomb factory in the Kasbah. Under hard questioning they gave away its location. A raid on the site yielded the store of Yacef's bombing material and, temporarily, broke the back of his campaign. Quiet settled over Algiers, and Bigeard's 3rd Regiment was reassigned to the outback.

Most of the FLN's political leaders had taken flight, not just out of the Kasbah, entirely out of the country. Now Ben M'hidi slipped away to a safe house in Algiers, but it was not safe enough. The French caught him there while looking for someone else. Within days he died in custody. The authorities reported that he hanged himself. His Algerian friends were always skeptical about suicide, but for forty-four years that was the official French line. In 2001, Aussaresses, who had retired as a general, admitted in his memoir that he had murdered Ben M'hidi with his own hands.[20] Another prominent Algerian who required special treatment, a lawyer named Ali Boumendjel, was pushed off a bridge connecting two buildings six stories above the ground. His death, too, was listed as a suicide.[21]

M'hidi's death left Yacef on his own, isolated from the FLN's high command, and totally in charge of the Algiers network. He spent his time trying to put the pieces back together. He thought the network would shatter again in April when Djamila Bouhired was stopped by a French patrol in the Kasbah. Yacef, walking a few paces behind her dressed as a woman, drew his submachine gun and shot her because he feared that she would talk under torture.[22] She survived, however, and revealed the location of a large bomb cache without being tortured.[23]

In May, madness descended once again on the city. Terrorists shot down two paras returning from a movie. In a spontaneous reaction, some of their comrades followed an informer to a Turkish bath, which he alleged to be an FLN hideout. The paras went in, guns blazing, and mowed down seventy to eighty Muslims, including homeless beggars taking shelter for the night. French officials took no action against the killers, but Yacef responded with a novel idea for killing innocent people. On June 3, men dressed as utility workers and led by Ali la Pointe, placed explosives in small inspection compartments at the base of street lamps near bus stops in the city center. Timed to explode during the rush hour and designed to scatter metal shards from the lampposts, they caused eight deaths and injury to ninety people, but because half the victims were Muslims, the incident did not sit well in the Kasbah.[24]

So to spare Muslims, Yacef tried something different. His target this time was a casino on the western outskirts of Algiers, a *pied noir* hangout. The bomb was set to go off about 7:00 p.m. on June 9, and a fifteen-year-old Muslim employee at the casino placed it beneath the orchestra platform. The dance floor was beginning to fill up when it buckled from the explosion. After the debris stopped flying and the dust settled, bodies and body parts were scattered about. The final casualty toll was nine dead and eighty-five wounded. When General Raoul Salan, the French army commander, heard of the disaster, he rushed to the scene. "There were still fragments of feet in the slippers of the young dancers," he said. "One had to have seen such a spectacle to understand our reactions toward these assassins."[25]

After the dead were buried two days later, the *colons* went berserk. They killed five, injured fifty, smashed a hundred Muslim shops, and destroyed several cars. Some used meat hooks on their victims looted from Muslim butcher shops. Police and soldiers were largely passive. Two hundred European rioters were arrested, but only four were detained—and they were soon released. Ten thousand furious *colons* surged into central Algiers, but were diverted to the monument for the dead, where General Salan led them in singing the *Marseillaise,* and asked them to disperse, which they did.

In July, having carried out his gruesome assignment for six months, Aussaresses was entitled to transfer out, and he left Algeria. Godard took control of intelligence in Algiers and set up a different system. He dispersed FLN turncoats in the Kasbah as undercover agents, who were returning with accurate information.

On August 26, the paras, acting on undercover intelligence, trapped the two top men in Yacef's new bomb squad in a second-floor apartment at the dead-end of a narrow passageway, a scene also depicted in the movie, *The Battle of Algiers*. The French captain wanted them alive, hoping to persuade them to give up Yacef, so he offered to guarantee their lives if they would surrender. They asked for confirmation in writing, and said they would lower their own written terms in a basket. That was agreed. What they actually put in the basket was a bomb, which exploded on the way down and injured three paratroopers, including the battalion commander. The two Muslims were killed trying to make their escape.

A month later, the paras cornered Yacef and Zohra Drif. When the soldiers came to their hideaway at 5:00 a.m. on September 24, the two Algerians secreted themselves in a space between the bathroom and the staircase. But the soldiers discovered it from the hollow sound while tapping on the wall. When they broke through, Yacef greeted them by throwing out a hand grenade while Zohra Drif burned vital documents. Godard arrived on the scene, and set charges. He gave Yacef ten minutes to come out or be blown up. Yacef and Zohra Drif surrendered. In captivity, Yacef was not mistreated. Three times, military tribunals condemned him to death, but the order was never carried out and he was amnestied when de Gaulle became president.

Ali la Pointe and two companions, Hassiba Ben Bouali, a woman, and Yacef's twelve-year-old nephew, Petit Omar, continued to hide out in the Kasbah. But one of Godard's spies found out where, and on the evening of October 8, paras surrounded the building. Ali was called upon three times to surrender. He never answered. The hollow charges laid were supposed to be just powerful enough to knock out the partition behind which the three were hiding. But they were so powerful that they leveled the building and caused adjacent houses to collapse. The three fugitives were found dead in the ruins. Seventeen innocent Muslims died in the other buildings, including four small children.

Apologists for the Bush adventure in Iraq a half-century later often trumpet the French victory in the Battle of Algiers as an object lesson in counterterrorism, but France went on to lose the war for Algeria.

Turning the Tide

Not only did the French army win in Algiers, it also had the upper hand in the countryside. Along the Tunisian border, it built a 200-mile barrier consisting of an electrified fence, barbed wire, and land mines, and defended by 80,000 troops, which severely reduced the flow of arms to the FLN. It was called the Morice Line, after the French Minister of Defense, Andre Morice.

To isolate the FLN from a natural source of recruitment, the French uprooted a million peasants from their villages and moved them into barbed-wire encampments where they lived idle lives off inadequate provisions in overcrowded conditions. Children went hungry, and sometimes starved. The young men who survived slipped out of camp by the thousands and made their way to Tunisia and Morocco to join the FLN. *Regroupement,* as the French called it, succeeded brilliantly in separating the peasants from the FLN, but created such resentment in the internment camps that it converted people with narrow tribal loyalties into Algerian nationalists with an ax to grind.

For a number of reasons, French public opinion soured rather early on the Algerian war. One incident brought it home in the harshest possible way. In May 1956, a regiment of reservists from the environs of Paris arrived in Algeria. Two weeks later one of its patrols, numbering twenty-two men, was caught in an ambush fifty miles southeast of Algiers. Only one of them survived; twenty-one died. It was shocking news in the Paris media, and it pressured then-Governor General Robert Lacoste into adopting tougher measures, including the execution of Zabane and Ferradj, which ignited the FLN's terrorist campaign in Algiers.

Despite the success of the paras in Algiers, their resort to torture had negative repercussions in France. Voices of conscience were raised as early as 1957. One of the first was a distinguished French general, Jacques de Bollardiere, known for his deep commitment to human rights. He proudly marched into Algiers with the paras in January, but soon began hearing complaints from Muslim women about the disappearance of their husbands and sons. He spoke with Massu, not knowing that Massu was in it up to his nostrils. Getting nowhere, he soon asked to be reassigned. Back in France, de Bollardiere wrote a letter to the leftist journal *L'Express,* warning against losing sight "of the moral values which alone have. . .created the grandeur of our civilization and of our army."[26] By September, more than three thousand Algerians had disappeared, according to Paul Teitgen, secretary-general at the Algiers Prefecture, who resigned. Teitgen was in almost daily contact with Major Aussaresses, who conceded in his book that Teitgen was unaware of the major's nighttime activity that would account for the missing persons.[27] Critical reports were published in the leading French newspapers, *Le Monde* and *Le Figaro.* The National Assembly created the so-called Safeguard Committee for Individual Rights and Liberties to investigate the problem. Its report achieved some moderation, but did not stop the abuses, which Massu justified as necessary for the preservation of *Algerie francaise.*

Eventually, they had the opposite effect. They contributed to its demise. Aussaresses' candid report four-and-a-half decades later admitting torture but reducing its importance to the paras is historically interesting, but largely irrelevant. What counted was the French people's perception in real time of the widespread torture of Algerians. That intensified their negative feelings about the war and more than nullified the French victory on the ground.

An incident on the Tunisian border further damaged the French position. On February 8, 1958, in a reprisal raid ordered by an unidentified air force colonel allegedly without higher authority, the French bombed the Tunisian border town of Sakiet, leveling an FLN base, a busy market, a hospital, and a school. About eighty people, including women and children, were killed. "An idiotic act," said the *New York Times* correspondent C.L. Sulzberger, "staged at the precise instant of maximum embarrassment with minimum chances of gaining anything."[28]

The international furor that followed led to the fall of the latest French premier, Felix Gaillard, who trampled on French sensitivities by accepting an Anglo-American offer to mediate the dispute. He was voted out of office in April. With tensions rising on all sides and a vacuum of government in Paris, the governor-general of Algeria, Robert Lacoste, ordered the execution of three more FLN terrorists. The FLN retaliated by executing three captive French soldiers in a move that was purely tit-for-tat without any semblance of justice for the hapless victims. With that, the enraged French army lost its poise and its top generals gradually let themselves become players in a tangled plot that would lead to the return of de Gaulle to power, who most of the plotters hoped would save *Algerie francaise.* Lacoste slipped quietly out of Algiers and returned to Paris. That made the government leaderless in both Paris and Algiers.

May 13 was an eventful day in French history. After a fitting tribute at the monument for the three murdered French soldiers, a young agitator named Pierre Lagaillarde led a mob of youths up a flight of stairs and across a large plaza to the *Gouvernement-Generale* (government building). As police and paratroops stood by and idly watched, several hundred rioters stormed the building and mindlessly turned government offices inside-out by smashing windows and tossing files through the broken glass. Massu, unable to control the crowd, agreed to form an emergency Committee of Public Safety that included Lagaillarde and other rioters. Later Salan arrived on the scene and appealed for calm, but the rioting was already over, and the only way he could exercise command was to go along with the crowd. Paris gave Salan general powers for the maintenance of order in Algiers while he was a virtual prisoner in his own office.[29]

In Paris, a worried National Assembly installed Pierre Pflimlin as the sixth French premier in the three-and-a-half years since the Algerian War began. The right-wing plotters in Algiers feared that Pflimlin would negotiate with the FLN. Pressure grew for de Gaulle's return to power. On May 28, after two weeks in office, Pflimlin stepped aside, and on June 1, the National Assembly voted de Gaulle in.

⁓

After Mendes-France declared Algeria to be an integral part of France (*Ici, c'est la France!*), the premiers who followed him, including liberal socialists like Guy Mollet, kept repeating the mantra, *Algerie francaise,* and sought futilely to embrace that phantom. Pro-*pied noir* factions deceived themselves into believing that de Gaulle was also on their side.

De Gaulle's first task, which he accomplished in his first four months, was to restructure the French government, especially to strengthen the presidency. A new constitution that delineated a greater separation of powers was approved in a referendum on September 28, 1958. In November, de Gaulle, the last premier of the Fourth Republic was elected president of the Fifth Republic, and took the higher office in January 1959.

His next priority was the French army. He wanted no more Dien Bien Phus, the symbol of French defeat in Vietnam. He purged those officers involved with the *pieds noirs* in the crisis of May 13, 1958, ordering them to withdraw from the Committee of Public Safety and warning them to stay out of politics. Massu he promoted and reassigned to command of a corps that controlled the entire Algiers area. Salan, who had been all-powerful in Algiers, exercising both military and civilian control, was recalled to Paris for what de Gaulle led him to believe was a promotion, but turned out to be a sinecure of insulting triviality, military governor of Paris. Salan served out his time to his sixtieth birthday, and then retired from the army—but not from politics.

The FLN did not make things easy for de Gaulle. It greeted his return to office by renewing the terrorist offensive with a rebuilt terrorist organization in Algiers. On June 20, a grenade thrown into an Algiers café claimed nineteen lives, seventeen of them Muslim. In the months that followed, terrorist incidents in Algeria, especially bombings and assassination attempts, rose into the thousands. The FLN also carried out terrorism in France after an earlier failure. Initially, it victimized Algerians who belonged to rival organizations, but eventually it got around to hitting the French as well. On August 24, the FLN struck throughout France against military and police targets. Police stations were attacked in Paris and Lyons, killing four gendarmes. Several fuel dumps were blown up, destroying a day's worth of France's oil supply. The next month a para captain was shot and wounded in Metz, and in Paris, an attempt was made on the life of Jacques Soustelle, former governor-general of Algeria. The attack failed and the would-be assassin was caught. There were other failures, some of them spectacular. For example, a bomb in the ladies lavatory atop the Eiffel Tower was defused, and an attempt to blow up a battleship in Toulon harbor failed. The wave of terrorism in France generated a furious backlash and a determined police crackdown. On September 28, the FLN called it off. Shortly thereafter, acting from a position of strength and deeply conscious of the pressing need to deal with the Algerian problem, de Gaulle began reaching out with peace feelers, only to have them spurned by the FLN.

In Salan's place as the military commander in Algeria, de Gaulle appointed Air Force General Maurice Challe who brought new life to the war in the countryside. Challe mounted vigorous offensives against guerrilla units in their separate Wilayas. He even penetrated FLN strongholds where French troops had never before set foot. After several months of this, Challe had the FLN reeling on the edge of defeat.

Despite Challe's success, de Gaulle became convinced, after a great deal of thought and consultation with his closest advisors and foreign leaders, that the only way out of the Algerian problem was a negotiated settlement. On September 16, 1959, he addressed the nation and for the first time uttered the term "self-determination" for Algeria. He offered the Algerians three choices: total independence, total integration with France, or a federation in which Algeria would be internally independent but tied to France "as regards the economy, education, defense, and foreign relations." The last choice was the one de Gaulle favored.[30] He hoped that way to end the conflict and retain close ties to Algeria while avoiding negotiations with the FLN. Nice try, but the Algerians opted for the first choice, total independence.

The speech actually sent a chill up the spine of the *pieds noirs*. Afterward when de Gaulle visited Algeria, crowds booed him and held up signs saying, "Down with de Gaulle." He was already marked for assassination. Conspirators devised approximately thirty plots to kill him, but they all fizzled for one reason or another. The first reportedly came on June 4, 1958, three days after his investiture on his first visit to Algiers as premier. As he stepped out on the balcony of the government building to deliver a speech, a hit man in a facing apartment drew a bead on him through a telescopic sight. When de Gaulle opened his speech with a dramatic bridge to his listeners, "*Je vous ai compris!* (I understand you!)," the gunman put down his rifle and listened to the rest of the speech.[31]

That reprieve gave de Gaulle some time to think out the Algerian problem, but once he spoke of self-determination for Algeria, the honeymoon was over. Meantime, he faced one major crisis after another—including a general's putsch that entangled the noble Challe and a bloody rebellion by the white colonists. De Gaulle survived them all. In his heart he wanted to preserve French Algeria, or at least to retain close ties to an independent Algeria, but he could see that it was not to be and knew the time had come to give up the past. No other Frenchman of that era could have pulled it off.

Algerie Algerienne

The cease-fire at Evian in March 1962 formally ended the Algerian War, but it did not end the fighting. Thousands of Algerians died at the hands of the colon terrorist organization known as the OAS (*Organization de l'Armee Secrete*), and the FLN responded in kind against the colons until, finally, on June 17 out of sheer exhaustion the parties agreed to a truce. In the main, except for a few isolated incidents, the bloodshed ended and an exodus of Europeans accelerated. They departed in the hundreds of thousands, people born and raised in Algeria, taking only what they could carry in two suitcases and leaving behind most of their worldly possession, even burning their furniture in the streets in a final act of ill-will toward the Muslims. Most of them returned to France penniless, but they were luckier than the Algerians who had served in the French army and remained after the exodus. Anywhere from 30,000 to 150,000 of these *harkis,* as they were called, died horrible deaths at the hands of the vengeful FLN.[32]

However, independent Algeria has not had a smooth ride. The unity that marked the FLN's war against France fell apart after the Algerians took control of the government. While the Algerians' history is a tragic one, it is theirs alone, not imposed from the outside. They have the right to be burdened with their own problems.

CHAPTER 4

Malaya and Kenya: Dying Gasps of Empire

> Britain will be honored by historians more for the way she disposed of an empire than for the way in which she acquired it.
>
> —David Ormsby Gore (Lord Harlech, 1962)

History offers no guarantees. Insurgents have not always won. They can be sure only that they will suffer, and those who contemplate armed rebellion do so only because they feel that living under the heel of a foreign occupier is a fate worse than death. This seems a good place before leaving the colonial period to briefly offer two examples of insurgent military losses, in Malaya and Kenya, which ultimately turned into political triumphs.

Malaya

Historians often cite the British put-down in the 1950s of a communist uprising in Malaya as a prime example of successful anti-insurgency. That would seem to contradict the argument in this book that foreign occupation is a losing game, but the way the British went about their task actually strengthens it because, while the British won a military victory, Malaya won its independence. What could be better for an occupied country than to be rid of the occupier?

Malaya was a wealth-generating British colony before World War II, rich in rubber and tin. Deep in debt from the effects of the war, Britain hurried back afterward to reclaim their southeast Asian colony to help bolster their economic and fiscal recovery. In the unjust colonial system, the colonial power expropriated the colony's wealth. From 1946 to 1950, Britain derived $700 million (about $4.9 billion in

2005 money, according to the U.S. Bureau of Labor Statistics) just from the export of Malayan rubber to the United States.[1]

The Malayan population included two major ethnic blocs, Malay and Chinese, along with a smaller number of Indians and aborigines. Although the Chinese (42 percent) were slightly more numerous, the Malays (40 percent) held the important political offices under the British, and dominated the police and military. The exclusion of the Chinese ethnics made them more susceptible to recruitment by the Communist Party. An open Communist rebellion broke out in 1948 and quickly gained momentum. The insurgents waged war from the jungles largely with attacks on rural villages and occasionally on British colonial targets. They struck their heaviest blow in 1951 with the assassination of the British high commissioner, Sir Henry Gurney, and then probably wished that they had not, because Gurney's replacement, General Sir Gerald Templer, turned the tables on them.

A solid beginning in counterinsurgency had already been made with training programs for Malay police and military personnel and the establishment of "new villages" for ethnic Chinese as part of an effort to isolate the rebels from their source of support. About thirty-thousand Malay police trained as paramilitary "special constables" to help fight the rebels in the jungles. They were taught to secure a village, train local people in self-defense, and move out from there to secure a wider area. Recognizing that they were not waging a conventional war, the British took a humanitarian approach that combined military and political initiatives in what was called the battle for "the hearts and minds of the Malayan people." Templer persuaded London to commit to the struggle over the long haul. He beefed up the training programs with a special emphasis on counterintelligence and encouraged ethnic Chinese to join the security forces—with a modicum of success. About ten thousand alleged hard-core troublemakers, he deported to China. Meanwhile—and this is the important part— he scheduled elections and gradually turned the reins of government over to the Malays. Freedom day—*merkeda,* in the Malay tongue—came on August 31, 1957. Templer was long gone by then, and there remained the task of mopping up the insurgency, which essentially ended with a peace agreement in 1959.[2]

Military scholars have studied the Templer formula for counterinsurgency to a fare-thee-well. It was tried in Vietnam and fumbled by the Americans. But the military tactics of the counterinsurgency may have been less important to the British success than the politics of Malaya. Templer entrusted the Malays with the responsibility of governing themselves and did what he could to integrate the Chinese community into the Malayan power structure. The brilliant part of the Templer paradigm was the ultimate British withdrawal on favorable terms, leaving behind a stable society.

Kenya

While fighting in Malaya, the British scored another colonial victory over the Mau Mau insurgents in Kenya in an uneven struggle that pitted the post–World War II

British Army against lightly armed natives. The Mau Mau insurgents in that conflict were Kikuyu, the largest Kenyan tribe, largely poor and illiterate, and the most heavily impacted by British colonization. The Kikuyu honored their fighters as the LFA (Land and Freedom Army), because land and freedom were their principal issues.

The Mau Mau gained strength and unity from a traditional oath that Kikuyu have taken for centuries in times of crisis to meet the challenges to defending their tribe. The oath-takers ate the flesh or drank the blood of animals (sometimes drank the blood of humans) and pledged absolute loyalty to the cause. In the post–World War II era, the pledge to preserve the land and freedom meant that they would fight to the death to drive out the white settlers. The British colonial government estimated that the oath of unity against British rule was administered to 90 percent of Kikuyu men, women, and children—sometimes forcibly in mass ceremonies.[3] That seems like an exaggeration, because a fair number of Kikuyu professed loyalty to the British crown.

The white farmers had begun arriving late in the nineteenth century. They settled in the central highlands where the air was cool and the soil fertile, and pushed the Kikuyu out. By the mid-twentieth century, thirty thousand colonists occupied about twelve thousand square miles of the richest land, while 1.25 million to 1.5 million Kikuyu were squeezed into two thousand square miles of less desirable soil designated as the Kikuyu reserves. Many Kikuyu families scratched out a living as tenant farmers on white-occupied land. The whites considered them to be nothing more than laborers without rights to the land.

Kikuyu moderates tried to get justice through political activism and legal appeals in colonial courts. Among the moderates, Jomo Kenyatta benefited from a Christian missionary education and spent sixteen years studying and writing in Britain. His book, *Facing Mount Kenya,* celebrated Kikuyu values and made him an icon among his people. Upon his return to Kenya, he assumed the mantle of undisputed leader of the colonized and *bete noir* of the colonizers. The colonial government could not publicly acknowledge anyone who disagreed with their claim to absolute rule.

As much as he cherished freedom, Kenyatta was upstaged by radicals who had fought in the British Army during World War II and returned to Kenya expecting equal treatment with whites as just compensation for their service. When the white settlers continued to oppress them, they turned to violent rebellion. They drew on the traditional oath to recruit fighters and gain wide support among ethnic Kikuyu.

By 1952, Kenya had reached the boiling point. The Mau Mau were raising havoc among the settlers, killing cattle and burning crops, and had set out on a deliberate campaign to assassinate prominent Kikuyu who supported British rule. In October that year, they murdered Senior Chief Waruhiu wa Kungu, perhaps the most avid pro-British Kikuyu. The Mau Mau despised him as a traitor to his country. The new Kenya colonial governor, Evelyn Baring, declared a state of emergency and rounded up Kikuyu leaders, including Kenyatta. Most settlers considered Kenyatta to be the mastermind behind the uprising, a belief probably derived from his celebrity as an advocate for freedom. But it was a dubious conclusion in light of his conservatism. He and five other prominent Kikuyu were convicted of inciting a revolution in a rigged trial in which the prosecution bribed a key witness to fabricate testimony. The judge accepted the hefty sum of twenty thousand pounds to make sure the government won and the venue was shifted outside Nairobi far from the prying eyes of the press.[4] So Kenyatta spent the next eight years of Kenyan upheaval and tragedy in prison. Soon after his release in 1961, he became the first president of a free Kenya.

The arrest and trial of the Kikuyu leaders was part of a colonial strategy of nonlethal decapitation. By isolating Kenyatta and the others, the British thought they could nip the Mau Mau rebellion in the bud. But the get-tough strategy only raised the level of violence. Mau Mau guerrillas began attacking white settlers in addition to black loyalists. One white farmer was disemboweled. A white family that consisted of a six-year-old boy and his parents were hacked to death by their trusted servants. The entire settler community recoiled in horror and fear. As a political bloc, they were far to the right, like the *pieds noirs* of colonial Algeria and the apostles of apartheid in South Africa. Their demands for summary justice went to the extreme of calling for Mau Mau annihilation.

A contingent of British troops flew in and showed the colors in a parade through Nairobi on October 20, 1952, the day Governor Baring signed the emergency order. The Mau Mau, caught unawares, began preparing for guerrilla warfare. They gathered under cover of the thick forests in the foothills of Mount Kenya and the Aberdares range north of Nairobi to train and plan strategy. The following spring, the rebels went on the offensive, attacking outposts of the loyalist Home Guards posted in the Kikuyu reserves. Initially, they got the better of the loyalists. In the bloodiest battle of the war on March 26, 1953, Mau Mau raiders assaulted the village of Lari about twenty miles north of Nairobi. They lured a security patrol three miles outside Lari to investigate the killing of a loyalist whose body was nailed to a tree, and then attacked the undefended village. They torched the homes of loyalists and butchered inhabitants who tried to flee, killing or severely wounding about 120 Christian women and children. The raiders left untouched the homes of Mau Mau sympathizers. The patrol spotted the light of the flames from afar and hurried back to the village. What they saw sent them into shock. They went on a grief-stricken rampage and killed more than two hundred known or presumed Mau Mau sympathizers.[5]

The British military commander, General George "Bobbie" Erskine, called in troop and police reinforcement, the latter to bolster the defense of other vulnerable villages while the army pursued the Mau Mau in their jungle hideaways. It was slow going at first, but then, using prison labor, the British cut roads into the forests and established field camps that allowed them to penetrate ever deeper. They wore the rebels down in small skirmishes, killing or capturing a few at a time, and keeping the rest on the run. The Mau Mau fighting force in August 1953 of perhaps twelve thousand men organized in raiding parties was reduced by December 1954 to fewer than four thousand struggling to survive.[6] As time passed, the Mau Mau raids took on more the character of looking for food than punishing loyalists. The British employed other tactics that hampered the rebels' effectiveness. For example, again with the aid of forced labor, they dug deep trenches in key places at the edge of the forests, filled them with wooden spikes, and built Home Guard posts with tall watch towers to oversee them. The trenches were a nuisance to the insurgents, dangerous to cross at night. Another, more sweeping measure, Operation Anvil, dealt the Mau Mau a fatal blow by cutting them off from Nairobi, their main base of support and source of supplies.

Operation Anvil began in the early hours of April 24, 1954. One loyalist black African and five British battalions surrounded Nairobi sealing off streets and other passageways so that no black could leave or enter. Over the following month, they conducted house-to-house searches, assisted by Home Guard units, Kenyan police, and Kenyan Police Reserves, an auxiliary force of white settlers distinguished for their hatred of the Mau Mau and undisciplined brutality. With the aid of inform-ants, they rounded up more than twenty thousand known or suspected Mau Mau, along with any other Kikuyu who could not provide sufficient documentation, all of whom were carted off to prison in caged trucks. Another two thousand women and four thousand children were relocated to the Kikuyu reserves. Even Kikuyu men affiliated with Christian churches were caught in the sweep and, try as they might, white Christian prelates found it impossible to dislodge their black followers from their incarceration.[7]

Kikuyu outside Nairobi were also apprehended and consigned to the prison system, which consisted of more than a hundred facilities organized according to function—such as screening, labor, and reeducation—and prisoner attitude— whether moderate or militant. The British masters had one overriding goal: to extract from the prisoners confession that they had taken the Mau Mau oath. If they did not renounce their oath they would be held for "reeducation," and if they per-sisted in clinging to their anticolonial values they would be beaten and often killed.

Contrary to the proud boast of David Ormsby Gore that "Britain will be honored by historians" for the way she disposed of her empire, the Kenyan prison system known as the "Pipeline" hardly measured up to the high standards implied. In *Imperial Reckoning,* a powerful indictment of Britain's performance in Kenya, Harvard historian Caroline Elkins mentions the Kenyan labor camps in the same breath with some of the worst detention systems in modern history. "The British colonial government's work camps," she wrote, "were not wholly different from those in Nazi Germany or Stalinist Russia;..."[8] Nothing in the Kenyan system com-pares to the "final solution," the official Nazi policy authorizing the extermination of Jews. Yet tens of thousands of Kikuyu were exterminated without formal sanction by both white and black camp guards. According to Elkins, high British officials from the colonial governor in Nairobi to colonial cabinet secretaries in London knew the overall reality of the prison excesses and kept the lid on. The cover-up continued for a half-century until Elkins documented the horror by interviewing prisoners who survived the Pipeline.

They told of horrible beatings that drew blood and spattered brains; of unsanitary conditions and inadequate food that led to disease and starvation; of the castration of men and the rape of women; and of even more exotic forms of inhumanity. Hard-core Mau Mau who refused to talk and emitted a low droning sound to block out the orders of their guards might have their mouths stuffed with dirt and sand. One man told of squatting at an outdoor toilet to relieve his bowels when a guard pushed him down so that he was stuck rear-first in communal excrement. Within the guidelines for reeducation set by the colonial administration, camp officials enjoyed virtual autonomy in carrying out the policy. Some camps used harsher means than others. Those holding hard-core Mau Mau were particularly brutal. Refusal to confess and renounce the oath was given as justification for the abuse, but the beatings and torture, dished out with great frequency and little or no provocation, often seemed to be the true purpose.

Inmates sometimes recorded complaints and smuggled them out of the camps to family, friends, and sympathizers, who passed them on variously to the colonial administration in Nairobi and London, to Christian missionaries, the opposition Labour Party in parliament, and the British press. When the colonial bureaucracy was moved to make inquiries, they inevitably came to a dead end. The higher ups saw it as their duty to defend the guards and prison officials carrying out their policies—and to protect their own hides. They deflected attacks in parliament, press reports, and calls for independent inquiries of prisoner abuse as hearsay or isolated incidents—until eleven prisoners were beaten to death and many others injured at the Hola camp on March 3, 1959. Initial reports from Hola put contaminated drinking water as the cause of death. But the autopsy revealed death from blunt instruments, and when made public it exploded into a political scandal.

Paul Mahehu, one of about a hundred men assigned to dig for an irrigation canal, told his story to Elkins. They had been warned that they would be beaten that day and, to avoid the clubbing, they were determined to comply with their work order. But the assignment—that every man should dig a hundred cubic feet of earth in two hours—was more than they could possibly accomplish. Three times, a British officer gave the order, and three times the men appealed to reason. Upon the third refusal, the officer blew his whistle and five hundred black guards set upon the hundred-man work crew and beat the men with heavy sticks. "I cannot understand how I escaped death on that day," said Mahehu. "The [guards] were so many, their clubs would hit against each other as several [of them] would try to hit the same detainee. I was hit and I fell down. The detainee who fell over me had his skull broken, and I was covered with his brains and blood. I pretended to be dead. Other detainees continued to be beaten long after they had died."[9]

This was the beginning of the end of the colonial reign in Kenya. The Conservative government did not fall that year, but realized it had only one way to go. The detention camps were closed and the prisoners released. London lifted the state of emergency the following year and granted Kenya independence in 1963.

Despite the gory tales of rebel massacres of white farmers and their families, the Mau Mau killed far more loyalist blacks than whites, thirty-two white settlers against more than 1,800 African civilians. Several hundred more Africans disappeared and were never accounted for. Officially eleven thousand Mau Mau fighters were killed in combat, but Oxford historian David Anderson puts the number at more than twenty thousand.[10] Elkins argues that the full impact of the war and detention on the Kikuyu was far greater than that. Taking into account all the deaths and a birth rate lower for Kikuyu than other tribes due to malnutrition, disease, and absence of the male partners, Kikuyu population growth between 1948 and 1962 was 130,000 to 300,000 births lower than could be reasonably expected.[11]

Certain pieces of successful insurgency were missing in these two examples. The overwhelming superiority of British arms in Malaya and especially Kenya has been mentioned. Furthermore, these rebels had no cross-border sanctuaries where they could heal their wounds and replenish supplies. Such sanctuaries were available to the Algerian, Vietnamese, and Afghan rebels, and it can be plausibly argued that the indigent populations and outside activists provided sanctuary for the Zionists in Palestine and the Shia in occupied Lebanon.

A more important point was a cataclysmic shift in global relationships in what is called here the age of self-determination. The conflicts in Malaya, Kenya, Palestine, and Algeria were the dying gasps of colonialism. The Zionists showed how a colonial power could be defeated—in this case, transplanted Europeans against a European power. The Vietnamese and then Algerians against the French sealed the doom of colonialism—third world rebels against a European power. Failed insurgencies in Malaya and Kenya were rendered moot in a new political atmosphere. In Malaya, Britain pursued an enlightened policy of relinquishing power. The conflict in Kenya was more of a sheer power play until public disclosure of British torture reversed the victory of British arms. Since then, neocolonialist powers—the United States, Soviet Union, and Israel—have intervened in the internal affairs of smaller nations, only to taste the bitter lesson of defeat in irregular warfare. First up is the American defeat in Vietnam.

CHAPTER 5

VIETNAM: SELECTIVE TERRORISM

To win in Vietnam, we will have to exterminate a nation.
—Benjamin Spock (1968)

Anyone who isn't confused doesn't really understand the situation.
—Edward R. Murrow (1969)

Vietnam was America's fourth major war of the twentieth century, different from World Wars I and II and Korea in that there were no front lines. Previously, an army's progress could be measured in territory gained or lost, or by cities and towns captured or surrendered. Vietnam was always more fluid. The Saigon government controlled the cities; the enemy controlled much of the countryside. In disputed villages and hamlets, the government ruled by day, the Vietcong by night. No area under government control, rural or urban, was entirely safe from guerrilla or terrorist attack. No enemy sanctuary within Vietnam was entirely safe from American bombs or combined American/South Vietnamese military sweeps. Against larger North Vietnamese and Vietcong forces in the thick forests and rugged mountains, the Americans would probe for contact, and when made, they would rapidly deploy first-rate troops by helicopter for pitched battles and bring to bear their massive air, artillery, and infantry firepower. When the enemy had had enough, he did not so much retreat as disappear, and the measure of progress would not be in territory, but in body counts. America claims to have won every such battle, but if that is so, the victories were not cheap, because 58,000 Americans died in Vietnam.

With all of its great power and prestige, America trapped itself in what was essentially the occupation of South Vietnam. Some might consider the use of the term "occupation" a stretch in this context. But America, the outsider, came to save what it could from the indigenous communist bad guys. The South Vietnamese anticommunist government was an American creation that grew out of the psyche of the Cold War. In those days, America followed a policy of containing the spread of communism. In Cold War language, it feared the "falling dominos" of Asia. On the heels of the communist takeover of China and the communist aggression in Korea that ended in stalemate, America believed that the loss of Vietnam to communism would lead to the fall of the other nations of southeast Asia. So as the Viet Minh were defeating the French in 1954, America rushed into South Vietnam to bolster the dominos left in play.

For the next two decades, the American response to the communist challenge in Vietnam reflected the styles of four American presidents. Dwight D. Eisenhower, the ex-five-star general who knew enough about war to try to avoid it, chose covert action. He sent an esteemed American undercover agent, Edward Lansdale, to South Vietnam to tutor a hand picked Vietnamese strongman, Ngo Dinh Diem, in anticommunist nation building. John F. Kennedy focused on reforming the American military so it could fight brushfire guerrilla wars while maintaining a powerful deterrent to the main Soviet threat. During his two years and ten months in office, he assigned thousands of specially trained American advisors to South Vietnam to implement and guide counterinsurgency programs. Lyndon B. Johnson introduced combat troops and plunged headlong into war. Richard M. Nixon, contemptuous of the American role in Vietnam, fixated on ending the war with honor. He had higher priorities in mind, namely, America's strategic posture vis-à-vis the Soviet Union and China. In the end America gave up, and left South Vietnam dishonorably.

America lost because it proved unable to cope with a people's war. While American troops were winning most of the large-scale pitched battles, often with heavy casualties, the Vietcong maintained a strong presence in the countryside with a combination of propaganda, intimidation, and selective terrorism. The communists waged a campaign of decapitation at the village level in the early 1960s, killing off political leaders loyal to the Saigon government and other influential men and women who opposed them, usually leaving their victims on display for villagers to see and think about. Fear kept the apolitical peasants in line while the insurgents filled in the leadership gaps they had created with communist cadre, political propaganda, and respect for the rural ethos. American advisors, recognizing the power of the Vietcong terrorist strategy, created a variety of programs to meet the challenge, even to the point of organizing their own decapitation campaign with teams that invaded enemy villages to capture or kill Vietcong leaders. In the end, all the American efforts fell short. America suffered a humiliating defeat.

America's Little Dictator

At a high-level meeting in Washington early in 1954, President Eisenhower's top foreign policy advisors told Lansdale he was going to Vietnam. Lansdale asked Secretary of State John Foster Dulles what he was supposed to do there. "Do what you did in the Philippines," Dulles replied.[1] What he did in the Philippines—or so he is credited—was to roll back the tide of communism. Lansdale, a master of covert action, was so skilled in dirty tricks that he became the model for the fictional hero of a popular Graham Greene novel of the time, *The Quiet American.* Only a few years earlier in the late-1940s, the communist-led Hukbalahap movement had been on the ascendancy. With about 15,000 guerrillas and a million sympathizers, it had expected to take control of the government by the early 1950s. To reverse the tide in the former American colony, the CIA sent Lansdale to Manila. He was considered the man for the job because of his familiarity with the "Huks," having studied their movement during an earlier tour as an Air Force intelligence officer. He befriended the defense secretary, Ramon Magsaysay, and coached him in no-holds-barred counterinsurgency. Magsaysay was an excellent student. With Lansdale's counseling, he infused discipline in the Philippine army, created a ruthlessly efficient secret service, and without the infusion of American troops crushed the communist rebellion. In 1953, Magsaysay was elected president and Lansdale returned to Washington.

It was not until after the fall of the French fortress of Dien Bien Phu that Lansdale arrived in Saigon—on June 1, 1954. By then the situation was urgent and going downhill. Lansdale tried, but could not work his miracle a second time.

He set out to groom an up-and-coming anticommunist Vietnamese stalwart in counterinsurgency the way he had groomed Magsaysay. This time he chose badly or, better to say, the policymakers in Washington chose badly for him. Diem, a Catholic, brother of a Catholic bishop, and son of a mandarin (high government official), had spent time in America, and had impressed some Catholic notables, such as Francis Cardinal Spellman and Senators Kennedy and Mike Mansfield. For the Eisenhower Administration, Diem had two things going for him: his staunch anticommunism and his disdain of the French. The 1954 Geneva accord between France and the Viet Minh left a divided Vietnam pending a unifying election two years later. The Americans moved quickly to persuade the Emperor Bao Dai, the last French-influenced sovereign languishing in comfortable exile on the Cote d'Azur, to appoint Diem as premier of South Vietnam.

Of course, neither Diem nor the Americans had any intention of going through with the election, which everybody knew Ho Chi Minh's communists would win hands down. Up to 700,000 Catholics had fled from north to south after the breakup of Vietnam, and the Catholics were Diem's principal base of support in the south and recipients of government jobs and largesse. But Buddhists were in the majority in South Vietnam, and Diem's prospects in a free election, even with the communists factored out, were virtually nonexistent. So he proceeded to crush the opposition—with Lansdale's advice and support—by taking decisive action against the Binh Xuyen crime syndicate and the militias of the fringe religious sects, Cao Dai and Hoa Hao. The Buddhist hierarchy remained politically passive for the time being.

Not only did Diem prove to be an ardent anticommunist, he was anti-everybody who showed the slightest opposition to his rule, driving them into the arms of the communists. While he toyed with the trappings of democracy, in his heart he was an unreconstructed dictator and had not a shred of political talent. Lansdale, who put fighting communists ahead of the niceties of democracy, engineered Diem's early moves. First, to rid himself of the emperor's clothes, Diem pushed through a referendum that made South Vietnam a republic and extinguished the Bao Dai legacy. He also rigged the election for South Vietnamese president to give himself 98.2 percent of the vote. In elections for a national assembly, he declared that only members of the National Revolutionary Movement, headed by his brother, Ngo Dinh Nhu, could participate. When two non-NRM candidates won seats anyway, these results were nullified.[2] Diem also gained control of the secret police and used it to torture, imprison, and ultimately liquidate his enemies. He became so paranoid and dictatorial that even Lansdale objected, only to find that the policymakers in Washington who had originally assigned him to Saigon were willing to go along with his protégé's excesses.[3]

With no room in the Diem government for open dissent by a loyal opposition, the resistance consequently grew in ways secret and disloyal. Some who opposed Diem aligned themselves with the communist movement and formed the NLF (National Liberation Front) at the end of the decade. Late in Diem's tenure, an alliance materialized between the Buddhist hierarchy and increasingly militant youth as young as preteen. Both were anti-Diem and anti-NLF. The Buddhists devised the strategy for protest and the youth provided the bodies to make it happen, and their energy was a major cause of Diem's ultimate downfall.

Lansdale stayed in South Vietnam about a year until Diem had solidified his power, and returned periodically for consultations. In Washington, he was kept busy defending Diem against American detractors. If he could have had his way, Lansdale would have established an American presence throughout the Vietnamese bureaucracy to facilitate his big ideas on aggressive covert action. As it was, the number of American military advisors in Vietnam continued to grow through the 1950s. It stood at 685 when Eisenhower left office in January 1961, despite a Geneva-dictated cap of 342. (America was not a signatory to the Geneva agreement, so it felt under no obligation to comply with it.) As the Vietcong began to assert itself, President Kennedy upped the ante with helicopter support units, disguised air force combat units, Green Berets, etc., until the level reached 16,000 at the time of his death on November 22, 1963. Three weeks earlier, the Kennedy Administration had given up on Diem by signaling its acquiescence to a military coup, which, to Washington's embarrassment, resulted in the murder of Diem, his brother, Nhu, and Nhu's wife.

More than a decade after Lansdale first arrived in Saigon, the Johnson Administration sent in combat troops. The force grew to more than a half-million ground troops by 1969 supported by America's Herculean air and sea power, and it was never enough.

Vietcong Atrocities

The NLF came into being in December 1959 in an area known as the Parrot's Beak deep in the jungle near the Cambodian border northwest of Saigon. For more than a year before that, like-minded people who dared not speak out publicly held a myriad of clandestine meetings to map a course of underground political opposition to Diem. "Had Ngo Dinh Diem proved a man of breadth and vision," said Truong Nhu Tang, one of seven members of the mobilization committee, "the core of people who filled the NLF and its sister organizations would have rallied to him."[4] Truong, a corporate executive and not himself a communist, believed this even after he discovered that four of the mobilization committeemen belonged to the PRP (People's Revolutionary [Communist] Party), and that three of the four made up the leadership group responsible for organizing the details of the NLF's founding, one of whom traveled twice to Hanoi prior to that first general meeting in the jungle. That made Truong one of the minority noncommunist members on the mobilization committee, although he never thought of himself that way.

Nevertheless, they agreed on guiding principles that included self-determination, private property, pluralism, and unity with the North through negotiations. Truong suspected that these principles, based on their depth and grasp of politics, psychology, and language, contained "the delicate fingerprints of Ho Chi Minh."[5] In other words, not all NLF members were communists, but the communists effectively controlled the movement, and Truong, who was well versed in the elements of Western political thought from his studies in Paris, had no illusions about what lay ahead. The road to freedom would be violent!

Such distinctions were frivolous to Diem and his American mentors, who defined the NLF as a communist front. Indeed, it amounted to no more or less than the political arm of the VCI (Vietcong Infrastructure), the hierarchy of hard-core communists who filled the management positions of the insurgency. Within the VCI, an executive committee known as the COSVN (Central Office of South Vietnam) directed operations. COSVN was answerable to Hanoi's Communist Central Committee, and, in turn, managed the activities of the PRP, NLF, and the Vietcong Liberation Army in seven regional zones, including Saigon as the capital zone. The orders from Hanoi filtered down through COSVN to district to village to hamlet to the fundamental organizational unit, the cell.[6]

The VCI was well positioned for the struggle against the American-backed government in Saigon, with 60,000 main force fighters, trained and equipped like regular infantry, and 180,000 regional and local guerrillas. They could fight pitched battles, carry out guerrilla raids, or wage terrorist campaigns. By 1963, whether through outrage at Diem or intimidation by the Vietcong, half the population of South Vietnam supported them, although that support shifted somewhat in subsequent years to the Buddhist struggle against the Saigon regime.[7]

The basic fighting unit of the Vietcong was the three-man cell, and the most feared of these was the special activity cell, which carried out assassinations, acts of sabotage, and other daring military and paramilitary operations. The units would often be larger, depending on the mission.[8] The armed propaganda teams were a key element for the purpose of recruitment. Typically, they would enter a village at dusk, introduce themselves to the local people in a friendly way, and then gather everyone together for entertainment and lectures on alleged GVN (South Vietnamese government) corruption and American atrocities. Finally, they would get to the main business, recruitment. One visit was rarely enough. As a last resort, if their recruitment efforts did not yield enough volunteers, they would draft able young men. Terrorism would come into play only if the villagers resisted their advances. Then a special activity team would make an example of someone from the village, possibly a corrupt village chief or secret Saigon agent.[9] In a real-life example, on September 30, 1961, a farmer named Truong Van Dang of Long Tri village was seized and tried in a jungle clearing before about fifty villagers for ignoring NLF orders to turn over his rice fields to the tenant farmer who actually worked them. Dang was convicted, of course, and then taken to one of the rice fields for the execution.[10]

Cell leaders were usually Viet Minh veterans or North Vietnamese communist cadre. Rank and file members were drawn from the villages of South Vietnam and ranged in age from about twelve to twenty-five. The optimum age was eighteen.[11] Kids who should have been working in the rice paddies or playing soccer were learning communist dogma, jungle warfare, and terrorism. Their primary terrorist targets were the natural leaders who stood in the way of the Vietcong, those with people skills that villagers turned to for advice. "Potential opposition leadership is the NLF's most deadly enemy," said author Douglas Pike in 1966. "Steadily, quietly, and with a systematic ruthlessness, the NLF in six years wiped out virtually an entire class of Vietnamese villagers."[12] In a later assessment published in 1988, he added, "The assassination rate declined steadily from 1960 to 1965 for the simple reason that there were only a finite number of persons to be assassinated. Many villages by 1966 were virtually depopulated of their natural leaders."[13]

From the Vietcong's birth in the closing days of 1959 to the waning years of the war in the mid-1970s, the political decapitation of the rural opposition was a major communist strategy and its successful outcome a major reason for the communist victory. This strategy of "selective terrorism" the Vietcong inherited from the Viet Minh and earlier nationalists who fought the French going back a hundred years. Knocking off local government workers who lived in the neighborhood had a direct intimidating impact on the people the Vietcong wanted to control, far more than would the assassination of high-ranking officials in the remote cities.[14]

In what Pike calls a routine mission, a guerrilla force of about a dozen entered the village of Phuoc Trach in Tay Ninh province at dawn on February 2, 1961. They killed at least three defenders, including the target of the raid, seventeen-year-old Phan Van Ngoc, a lay priest of the Cao Dai temple who had condemned the NLF from the pulpit as antireligious. After stabbing him to death, the guerrillas withdrew. Not only had they silenced a critic, they had intimidated the entire village and other villages in the region.[15] The Vietcong had little, if any room for religious tolerance. On September 28, 1961, Father Hoang Ngoc Minh, a revered Catholic priest in Kontum parish, was stopped at a roadblock outside Kondela village, taken to a nearby field and dispatched with bamboo spears and a pistol shot to the brain.[16]

Intimidation was especially important in the realm of education, but it did not necessarily involve the murder of the educators. On August 23, 1961 in Phong Dinh province, two schoolteachers, Nguyen Khoa Ngon and Miss Nguyen Thi Thiet, were forced at gunpoint to accompany two NLF guerrillas to their school, Rau Ram, to witness the execution of two farmers, one of whom was shot and the other beheaded. The teachers inferred that they were being taught a lesson not to take an anti-Vietcong attitude with their own students.[17]

The Vietcong wanted the people to understand that the murders were aimed only at those who worked against the revolution, and if it could be achieved with less bloodshed, so much the better. In Quang Nam province in 1962, the guerrillas tacked up messages on the walls and trees of villages warning them not to obey the orders of the Saigon government and to support the revolution: "If you obey our orders you will be forgiven by the people and the Liberation Army....If you work for the enemy you will be punished according to the [Vietcong] law...."[18] Usually, before someone was marked for assassination, he/she would be warned to cease pro-government, anti-VC conduct. After an execution, the executioner would take pains to explain the victim's "crimes" as perceived by the VC, thus attaching a claim of legitimacy to the killing.

In a pertinent example in 1968, Trinh Duc, a committed member of the PRP, had worked his way up to the Xuan Loc district Party branch secretariat and was put in charge of three villages about fifty miles northeast of Saigon. A village covered a fairly large area and contained several hamlets. Some of Trinh Duc's hamlets were contested, loyal to the GVN by day and to the Vietcong by night. Even if the hamlet chiefs were government appointees, Trinh Duc usually left them alone as long as they did nothing against the VC and were not corrupt. Otherwise, they paid the price. For example, the chief in the hamlet of Vinh, whose name was Thuan, was overstating the hamlet's population under Saigon's rationing program to gain extra rice, which he would mark up and sell on the black market. Trinh Duc even did business with Thuan, but then decided that the price was exploitive. He told Thuan he would pay no higher than the government price, but Thuan refused to mark it down. "As far as I was concerned," said Trinh Duc, "this was a frontal challenge. The price wasn't even that important. But if I let him do this, it would have proved he was stronger than I was. The revolution would have lost face in the hamlet."[19] The party decided to execute Thuan, but in a rather formal way consistent with Vietcong procedure. A hit team captured him and brought him back to Trinh Duc, who first explained why he was being executed (as if that would make him feel better about it). Afterward, they pinned a written explanation on his shirt, and carried the body back to his hamlet for display—and saved face for the revolution.[20]

Killing up close and personal is a grim business that repulses most people. Even when one considers it a duty, it requires some getting used to. Nguyen Van Thich, a Vietcong platoon leader whose unit was assigned assassination duty in May 1967, admits to taking the lead in about thirty killings over several years. "It was explained to us," said Thich, "that assassinating and kidnapping GVN officials would help South Vietnam be liberated even faster. Destroying the government infrastructure would help the Party mobilize people to fight.... The motto we used was 'Kill the Wicked and Destroy the Oppressors to Promote Mobilization of the People.'"[21] Originally, their targets were policemen, informers, and hamlet or sub-hamlet chiefs. By 1970, they were giving top priority to former Vietcong working for government propaganda teams, who knew the VC from the inside and were capable of doing serious damage to the organization.

Meticulous planning that might take several weeks and involve a wider network went into the executions. The unit's first victims were two policemen guarding a bridge. The hit squad crept up on them and shot them, killing one and seriously wounding the other. Thich said he had nightmares afterward, but got used to the assignments. "Regardless of what a person might be like," he reasoned, "the order came from above and I carried it out." But he still came to regret some of them. One of his team killed a hamlet chief in the line of duty, by stabbing him in a local shop during daylight hours. Later he visited the chief's widow and learned to his dismay that she was destitute with five children and no way to earn a living. Another case that bothered him was the assassination of a pregnant twenty-one-year-old woman, a former VC who after being arrested by the GVN denounced her former network. The Vietcong sentenced her to death. When she faced the Thich hit team, she accepted her sentence and did not beg for mercy. Thich regretted that he had not postponed the execution until after the baby was born.[22]

～

There was another aspect to Vietcong terrorism, not always so precise or confined to influential people in the rural culture. Large sapper units, composed of hard-core communist cadres organized along military lines, engaged in high profile terrorist acts. The ambush was one such tactic. Again, it involved careful preparation for different stages that included, first, an attack against possibly a civilian target, like a village or a supply convoy or river barge, followed by the entrapment of a relief force. One notorious ambush on March 22, 1961, started with a roadside barrage on a truck, unarmed and without escort, carrying twenty girls belonging to the Republican Youth Corps. The girls were returning home from a celebration in Saigon organized by Diem's notorious sister-in-law, Madam Ngo Dinh Nhu. Nine girls were killed in the initial fusillade. A nearby civil guard unit, responding to the sound of gunfire, was ambushed as it approached the truck. Then a larger civil guard force was called in. The guerrillas fled in apparent disorder across an open rice field into a mangrove swamp with the guards in hot pursuit. No sooner did the pursuers enter the swamp than they, too, were waylaid. Six guardsmen died in the two ambushes.[23]

Harassing fire into villages was a tactic that kept the Saigon forces guessing. It took only a few men to fire a few random shots into a village in the dead of night and call in loud taunts by bullhorn. Casualties seldom resulted, but at the very least it kept the villagers on edge and disrupted their sleep. GVN military units stationed nearby would not know whether to respond to the shooting and risk an ambush or let it pass. The latter decision was militarily correct, but it could also be risky because the shooting might be the precursor to a full-scale attack on the village. Not responding to the original harassing fire could make the villagers feel vulnerable, if not terrified.

In the cities and other areas where government controls were tight, the Vietcong directed much of its energy to espionage and the infiltration of undercover agents into South Vietnamese ruling circles. At the same time its agents committed less frequent, but more spectacular and messier terrorist acts than occurred at the village level. Sapper units engaged in sabotage against military and dual-purpose military-civilian targets, such as Saigon hotels where Americans were billeted, ammunition dumps, roads, railroads, bridges, and communications equipment. Leaflets would warn travelers not to board trains carrying American or South Vietnamese military equipment or personnel. The grenade was a common weapon in the cities, often delivered by boys on bicycles to cafes or cars pausing at traffic lights. Sometimes the bicycle itself, packed with explosives, would be left alongside a building marked for destruction.[24]

Any prominent South Vietnamese who worked against the interests of the Vietcong had reason to watch his back. A world-class cyclist, Le Thanh Cac, was assassinated in 1962 while training outside Saigon because he was forming an athletic organization that it was feared would be anti-Vietcong. The VC tried twice to execute Nguyen Van Bong, director of the National Institute of Administration, which trained South Vietnamese bureaucrats. It succeeded in 1971 by planting *plastiques* explosives inside his car. The South Vietnamese minister of education, Le Minh Tri, was killed in 1969 when a motorcyclist tossed a grenade into his car. A newspaper editor, Ta Chung, was gunned down outside his home in 1967 after ignoring warnings to stop writing editorials critical of the Vietcong. The paper, *Chinh Luan,* continued the editorial attacks, and a year later, sappers were caught trying to sneak into the newspaper office to plant a bomb.[25]

The Vietcong also targeted Americans who could never be quite sure on the bustling streets of Saigon and other cities who were friends or who were foes. One of the first attacks aimed primarily at U.S. personnel occurred on Christmas Eve 1964 at the Brinks Hotel in Saigon where American Army officers were billeted. Two were killed and fifty-eight wounded. On March 30, 1965, a car bomb that exploded outside the U.S. embassy in Saigon claimed 160 American and Vietnamese casualties, including two embassy personnel killed. At that time, the embassy fronted directly on a busy street. The powerful 250-pound blast wrecked the embassy interior and shops on the opposite side the street. Most of the victims were shoppers and casual passersby.[26] On June 26 that year, thirty-one people were killed when two bombs went off simultaneously at the dinner hour outside the My Canh floating restaurant on the Saigon River, patronized largely by U.S. servicemen and wealthy Vietnamese. Nine of the dead were Americans. The mastermind of all three bombings was a Vietcong operative named Nguyen Van Sam, who was later apprehended. Another important Vietcong agent, Nguyen Van Troi, plotted several other Saigon bombings. He was caught mining a bridge near Tan Son Nhut Airport over which U.S. Secretary of Defense Robert McNamara was scheduled to pass on a visit to Vietnam. Troi was executed by a firing squad.[27]

At Hue during the Tet offensive of 1968, Vietcong and North Vietnamese assassination squads raised the bar for atrocity. Tet began with assaults on cities and towns throughout Vietnam in the predawn hours of January 31, including one attack that penetrated the rebuilt and relocated U.S. embassy grounds in Saigon. The most determined attack was at the imperial city of Hue, where nearly ten thousand North Vietnamese troops and Vietcong guerrillas occupied the greater part of that ancient city of 140,000, including most of the walled citadel. In the three-and-a-half weeks of fierce fighting that it took for the American Marines and South Vietnamese forces to regain control, the Vietcong terrorists exacted a particularly bloody toll on the political, religious, and intellectual leaders of the city. Although Hanoi has always denied it, American and South Vietnamese historians agree that up to three thousand civilians died in a deliberate campaign of mass assassinations. A captured document, which laid out the North Vietnamese plan for administering Hue after its capture, set as one of its goals the total disruption of the South's government machinery. In hunting down their victims, the special activity cells apparently worked from a prepared list of the names and addresses of their intended victims, prepared with the help of Hue's former police chief who left in 1966 and turned up in 1968 as the Vietcong's chief administrator. The exact number of assassinations has never been verified. But after the battle, about 3,500 citizens were missing. Between 2,300 and 3,000 bodies were exhumed, many from mass graves with their hands tied behind their backs and their skulls crushed or marked with bullet holes and some who had apparently been buried alive and left to die. The remainder who were unaccounted for may have been secret Vietcong infiltrators who departed with the defeated enemy.[28]

Vietnamese Catholics seemed to be a prime target. Nineteen months after Tet, Vietcong defectors led American troops to a creek bed in rugged mountain terrain ten miles from Hue where lay the skeletal remains of 428 South Vietnamese servicemen, students, and civil servants from Hue's Catholic neighborhood of Phu Cam. Three hundred more victims were found later in the coastal flats, among them Father Buu Dong, a prominent Catholic leader. He had tried to steer a neutral course between the warring sides. In his room, according to local people, he kept a picture of Ho Chi Minh and prayed for the North Vietnamese leader while also accepting American aid for his parishioners. Five-and-a-half weeks before Tet, he is said to have entertained Vietcong and South Vietnamese soldiers together for Christmas dinner.[29] His efforts at conciliation did not save him.

Several Americans and other Westerners were among the Hue victims, some murdered and some marched away as prisoners. High on the list was the senior civilian American advisor in Hue, Philip W. Manhard, of the CORDS (Civil Operations and Revolutionary Development Support), the American pacification agency.

Manhard and about thirty CORDS personnel were missing when the Hue standoff ended. Many of them, including Manhard, turned up in prisoner exchanges at the end of the war.[30] Stephen H. Miller, a twenty-eight-year-old Foreign Service officer, was not so lucky. The Vietcong occupied his house and found him hiding in a closet. His body was recovered a few days later, hands tied behind his back, in a field behind a Catholic seminary. Dr. Horst Gunther Krainick had come with his wife, Elizabeth, from Germany to help found a medical school at Hue University. When the communists occupied Hue, the couple emphasized that they were German and expected no trouble from them. But Germans were on the VC hit list, and on the fifth day of the occupation, the couple was taken into custody. Later, they and two other German doctors were dug out of a shallow grave in a nearby potato field. Two French Benedictine priests who had always got along with the Vietcong were also executed. Father Urbain was bound hand and foot and buried alive. Father Guy was shot in the back of the head.[31]

American Atrocities

Once the United States had committed combat troops to the Vietnam struggle in 1965, a series of major engagements generated the bulk of the headlines back home. The battles were generally fought in jungles with double or triple canopies that neutralized American air power and made it virtually impossible for senior officers to exercise effective command from low-flying aircraft above the battlefield. The enemy also made American artillery a risky call by moving in for close-quarter combat. American strategy hinged on the belief that this war of attrition would reach a point where the North Vietnamese and Vietcong would lack the manpower to replenish their losses, and sue for peace from a position of weakness. This strategy did not take into account the enemy's deep resolve, nor did it recognize the political realities of their stubborn struggle for self-determination.

Tet was the turning point of the war. On the battlefield, the American/South Vietnamese side won Tet hands down, sooner or later retaking every stronghold the communists had occupied in their initial thrust, driving them out with heavy losses. The Vietcong suffered up to 50 percent casualties. It took two years for them to rebuild their forces. Behind the bravado from Hanoi about "an unprecedented victory of scientific quality" at Hue, Vo Nguyen Giap, the North Vietnamese defense minister and master military planner, came under severe criticism from within his own hierarchy for exposing his finest troops to America's devastating firepower.

But appearances trumped the reality. The fact that the communist forces were able to mount such a wide-scale attack throughout South Vietnam and inflict substantial casualties on U.S. troops shook America's political resolve. The antiwar movement gained momentum. President Johnson soon announced that he would not run for reelection. Chicago was racked with antiwar protests during the 1968 Democratic nominating convention. In a historic comeback from the political graveyard, Republican Nixon was elected President that year, and after taking office in

January 1969, he declared a policy of gradual American withdrawal and the "Vietnamization" of the war. It was downhill from there.

From the beginning of the "hearts and minds" battle, long before the arrival of American troops, the advisors wrestled with the problem of Vietcong control in the countryside, and came at it from several different angles. Back in the mid-1950s, Lansdale persuaded Diem to adopt "civic action" programs to win the peasantry's allegiance to the central government—programs such as building roads, bridges, schools, health facilities, and community projects, and introducing the latest crop technology, all seasoned with pro-government propaganda. Diem's efforts at "pacification" were halfhearted. Unable to see beyond his own political survival, he gave the peasantry short shrift. He kept his best troops around Saigon as a kind of palace guard and rewarded them for loyalty to him.

In the early 1960s under American prodding, the GVN introduced the strategic hamlet program to separate the Vietcong from the rural people (isolate the fish from sea, to use Maoist terms). Initially, under CIA management, the Americans adopted the politico-military tactics that proved so effective for the British in Malaya. They deployed small teams of military professionals to an area of Darlac Province, fortified the villages, taught the local people self-defense, and trained a local militia to come to the aid of any neighboring village under attack from the Vietcong. The program earned early success, and the CIA wanted to expand it.[32]

But the U.S. Army high command argued successfully in Washington that the program should be put under its control. That led to its undoing, because the army paid less attention to the "hearts and minds" program and shifted the emphasis to military force. Under the Army's management, the Special Forces relocated farmers to defensible hamlets ringed with barbed wire and moats and fortified with ramparts for which fields of fire were cleared. American Green Berets were assigned to the hamlets to lead the defense. Villagers resented their relocation, their sense of imprisonment, the overcrowded conditions, the destruction of ancestral homes, the longer walks to the fields, and the corrupt Saigon officials who charged them for materials that should have been free under the terms of American aid. The net result was to drive more of them into the arms of the Vietcong who found ways to contact the people in the fields and often slip into the hamlets by mingling with them when they returned at dusk. After the American military buildup in 1965, the army conducted "search and destroy" missions into the countryside that further alienated the local villagers.

Other ideas percolated up through the growing American bureaucracy of counterinsurgency fostered by President Kennedy. American-led, deep-penetration patrols began showing up in villages to compete with the Vietcong in propaganda and infrastructure support. These so-called political action teams consisted largely of VC and NVA (North Vietnamese Army) defectors recruited through the "Open Arms" program.

Soon the CIA was putting together deep-penetration teams with more violent objectives. Some went "over the fence" to Cambodia, Laos, North Vietnam, and the demilitarized zone, chiefly to monitor the Ho Chi Minh trail, but also to kill or capture VC and NVA cadre. Not only was the mission more violent, the patrols were of a tougher breed that included paid Montagnards, ethnic Chinese and Cambodians, and even hardened criminals, prison troublemakers reportedly induced to volunteer for these dangerous missions with time off for bad behavior, i.e., reduced terms for using their murderous skills to kill communists. Dressed like peasants in black pajamas and difficult to distinguish from the Vietcong, they moved about deep in enemy territory without precise orders, looking for opportunities to capture or kill somebody important. According to one SEAL's account, they were told to ignore the rules of engagement about who was or was not fair game.[33]

This idea grew out of a CIA station chief's experience with Vietcong tactics. Soon after his arrival in Vietnam in December 1963, Peer DeSilva witnessed a particularly atrocious scene. As he described it years later in his memoir, a Vietcong team had impaled the bodies of a village chief, his pregnant wife, and a young boy on sharp poles. The woman had been disemboweled and the fetus, spilled onto the ground. Although horrified by the sight, DeSilva could also see the intimidation value of the act. "A bloody act of terror in a populated area," he wrote, "would immobilize the population nearby, make the local inhabitants responsive to the Vietcong and, in return, unresponsive to the government requests for cooperation."[34]

DeSilva wanted hunter–killer patrols in every province of South Vietnam to go after the VCI. These patrols were called PRUs (Provincial Reconnaissance Units). They set out to win the war by a form of decapitation and disembowelment of the Vietcong. It was their job to eliminate the enemy's infrastructure, which consisted of political leaders, hard-core communists, tax collectors, supply managers, local military officers, etc., the people essential to the smooth functioning of VC villages and military operations. It boiled down to a strategy of trying to beat the enemy at its own game of intimidation and selective terrorism.

PRUs worked best when they had precise information about their targets. So the CIA built PICs (Provincial Interrogation Centers) to which VCI suspects would be brought for questioning. The PICs, typically compounds of one-story concrete block, cement, and wood buildings, were put up in every province and manned by Vietnamese interrogators whose questioning routines were established by the Americans. Torture would often be used to loosen VCI tongues. From the information acquired, "blacklists" were compiled and turned over to subsequent PRUs for targeting more VCI suspects. PICs and PRUs became the heart of the Phoenix Program under CORDS, the pacification agency created in 1967 with a military commander, General William C. Westmoreland, and a CIA man, Robert W. Komer, as his second in command. Komer ran the show on a day-to-day basis. In July 1968, he persuaded South Vietnamese President Nguyen Van Thieu to order his police and intelligence agencies to participate in the program, thus expanding the network of hunter–killer, intelligence gathering teams to include South Vietnamese police and military forces.

With all these patrols out hounding the Vietcong, the South Vietnamese questioners at the interrogation centers were kept very busy, and despite (or because of) CIA coaching on interrogation techniques, their methods of persuasion hardly measured up to the standards of the Geneva Convention. At least, Americans tended to look the other way when it came to torture. According to John Patrick Muldoon, the first director of the PIC program, "You can't have an American there all the time watching these things." "These things" included rape, murder, electric shock, water treatment, body suspension, beatings, and the use of attack dogs.[35] A wide variety of people went through the interrogation centers, and not all of them were tortured. But many were.

Truong Nhu Tang, who helped organize the NLF, has given personal testimony of what it was like to be at the mercy of South Vietnamese interrogators. He was betrayed in June 1967 (prior to the implementation of the Phoenix Program) and taken to an interrogation center in Cholon, Saigon's Chinatown, which once served as a headquarters, casino, and drug distribution center for the Binh Xuyen criminal empire. In one corridor of the building, he saw the worst horrors of man's inhumanity to man: "Sprawled out on the floor were...people chained together by the ankles. Many of their faces were bloody and swollen; here and there, limbs jutted out at unnatural angles. Some writhed in agony; others just lay and stared dully."[36] One day soon he would be part of that scene.

He was ordered to confess that he was a communist. When he refused (because he was not) he was subjected to water torture. He was strapped to a bench, face up, a compress over his eyes and nose, his mouth pried open, and soapy water poured into his mouth. Unable to breath, he gagged and lost consciousness. When he woke up a guard was pressing on his stomach to force out the water. He struggled to avoid suffocating in his own vomit. Days later, after refusing once again to admit that he was a communist, guards attached electrodes to his nipples and cranked up an electric charge. The shock burned his eyes and knocked him out once again. He woke up among the twisted bodies that he had seen on the first day. Between tortures, he was confined to a bare cell without furniture or amenities. He could only lie on the cold cement floor, and had to rely on guards to bring him rice with dried fish and provide escort when he needed to go to the toilet. At times, he wished for death. Eventually, his wife came for a visit and persuaded him to confess that he was a communist just to get out of there, which he did. He learned later that she paid a $6,000 bribe to the "butcher" who was in charge of the torture chamber.[37]

Given Truong's experience, it is not hard to imagine what the PICs were like for captured VCI suspects. In sharp contrast, however, defectors who came through the Open Arms program and gave information voluntarily would be returned without being tortured to their homes and families, if that could be done safely. But if the Vietcong found out about the defections, the defectors' chances of surviving would be greatly diminished.

The PRU recruits, trained by the CIA at Vung Tau on the coast east of Saigon, were better organized under the Phoenix Program. To put the official face on it, information was the key to success. Therefore, it made more sense to capture than to kill a VCI, and bring him/her into an interrogation center for questioning to obtain information for future patrols. At its best, that was the way it worked. American leadership of the PRUs was entrusted principally to highly trained Navy SEALs and Army Special Services (Green Berets), with Marines assuming that role in I Corps, the northernmost zone of South Vietnam.

As the SEALs tell it, their operations under the Phoenix Program were very successful. The SEALs, of course, gained fame for underwater demolition in beach clearing operations during World War II. When President Kennedy called for the armed services to meet the challenge of guerrilla warfare, the Navy created SEAL (sea, air, land) teams for special operations. In Vietnam, the SEALs were assigned to the Mekong Delta south of Saigon, and some of the best men among them were given the opportunity to lead PRUs on special missions into Vietcong territory. According to Kevin Dockery who authored a history of the SEALs, "The successes of the PRUs under SEAL leadership were remarkable.... In some provinces, the Vietcong ceased to be a functioning entity because of the actions of the PRUs and their SEAL advisors."[38]

Chief Warrant Officer James Watson became a legend in SEAL history. He jumped at the chance to lead PRUs, which in his area of operations were mercenaries, mostly VC and NVA defectors from the Open Arms program, who knew how to fight. After a few missions together, Watson and his PRU teammates learned to trust in each other and developed a mutual admiration society. Acting on time-sensitive intelligence (so-and-so will be at such-and-such a place at a certain hour), they might start out at a moment's notice, and they never flinched from a fight. On one very difficult operation, Watson took along First Class Radioman Jack Rowell, not because Rowell was a good radioman, but because he was good with a Stoner, a light, rapid-fire machine gun that spewed out bullets at roughly 800 rounds per minute (13 rounds per second). As Rowell described it in an oral history, the unit came into its target by helicopter to a hot landing zone that was under fire from the moment they hit the ground. While Watson and two PRUs headed for the "hooch" where intelligence had located his VCI target, Rowell trained his Stoner on the tree line from which the VC fire was coming. His job was to lay down suppression fire while the rest of the unit carried out their assignments. Before long, the VC opened up from another tree line, and a PRU took a bullet in the leg. So now Rowell had to fight off enemy fire from two directions until Watson came back with his captive. The chopper swooped down for the extraction, and as they all piled on board, including the wounded PRU, Rowell kept firing. At liftoff he stood on the strut, held on with one arm, Rambo style, and kept the Stoner busy with the other. The entire operation took only fourteen minutes. The prisoner, as it turned out, was a VC commander, making it a successful operation.[39]

In his comprehensive book, *The Phoenix Program,* Douglas Valentine chronicles several Phoenix operations—some heroic, some tragic—but most of them were run of the mill. A typical operation would begin at the village level with information provided by a paid informant to the DIOCC (District Intelligence and Operations Coordination Center). Infantry would usually be deployed around a village while PRUs or other commandoes entered it to snatch the VCI suspect who would then be taken to an interrogation center. In one atypical operation in October 1969, Captain Frank Thornton, an American PRU advisor in Long An near Saigon, went in alone to capture Pham Van Kinh, commanding officer of four VC battalions. For backup, two SEALs and four PRUs cruised nearby in a Cobra helicopter. Thornton got his man and successfully radioed for extraction. Another atypical "op" turned into a bloody mess. In this case, a PRU team targeted a VC district official near the Cambodian border on his wedding day. When a PRU burst in on the wedding party, a VC reached for his gun. The PRU opened fire and two or three more PRUs entered the room, guns blazing. Twenty of twenty-two people in the wedding party were killed with no PRU casualties.[40]

In still another atypical operation, a spurned lover gave information that led to the killing of a district Communist Party first secretary, To Van Phoung. The U.S. Army's 1st Division had distributed wanted posters offering 100,000 piasters ($1,000) for Phoung's capture. The woman who was pregnant with his baby came forward to report that Phoung would be meeting with a party official in a tunnel near Binh An Village the following afternoon. A PRU team and its American advisor, Captain John L. Cook, assisted by the South Vietnamese National Police, descended on the site and quickly located the tunnel. After the target refused to surrender and a PRU lowered to negotiate was shot and wounded, Phoung was dispatched with a grenade thrown into the tunnel. His jilted ex-lover identified the body.[41]

While Kinh and Phoung were precisely the kind of hard-core Vietcong operatives the Phoenix Program was created to eliminate, most of those killed at the wedding party were unlikely to have been VCI. But chances are they were counted as such. In fact, most of those reported killed under the Phoenix Program were probably not VCI either, but rather ordinary people living in areas under Vietcong control. CORDS reported 20,587 VCI killed from January 1968 through May 1971. Not to be outdone, the Saigon government reported 40,994 killed in a similar but slightly smaller time frame, August 1968 through mid-1971s.[42] Both figures appear to be exaggerations—the South Vietnamese officials being bigger liars than the American officials.

The incentive for making inflated claims grew out of a quota system initiated by the first CORDS director, Komer, who set province-by-province goals for the elimination of VCI that came to about 1,800 a month for all of South Vietnam. Pressure to fulfill the quotas led to manipulation of the figures, according to an analysis by Professor James William Gibson of Southern Methodist University, who cited CORDS statistics that from January 1970 to March 1971, 87.6 percent of VCI killed were actually combat casualties. Only 12.4 percent, 616 suspected VCI, were victims of Phoenix teams. He also reported the testimony of American intelligence officers that many, if not most of the dead listed as VCI were probably civilians.[43]

There seems little doubt that Phoenix teams deliberately assassinated VCI. The questions are, to what extent, and on whose authority? William Colby, later director of central intelligence, claimed in his autobiography that when he took command of CORDS in 1969, he issued a memo making it clear that assassinations were "specifically not authorized." In testimony before Congress, however, he hedged somewhat, saying he could not rule out the possibility that individuals under his command carried out unauthorized assassinations. But as one low-level intelligence officer testified, those higher up the chain of command had "real reason not to know" how VCI suspects were neutralized, and neutralization became "a sterile depersonalized murder program."[44]

To look at this issue in its darkest light, it is not totally out of bounds to assume that the five hundred victims of Task Force Barker (Americal Division) at My Lai and earlier predations of Tiger Force (101st Airborne Division) in the same general area of Quang Ngai Province were counted as VCI. Both units operated in "free fire zones" with permission to shoot anything that moved, resulting in some of the worst American atrocities of the war.[45] "Indeed," said author Valentine, "the My Lai massacre was a result of Phoenix.... Under the aegis of neutralizing the infrastructure, old men, women, and children became the enemy."[46] In other words, the implicit tolerance for assassination in Phoenix carried over to the loose rules of engagement that rationalized the murder of innocent women, children, and old men in Quang Ngai Province. In wartime, fearful and desperate men facing death can lose their moral compass.

In the end, the Phoenix Program failed. For all the good ops, there were plenty of bad ones. Innocent people died. The PRUs did not always mesh. The Vietnamese often resented their American advisors. VCI often gave false information at the interrogation centers, sometimes telling their interrogators only what they thought their captors wanted to hear, sometimes giving names for the blacklist of people with whom they had personal grudges. More fundamentally, Phoenix failed for the same reason that the Americans lost the larger war—because Americans did not belong there. The Vietnamese communists may have been bad guys by American standards, but it was more important to the outcome of the war that they were Vietnamese.

Vietnam for the Vietnamese

Truong was a Western-educated man who loved freedom. Although not a communist, he joined the NLF to fight for Vietnamese independence. He became the Minister of Justice in the Provisional Revolutionary Government, but after the war he discovered that his rank was meaningless because all power resided with the communist government in Hanoi. When Hanoi introduced a program of "reeducation" for southerners who had lived under and served the former Saigon government, he encouraged the civil servants in the old Justice Ministry to enter the program. Many of them were longtime friends. He drove two of his own brothers to a reeducation camp for what was to be a thirty-day period. The month passed, and more months followed, and they remained in detention. Eventually, Truong arranged to visit their camp. He was chauffeured around, but not allowed to speak with his brothers. He briefly spotted them, and their eyes met. What must his brothers have thought? A few months later he managed to get one of them freed. The other was transferred to a prison in the north and remained in detention for years. Disillusioned, Truong retired from government service, and escaped Vietnam on a boat to freedom. He returned to Paris where as a young man he had absorbed the writings of Western political philosophers, including Marx and Engels.

Truong's tragic experience is a metaphor for what ails the communist paradise. Communist orthodoxy turned Vietnam into a totalitarian state. Depending on one's point of view, that might be unfortunate for the Vietnamese people. Whatever the case, it is for them to live the experience and work out their problems. Vietnam is no threat to the United States, and never was. American policymakers recognized as much in 1995 by establishing diplomatic relations with the former enemy and exchanging ambassadors two years later. In the year 2000, the two nations signed a bilateral trade agreement, which took effect in December 2001. It has not been a perfect arrangement. Trade disputes have arisen, especially from American industries hurt by cheap Vietnamese labor. It is a genuine problem, common in today's world. The good news is the realization in American decision-making circles that we do not have to send half-a-million troops to Vietnam to solve the problem. We have learned to deal with communists in terms of mutual interest. Would it not have been better to learn that lesson without a tragic war?

CHAPTER 6

LEBANON: DOUBLE DEFEAT OF THE WEST

[W]e regard martyrdom [suicide bombing] as a Muslim's choice of the manner in which he seeks to die.
> —Naiim Qassem, Deputy Secretary-General, Hezbollah (1997)

The Iranian Revolution of 1979 was the triumph of a powerful religion-cum-political ideology, a version of Islam that its adherents revere as the unalterable formula for God's kingdom on earth. The revolution's leader, Ayatollah Ruhollah Khomeini, did not intend to end his makeover of humanity with the overthrow of the Shah. Ultimate fulfillment could come only with the establishment of divine rule on the widest possible scale. He realized that it was a daunting task in a wicked world, but he plunged ahead. He started by trying to export the revolution to neighboring Muslim countries, not by outright invasion and conquest, but by indoctrinating local Shiite peoples and undermining their secular un-Islamic governments—godless regimes like Iraq and opulent kingdoms like Kuwait and Saudi Arabia. The Israeli invasion of Lebanon in 1982 offered him another golden opportunity to act on the implementation of God's design.

Within days after the Israeli military juggernaut crossed the border into Lebanon on June 6, 1982, a thousand of Khomeini's Islamic shock troops, the Pasdaran, or Revolutionary Guards, slipped quietly into the inland Bekaa Valley to establish terrorist training camps and spread their extremist doctrine. A mixture of battle-scarred terrorists and callow youth, most of them Lebanese Shiites, flocked to the camps where the zealous Iranian teachers prepared them for *jihad* (holy war) and *shahada* (martyrdom). They believed that the heyday of the nationalist PLO (Palestine Liberation Organization) was fading fast, and that the torch of resistance to Israel and the West was passing to the soldiers of God. Before the year was out, a *shahid* (martyr) would personally deliver a horrible new weapon—a simple, inexpensive, dreadfully effective low-tech system known in the West as the suicide bomb.

The world has not been quite the same since. In pure destructiveness, the suicide bomb is nowhere near the nuclear bomb. But if you were a soldier on occupation duty, it would be unsettling in the extreme to think that while on patrol a man or woman in the street might blow you out of this world, or while comfortably asleep in your bed, a car bomber might see that you never wake up. Over time, living on the edge of doom, you are likely to take stock of your fears. It could also affect thinking at the highest levels of government. In the near term, spectacular suicide bombings persuaded the Reagan Administration to withdraw the American Marines from Lebanon, and over the decades-long Israeli occupation of Lebanon, the suicide bomb was one important weapon in a relentless guerrilla campaign that the Shia waged to drive the Israelis out, arguably the first military defeat in Israel's brief history.

Professor Augustus Richard Norton has described Lebanon as "a complex weave of families, clans, and factions for whom political ideology is only of modest importance in defining political behavior."[1] Lebanon in the early 1970s was a disunited nation that maintained an uneasy peace with itself. The growing populations of Muslim Shia, Sunni, and Druze sects resented the dominant political role of the Christian Phalange Party founded by Pierre Gemayel in 1936.[2] Being in power gave the Phalangists control over patronage and the nation's budget priorities. Obtaining power was in no small measure a function of ruthless strong-arm activity. One of the more effective political tools was assassination. To further complicate the picture, the PLO, which had been driven out of Jordan in 1970, had become a law unto itself in parts of Beirut and southern Lebanon.

In 1975, a modern reenactment of the ancient tribal vendetta triggered a civil war that raged on and off for fifteen years. Gunmen killed four Phalangists on April 15 in an attempted assassination of Gemayel. Later that day, Phalangists retaliated against the presumed perpetrators from the PFLP (Popular Front for the Liberation of Palestine) by attacking a bus and killing twenty-six people who were probably innocent of any crime except that of being Palestinians in the wrong place. The fighting spread. The war was on. Initially, the fighting raged between the Phalangists and the PLO. Although widely unloved in Lebanon, the Palestinians received help from small contingents of their Sunni and Shiite Muslim brethren. By the autumn of 1976, after more than a year of fighting during which the Muslims gained the upper hand, the desperate Phalangists looked beyond Lebanon's borders for support. In a move that shocked and angered the Muslims, Syrian President Hafaz al-Assad rescued the Christians by intervening militarily on their side. Relative calm returned to Lebanon with an agreement brokered by the Arab states, which left a sizable Syrian presence in the Bekaa Valley. Although a Maronite Christian was elected president that year, the Christians controlled only a small coastal enclave in the north and a few southern villages. Syrian forces took over most of the north and the upper Bekaa Valley in the east, while Shiites, Sunnis, and the PLO held sections in the south. The Druze retained their traditional homeland in the Chouf mountains, while a de facto border, the "Green Line," separated Beirut into Muslim and Christian sectors.

Yasser Arafat turned his attention back to the PLO's campaign of cross-border incursions and artillery bombardments against Israel. In March 1978, Palestinian terrorists ambushed a bus near Tel Aviv, killing thirty-five Israelis and wounding more than seventy. Israel responded with a limited invasion of Lebanon, "Operation Litani," and pushed the PLO away from the border. The UN Security Council passed Resolution 425, which called on Israel to withdraw from all Lebanese territory. It also created an interim force, UNIFIL (United Nations Interim Force in Lebanon), to monitor the border. Because the IDF (Israel Defense Force) used American-made antipersonnel cluster bombs in Lebanon that were supplied for defense, then President Jimmy Carter threatened to cut off military aid to Israel.[3] The IDF pulled back in June after creating a "security zone" controlled by a Lebanese Christian militia friendly to Israel, the so-called South Lebanese Army under the command of Major Saad Haddad. However, these moves did not stop the PLO, which launched eighty-nine terrorist operations against Israel between 1978 and 1981, resulting in nine dead and fifty-seven injured. One foray struck a children's nursery at Kibbutz Misgav Am.[4] Long-range artillery and rocket attacks also continued, especially against exposed communities in the northern Galilee. At the Israeli border town of Qiryat Shemona, more than half the population of about fourteen thousand fled south between 1974 and 1981 to avoid the shelling. Those who remained spent considerable time in air raid shelters.[5]

On June 3, 1982, agents of Abu Nidal shot and wounded the Israeli ambassador to Britain, Shlomo Argov, in a failed assassination attempt. Mossad (Israeli intelligence) construed it as a provocation designed to bring Israeli retaliation against Arafat, whom Abu Nidal despised with a passion equal to, if not greater than that with which he hated Israelis. But the government of Menachem Begin ignored the subtleties of radical Arab politics, and launched air strikes against PLO targets in Beirut. PLO leaders opted to return the fire with artillery and rocket bombardments of the northern Galilee, which established the pretext Israel needed for the new invasion that came only three days after Argov's shooting.[6]

As far as much of the world knew, this would be another limited operation to drive the PLO out of artillery range. But Ariel Sharon, Begin's defense minister, had bigger ideas that he tried to keep to himself and his coterie of close right-wing followers, unsuccessfully, as it turned out, because Sharon's intentions were widely known and supported in Israeli political circles, right and left.[7] Sharon waged full-scale war against a weak PLO force that was no military threat to Israel, and covered the invasion with the Orwellian codename, "Operation Peace for the Galilee." He prepared the IDF for a lightening thrust to Beirut to link up with the Phalange, which actually had coaxed the Israelis to invade in its continuing bid for outside help to retain power.[8] Sharon's goal was to expel Arafat and the PLO from Lebanon once and for all. On the way to Beirut, he planned for the Israeli army to go out of its way to engage the Syrians in the Bekaa Valley, hoping to end Syria's influence on Lebanese politics.[9] And this time, the Israelis had the "green light" from the Reagan Administration in Washington.[10]

Militarily, he achieved all that he set out to do, although not as smoothly as planned. Along the way, the army ran into pockets of stiff resistance and took more casualties than expected. Politically, Sharon fell far short of his goals. Although he succeeded in driving out the PLO, he failed in his efforts to dominate Lebanese politics at the expense of Syria and impose a peace treaty favorable to Israel.

The nature of the war shocked many Israelis. "This was Sharon's war," a heavy-hearted Jacobo Timerman lamented. "For the first time [in Israel's history], war was not a response to provocation."[11] Many Israelis wept with Timerman to find that they were the aggressor nation, destroying homes, leveling cities, and killing combatants and noncombatants indiscriminately.

After a ten-week siege of the Palestinian stronghold in Beirut, highlighted by daily artillery bombardments, the PLO bowed to pressure from its Muslim allies and agreed to vacate Lebanon. A multinational peacekeeping force, led by American Marines and including smaller contingents of French and Italian troops, was brought in to guarantee safe passage. After the PLO's departure, the peacekeepers redeployed to troop ships offshore.

The peace turned to dust after the assassination of the newly elected president, Bashir Gemayel, the new Phalange leader and son of the party's founding father. Bashir, a tough-minded, iron-fisted leader, was the man Israel wanted for the job, and his election was partly indebted to the intimidating presence of Israeli troops outside Beirut. He was killed when a bomb planted by a Syrian agent blew up Lebanese army headquarters. The IDF then entered Muslim West Beirut, breaking a commitment to the Americans to stay out (after the Americans had made that promise to the PLO), and stood by as vengeful Phalange militiamen carried out the infamous slaughter of Palestinian men, women, and children at the Sabra and Shatila refugee camps. An Israeli investigative body, the Kahan Commission, was unable to establish an official death toll, but accepted an Israeli army intelligence estimate of seven to eight hundred. Red Cross officials estimated eight hundred to a thousand.[12] The Lebanese government said 762 bodies were actually recovered, but that approximately 1,200 more were buried privately by relatives.[13] Other estimates go higher, allegedly because the Christian militia covered up thousands of bodies before journalists discovered the atrocity.[14] The Kahan Commission concluded that Sharon bore "indirect personal responsibility" because he failed to order "appropriate measures for preventing or reducing the chances of a massacre...."[15]

Sharon was stripped of his Defense portfolio, but remained in the Cabinet. Begin never recovered from this mortifying political setback, and following the death of his wife, he lost all interest in governing. He soon resigned as prime minister and got out of politics entirely.

Less than a week after the IDF launched the invasion, Iran set in motion its bold attempt to export the Islamic revolution to Lebanon, which would soon expose the weak resolve of the United States and ultimately turn Israel's triumph into a series of humiliating withdrawals. Several hundred elite troops of the Iranian Revolutionary Guards flew on June 12, 1982, from Tehran to Damascus, then trekked some thirty-five miles over a back road used primarily by smugglers to the ancient city of Baalbeck at the northern end of the Bekaa Valley. There, they set up camps to preach the beatitudes of divine rule and teach the lethal skills of terrorism. The area was shut off to the outside world, which, in any case, was focused on the Israeli siege of Beirut. From the embassy in Damascus, the hard-line Iranian ambassador to Syria, Ali Akbar Mohtashemi, ran a forward base of support for the Baalbeck outpost. The Syrian President, Assad, disgusted with his Christian allies, incensed by the Israeli invasion, and anxious to retain his influence in Lebanese politics, found it in his interest to cooperate with the Iranian initiative.[16]

Baalbeck became a magnate for the revolution that drew a potent cluster of young Lebanese Shiites and other Arab militants, which originally operated below the radar of Israeli and Western intelligence. From Amal, the mainstream Lebanese Shiite movement, Hussein Musawi led a coterie of rebellious followers to Baalbeck to make common cause with the Iranians. He formed his own breakaway organization, Islamic Amal. From Force 17, the elite PLO security unit, a Shiite named Imad Mughniyeh from a village in southern Lebanon brought his thirst for revenge and his expertise in explosives to the Iranian camps. He eventually would have a hand in suicide bombings against the Israeli and international troops in Lebanon as well as other terrorist activities. From Iraq came surviving members of al-Dawa, a militant group that had formed around the ideas of Khomeini during his days in Najaf, and was crushed in late 1970s and early 1980s by Iraqi President Saddam Hussein. They were only some of the dedicated, tough-minded men who came to the Iranian camps to learn how to fight irregular warfare against Israel and the West. Before the formal emergence of Hezbollah, they were loosely organized as the Lebanese National Resistance and covertly referred to as Islamic Jihad.

On November 11, 1982, five months after the Iranian Revolutionary Guards arrived on Lebanese soil and two months after the departure of the PLO, seventeen-year-old Ahmad Qassir, a member of the Lebanese National Resistance, rammed a white Mercedes filled with high explosives into Israel's military headquarters in Tyre. The blast killed 141 people, including seventy-five Israeli troops and Christian militiamen, and destroyed the eight-story building.[17] The Lebanese journalist Hala Jaber credits Iran for inspiring this creative form of martyrdom.[18] For her it invoked images of the Iran–Iraq War when the Islamic extremists sent teenage and preteen "martyrs" running through enemy minefields to clear the way for Iranian soldiers to advance. The crazed children wore white headbands, and shouted, "*Shahid, shahid*" (martyr, martyr), as, in American correspondent Robin Wright's expression, "they literally blew their way into heaven."[19]

Qassir's violent act was only the beginning. After the Sabra and Shatila incidents, the American-led multinational peacekeepers had returned to Lebanon, allegedly to stabilize Lebanese politics. Thomas L. Friedman of the *New York Times* argues that the reimposition of the American troops was a knee-jerk response to the Sabra and Shatila massacre, conceived in naiveté about Lebanon's tribal politics. The impulse for this policy, said Friedman, "came out of something very deep in the American psyche: a can-do optimism, a conviction that every problem has a solution if people will just be reasonable."[20]

At first, it seemed to work. The Marines mingled easily with Lebanese Muslims and Palestinians, and an ingenuous American optimism took hold in Beirut that all was well. The policymakers in Washington, looking at Lebanon through an American prism, determined that the way to long-term stability was to strengthen the central government of Amin Gemayel who had succeeded his murdered brother, Bashir. They did not see his party as just one faction in a brutal civil war. When Gemayel asked them to equip and train the Christian-dominated Lebanese army, the Americans jumped right in, and became identified in Muslim eyes with the Christians. Gemayel, a poor excuse for a politician with all the wrong instincts for coalition building, began using his U.S. connections to browbeat the Muslims.[21]

The Reagan Administration had argued internally over the reentry of the Marines. Ideologues in the State Department and on the White House staff favored it. The Pentagon brass, and particularly the Joint Chiefs of Staff, firmly opposed it. The ideologues won the president's support.[22] The American force of 1,500, even though supported by the big guns and significant air power of a U.S. Navy flotilla offshore, could only pretend to be powerful. Not intended as an occupying force, its purpose was intimidation, as if its mere presence was enough to calm the stormy seas of Lebanese politics. To make matters worse, the Marines bivouacked at the international airport on terrain that offered weak defenses, and the troops were constrained by tight rules of engagement, their M-16s half-loaded (the clip attached to the rifle, but no bullet seated in the chamber).[23] The first hint that relations with the Muslim population were turning sour came when the children started throwing rocks at patrols instead of asking for candy. On March 16, 1983, a grenade attack left five Marines injured. From that point on, the Americans kept their weapons fully loaded.

A month later, on April 18, 1983, America made its first big down payment on the price of its support for Gemayel. Shortly after 1:00 p.m., a dark delivery van sped past the gate to the American embassy compound in East Beirut and crashed into the front wall. The explosion, equivalent to four hundred pounds of TNT, caused a wing of the seven-story building to collapse. Sixty-three people were killed and 120 injured. The dead included seventeen Americans, nine of them intelligence agents. The blast wiped out the entire Middle East contingent of the CIA, including Robert Ames, the former station chief and, at that moment, the agency's Middle East analyst. The timing was hardly coincidental; it was the product of a tip from Soviet intelligence to the Syrians who shared it with the Iranians. The bombing was plotted in meetings at the Iranian embassy in Damascus chaired by Ambassador

Mohtashemi. The key planners, Mughniyeh and Mustapha Badredeen from al-Dawa, paid close attention to details about embassy routines, security arrangements, and traffic in and out of the compound.[24]

In August, fierce fighting broke out in Beirut between Christians and Muslims. It started with the Phalange militia against the Shia, and soon escalated. Druze and Sunni Muslims joined the Shia. The Lebanese Army intervened against the Muslims, and Muslim soldiers deserted the Army in droves to join their brethren. A heavy house-to-house struggle raged for four days. The exposed Marines, whose position lay within the Shia district, got caught in the cross fire and took casualties, including two deaths. In September, the Israelis pulled back from the Chouf mountains, which overlook the airport, leaving Christians and Druze to fight over possession of the abandoned Israeli stronghold, which, historically, had been the Druze homeland before the IDF displaced them. Again, the fighting was heavy, even vicious, but the Druze gained the upper hand. And again, the Marines were in the line of fire and suffered casualties. Two more died. The Marines struck back with forays outside their perimeter and called in strikes from naval guns offshore, all justified as self-defense.

By now the Lebanese army was composed almost entirely of Christians. When it got down to its last stronghold in the mountains, the Gemayel government appealed to the Americans for help. Robert McFarlane, diplomatic troubleshooter for the Reagan Administration, happened to be in Lebanon trying to mediate the conflict. He responded to Gemayel's plea by ordering Marine Colonel Timothy Geraghty to call in naval artillery and air attacks against the Druze. It meant taking sides militarily for the first time, an abandonment of the Marines' neutrality. Geraghty objected. He worried about his exposed position. "We're sitting ducks," he told McFarlane.[25] But the order stood. The nuclear-powered cruiser USS *Virginia* fired more than seventy rounds on the Druze position, and the Christian lines held. The air strike was no longer necessary, and it was called off. A week later the fighting ended in a cease-fire, but the Muslim resentment over the American intervention burned hotter than ever. Shia sniping from the shantytown neighborhoods that abutted the airport became a regular activity.

At about 6:30 a.m. on October 23, a serene Sunday morning that found the Marines sleeping late, a big Mercedes truck turned into the airport parking lot, circled twice as it picked up speed, broke through several barriers, and crashed into the first floor lobby of the battalion headquarters building. The entire four-story structure collapsed in a powerful detonation equivalent to six tons of explosives. Marine and naval personnel were crushed beneath the rubble. Many died instantly; others suffered a slow, agonizing death as rescuers scrambled desperately to reach them. The final toll was 241 dead, dozens more wounded, some of the wounded maimed for life. The cost of American intervention was the highest since the Vietnam War.

Again, the planning by Mughniyeh and Badredeen had been meticulous. The Marine barracks had been under surveillance for months. The terrorists knew that on Sunday mornings the Americans slept late—as at Pearl Harbor. The bomb-laden truck that approached the checkpoint looked like any that delivered produce from a nearby market.[26]

Four miles away and twenty seconds later, another bomb destroyed a building occupied by a company of French paratroopers. Fifty-eight French soldiers died.

Ten days later, another suicide bomber rammed a bomb-laden truck into the headquarters of the IDF in Tyre, killing twenty-nine Israeli troops and more than thirty Palestinian and Lebanese prisoners. It was the second time within a year that Lebanese terrorists had blown up the Tyre headquarters of the IDF, this one in a different building at another location. Anonymous callers to the media gave credit for the three explosions to "Islamic Jihad," and promised to continue the bloodshed until all foreigners had left the country.

After the tragedy, the Marines literally dug themselves into holes. They gouged out trenches, lowered trailers into the ground, and filled in the dirt. They walked underground from post to post, like moles, and complained that they were sent to die for no good reason.[27] Still, when they emerged from the ground more Marines died from attacks on patrols and from sniper fire and occasional mortar rounds lobbed into their compound.

The policymakers in Washington shrugged it all off and discussed how to use the Marines as leverage in a peace settlement, and where the Marines might be relocated in Lebanon to assure their safety while negotiations proceeded. But Secretary of Defense Casper Weinberger had never liked the idea of sending American troops into a situation that exposed them to hostile fire and served no useful military purpose. He had reluctantly agreed to the first deployment to guarantee safe passage for the PLO's retreat, and strongly opposed the second. Now he wanted the Marines out. Public opinion was on his side. When Congress reconvened in January 1984, after hearing from constituents in their home districts, members began issuing resolutions for the Marines to withdraw. In the meantime, Lebanon was sinking deeper into chaos as the government continued to lose its grip on the situation. On February 26, the Marines withdrew to their ships offshore while the battleship USS *New Jersey*, with no forward spotters on the ground to help aim the projectiles, blindly covered them by firing powerful sixteen-inch shells the size of compact cars into the Lebanese countryside where it was presumed a few sheep and their sheepherders must have been killed.[28] Using the familiar language of denial, the Pentagon called the retreat a "redeployment," knowing full well that it was nothing like the elective American redeployment that followed the exit of the PLO some nineteen months earlier.

The American military retreat was complete, but the Islamists did not stop there. In September 1984, another suicide bomber driving a Chevrolet van penetrated the compound of the American embassy annex in East Beirut. The driver was shot before he reached the building, but the explosion still killed fourteen people, including two American military personnel, wounded more than thirty others, and did extensive damage to the building. A caller who identified himself with "Islamic

Jihad" said afterward, "The operation comes to prove that we will carry out our previous promise not to allow a single American to remain on Lebanese soil."[29]

"Islamic Jihad" never had shape in Lebanon, no organizational structure, no leaders or followers, only a voice at the other end of a reporter's telephone conversation. It has been suggested that "Islamic Jihad" was a cover name for Hezbollah,[30] which is probable. Even though Hezbollah did not formally exist until 1985, the Lebanese Shiite embryo was already out of its Iranian womb in the summer of 1982. The creature began emerging at meetings in Baalbeck of radical young Shiite clerics and laymen. They came together with a fundamental belief that the new party should reflect their deep faith in the sharia and adopt Iran's revolution as the model for Lebanon.[31]

These fervent young advocates for God who idolized Khomeini represented only a small minority of the Lebanese Shia. Amal, the mainstream Shia party led by Nabih Berri, had made compromises with Israel and America that had angered the militants, in particular, Berri's acceptance in May 1983 of an American-brokered agreement that, contrary to UN Resolution 425, created a larger (thirty-mile) Israeli security zone on Lebanon's southern border with Israel, which the IDF would patrol together with the Christian militia force that served as Israel's proxy. (UN peacekeepers remained on station.)

So the militants set out to transform the political landscape. They worked with the Iranian Revolutionary Guards to organize the military camps, and when the eager young trainees had absorbed their lessons in the techniques of violence, the leaders dispatched small groups to carry out suicide attacks. For the time being, Hezbollah fighters remained an underground force, not showing their faces to the outside world or claiming credit for their deeds. At the same time, they rallied the people in the Bekaa Valley and encouraged them to resist the Israeli occupiers in the south. Along with their Iranian mentors, they spoke wherever crowds gathered, at mosques and funerals and other events, to promote the Islamic state and to discredit Israel and the West.

After the Israeli army pulled back to their enlarged security zone behind the Awali River, Hezbollah agents moved into the Shia neighborhoods in the southern Beirut suburbs, an Amal stronghold next to the airport where the U.S. Marines were stationed. It was not long afterward that the Marine barracks were blown up. These were fetid slums where raw sewage ran in the streets and Shiite refugees who had fled ahead of the Israeli advance through southern Lebanon crowded into ramshackle housing. The Christian government ignored their plight. Even the high class Sunni Muslims turned up their noses at the sights and smells of the Shia ghettoes. By late 1984, as the Islamist exhortations took hold on the people, the neighborhoods underwent a transformation. Khomeini's benevolent image gazed out from posters plastered to the walls. Bearded militiamen—the moral police—openly patrolled the streets wearing green headbands with inscriptions such as "Allahu Akbar" ("God is Great"). Schoolgirls discarded their Western jeans and T-shirts for loose-hanging clothes that concealed their emerging feminine curves and wore scarves to cover their heads. Alcohol disappeared from shops and restaurants.[32] Friedman described a scene one evening at the Commodore Hotel bar in Beirut where Western newsmen and women nursed their drinks and swapped stories from a day's work. A young, bearded Shiite militiaman walked in with an M-16 slung over his shoulder, headed directly for the liquor hidden behind the counter and smashed every bottle in sight with his rifle, leaving a large pool of booze and shattered glass on the barroom floor and a stunned audience of journalists.[33] More importantly, Hezbollah, heeding one the pillars of Islam to give alms to the poor, introduced welfare for the needy and organized programs to lift the people out of their wretched poverty.

On February 16, 1985, Hezbollah went public with a manifesto that proclaimed Khomeini as its supreme guardian and identified itself, not as just another small, isolated group, but as a "nation interconnecting with all Muslims of the world... linked by a strong ideological and political connection—Islam."[34] Each adherent, it said, was "a fighting soldier when a call for jihad arises...." It identified Israel as the principal enemy, a Western imperial presence in Muslim land, and promised that Hezbollah would not rest until Israel "has been totally eliminated from existence."[35] "Only if and when [the Israelis] leave the occupied land," the manifesto stated, "will the problem finally be over, and by occupied, we mean everything that is occupied, not just Lebanon"[36]—clearly, including Israel itself.

With the departure of the PLO from Lebanon, Israel had achieved a primary goal of the invasion. But its desire to implant a strong pro-Israeli government in Beirut blew up with the bomb that killed Bashir Gemayel. That Gemayel's assassination resulted from a Syrian plot represented another bitter setback for Israeli policy, which aimed at eliminating Syrian influence in Lebanon. The abominable Sabra and Shatila massacres, with their negative impact on world opinion, cramped Israel's ability either to directly sway Lebanese politics or to weaken Syria's. When in September 1983, the IDF pulled back from Beirut and the Chouf mountains to a line behind the Awali River north of Sidon, Israel was responding to the political reality on the ground. In other words, it was acknowledging a failed policy.

The new line stretched eastward for about sixty miles into a region of craggy mountains and steep cliffs carved out by smaller streams that feed the Awali. Borrowing from the concepts of the Bar-Lev defense in the Sinai more than a decade earlier, the Israelis established a system of constant patrols, round-the-clock roadblocks, and sophisticated communications. It was state-of-the-art military defense, but it was no defense against so-called terrorism. In truth, the Israelis did not seem to understand what they were up against, as if the IDF had not read the history of the Irgun and LHI campaigns against the British in the late 1940s.

When the Israeli troops marched through the south in 1982 on their way to Beirut, the Shia greeted them as liberators, showering them with rice and rose water as a sign of welcome, happy to be rid of the PLO.[37] The Shia had been living as second-class citizens in their own land ever since the arrival of the PLO from their defeat at the hands of Jordan's army in 1970. The Shia were poor dirt farmers and lowly merchants, largely uneducated and politically disorganized, and the PLO, despite a huge disparity in numbers—about 80,000 against 560,000 to 700,000 Shia—took advantage by levying taxes on the locals and setting up roadblocks to shake down travelers. To make matters worse, when the PLO raided or bombarded targets in northern Israel, the Shia usually bore the brunt of Israeli retaliation. Their resentment grew, encouraged by a charismatic leader, Imam Sayyid Musa al-Sadr, who taught them self-awareness and the value of political cohesion. Even after the mysterious disappearance of Sadr on a trip to Libya in 1978, for which many Shia blamed the PLO, they became more assertive—to the point of occasionally instigating armed clashes with their tormentors. But that was then. In 1983 there was a new stranger in the land. While most of the indigenous Shia were willing to give Israel the benefit of the doubt, a few hundred of the half-million-plus took advance courses in assertiveness at the terrorist training camps in Baalbeck.

Before the invasion, the Israelis already savored at least one asset in the south: Haddad, the leader of a Christian militia known as the SLA (South Lebanon Army), who controlled a strip along the Israeli border. Not only did he enjoy friendly relations with Israel, he got along well with Shiites in his area (some of them actually joined his militia), and shared with the Jewish state the same enemies, the PLO and Syria.

Haddad's militia, however, was too small to cover the wider security zone, so Israel now advanced another plan. It wanted to bring the villages together in a loose confederacy, each with a consultative council to advise the *mukhtar* (mayor), and each with a sixty-man militia, trained by the Israelis and lightly armed, for local security. Because the plan seemed to undercut the political leadership of Amal and to challenge the political-religious authority of the local clergy, Shiite leaders called on their followers not to cooperate.

To implement the plan, the Israeli government brought in administrators experienced in occupation duty in Palestine and imbued with a very low opinion of Arabs. In the words of Israeli scholar Avner Yaniv, they thought of all Arabs as "more dangerous verbally than in practical terms, cowardly, submissive, greedy, untrustworthy, emotional, bribable, and easily intimidated into collaboration with any authority, Arab or not"—an attitude born not of racism, he said, but of their encounters with Palestinians in the West Bank and Gaza.[38]

With this mindset and unaware in the beginning that the Shia had more spine than they ever imagined, the Israeli bureaucrats began to apply pressure on reluctant local villagers to accept their plan. Some Shiites were jailed and intimidated. To others with relatives imprisoned in Israel, the Israelis dangled a carrot. They offered freedom for jailed relatives in exchange for their cooperation. When these measures failed, the Israelis flexed their muscles. They ordered Haddad's militia to march through the Shiite town of Nabatiyeh, escorted by Israeli tanks and armored personnel carriers. More arrests followed and tensions rose. In March 1983, Sheikh Rajib al-Hahreb, the Imam of Jibshit, was arrested for speaking out against the occupation. This touched off modest demonstrations that turned violent. In one village, three Shiites were wounded.

Things went downhill from there. The insult to a revered sheikh was just one provocation. The Israelis also built airstrips, encampments, and fortifications, thus giving every indication, despite repeated denials, that they were settling in for the long haul. To local people, the Israeli actions invoked images of the West Bank. Were religious settlements next? Would southern Lebanon become the "North Bank"? The Shiites assumed the worst.

The point of no return came on October 16, 1983, in Nabatiyeh, an important religious center. Shiites were celebrating the feast of Ashura, the anniversary of Hussein's death in 680, the holiest day on the Shiite calendar during which men often engage in bloody self-flagellation to honor their hero's martyrdom. They came from surrounding villages that day, and swelled the population of Nabatiyeh. In the midst of this highly charge atmosphere, an Israeli military column appeared on the scene. Fatigued from a lengthy patrol, the troops had decided to take a shortcut through the town against instructions from higher command.[39] As they edged through the crowd of about fifty thousand in the marketplace, the people angrily resisted. Devout celebrants poured out of the mosques, surrounded the convoy, and started burning tires to block its passage. Things soon got out of hand. Three IDF trucks were set ablaze. Israeli troops fired on the crowd. Two Shiites were killed and fifteen wounded. Word of the melee quickly spread. Before the day was out, the Higher Shiite Council in Beirut called for civil resistance against the Israelis, tantamount to a declaration of war.[40]

The attack on the Marine barracks and the French paratrooper compound came one week later, and ten days after that a suicide bomber blew up IDF headquarters in Tyre for the second time. But now the trained militants from Baalbeck were not alone. The entire Shiite population in Lebanon was up in arms, with Amal and its moderate leader, Berri, taking the lead.

Few of the attacks that followed through 1984 and into 1985 were as dramatic as those in Beirut and Tyre. The attacks came in a great variety of ways: hit-and-run ambushes, rocket-propelled grenades, car bombs driven into IDF convoys, roadside homemade bombs, Russian-made land mines or old artillery shells packed in bags of nails, some set off by remote control, some attached to trip wires along a beaten path. In 1984, there were more than nine hundred such attacks against Israeli troops.[41] Palestinians left behind by the PLO in the refugee camps of Sidon and Tyre probably contributed up to 10 percent of the carnage.[42]

The Israelis responded by turning up the pressure. They restricted trade and travel, set up checkpoints, and instituted car and truck searches, making it difficult for farmers to bring their produce to market, a boon for Israeli farmers who exported their own goods to fill the vacuum. Transit between north and south Lebanon was sealed off, except for the checkpoint at Baader-el-Chouf on the Awali River, where up to 750 vehicles had to wait as long as three days to get through. Farmers were often forced to unload fruits and vegetables so border guards could check for weapons and bombs. Twice, suicide bombers drove their cars into the checkpoint and blew themselves up, each time taking a few Israeli soldiers and Lebanese civilians with them.[43]

Before long, the Israelis were resorting to draconian measures in response to Shiite attacks. One early morning in June 1984, an IDF column of tanks, trucks, and armored personnel carriers surrounded Maarekeh, a prominent center of resistance. They entered the town, conducted house-to-house searches, rousted the occupants, herded all Shiite males into the schoolyard, and took away 119 prisoners. This was the largest of many such raids during the occupation.[44] Maarekeh itself was raided at least a dozen times, and many nearby villages experienced the same treatment. The IDF also arrested and deported key religious leaders. One of them, Sheikh Ragheb Harb, was assassinated. He was a revered cleric, and dangerous to Israel's perceived interests for his fiery denunciations of the occupation. He was shot three times in the head on his way home from watching television news at a neighbor's house. The crime was never solved, but Shiites widely suspected Lebanese Christian militiamen loyal to the Israelis, and they reacted with nationwide strikes.[45]

At times, Shiite individuals took matters into their own hands. Bilal Fahs, seventeen years old, a bodyguard for Amal leader Nabih Berri, left his post one day and traveled to Damascus to pray for guidance at the Tomb of Zeinab, a Shia shrine. When he returned he asked his friends for forgiveness of all past offenses, and then headed south. In his last act on earth, he drove a Mercedes packed with more than two hundred pounds of explosives into an Israeli convoy and blew himself up. He was the only one to die in the explosion. Five Israeli soldiers were wounded.[46] Rael Noureddin, age thirty, went south from Beirut one night with a small band of followers. They were looking for a fight with Israelis, the way American street gangs pick fights with rival gangs. They found what they were looking for, and in a half-hour firefight, they killed one Israeli and wounded another. Noureddin was also hit, and bled to death on the way home, where he was celebrated as a martyr.[47]

The approximately 4,500 Israeli casualties—about six wounded for every one killed—were not militarily significant. Psychologically, they were huge. This was a people's war. There was no front, no army to fight. The attacks came any day on any stretch of road from any rooftop, behind any bush, around any corner. The enemy was difficult to track down, because it could be anybody in the indigenous population. Israel was suffering the fate of unwelcome occupiers faced with the opposition of brave, committed people unafraid to die for their homeland. As one Israeli peace advocate put it, "It is a war people in Israel never experienced before. We never really fought with the population. We fought with the Jordanian, Syrian and Egyptian armies, but never with the civilians. During the Suez war, you knew that the canal was the front. That was where the danger was and nowhere else, but in Lebanon, wherever you step you are surrounded by the war."[48] (He could have been talking about America in Iraq two decades later.) As further testament to this Israeli mood, 140 IDF soldiers refused to serve in Lebanon, more than the total number of the conscientious objectors in all of Israel's previous wars combined.[49]

On February 16, 1985, the IDF withdrew from Sidon, the western anchor of the Awali line.[50] The withdrawal itself was no secret, but the actual date came as a surprise. It was a Saturday, the Sabbath, a day on which Talmudic law forbids travel, except in dire circumstances. The troops left stealthily and in great haste to lessen the chance of ambush along the path of retreat. But in the days that followed, two officers and a sergeant were killed in ambushes. The Israelis retaliated with a series of raids on the villages east of Tyre, imposed dawn-to-dusk curfews, and took measures against car bombs and suicide drivers.

This was the first part of a three-phase unilateral pullback and a painful admission of defeat. The last phase came on June 6 that year, three years to the day after Sharon's ill-fated invasion began, and it put them back where they had started. In those three years, the IDF suffered 645 dead and 3,873 wounded,[51] against the deaths of thousands of Lebanese and Palestinians, mostly noncombatants. Was it worth the sacrifice? The Israelis had achieved their goal of driving out the PLO—temporarily, at least, and created a new enemy, the Shiites of southern Lebanon. The elder statesman, Abba Eban, had already articulated the irony of the Israeli predicament. "If it turns out," he had said a few months earlier in the pearl-shaped words of his English accent, "that all we have done is traded the hostility of 7,000 Palestinians for the hostility of 700,000 Shiites, then I think we will have made a very poor trade."[52]

Israel settled for a buffer zone that ran three to twelve miles into Lebanon all along its northern border, but it was not okay with the Lebanese Shiites. Unwilling to cede a centimeter of their own land to the Israelis, they continued their attacks, and, in an all-too-familiar pattern, the Israelis and their Christian allies continued to retaliate, tit for tat. Israel usually committed about a thousand troops to the buffer zone to patrol alongside the Christian South Lebanese Army, which numbered about 1,500 men. Occasionally, the Israelis would launch more muscular incursions highlighted by heavy bombardments into Shiite territory to strike back at their tormentors.

The Shiites attacked, primarily, the Israeli army and its surrogate, the Christian militia—military targets, and occasionally lobbed rockets onto Israeli territory to avenge civilian deaths from Israeli bombs. By contrast, when Israel unleashed its big guns and air power north of the security zone, it had a hard time discriminating between civilian and military targets. Indeed, it has been accused of deliberately targeting civilians to provoke their anger against the militants and drive a wedge between them.[53] True or not, it is undeniable that the Israeli army fighting all-out on Lebanese soil could hardly avoid hitting civilians. To complicate the issue, Shiite civilians and fighters were often the same God-fearing person. Never much more numerous than 1,500, the fighters fought where they lived. They were totally integrated into the society with a network of family ties and local support. Like volunteer firemen in an American small town, many of them worked day jobs and answered the call to duty whenever it came. In all, they amounted to less than three one-hundredths of 1 percent of all the Shiite people in southern Lebanon. On occasions when the IDF went on the attack to eliminate the "terrorists" with indiscriminant bombardments and air raids, the suffering would inevitably fall much heavier on the civilian population. The larger question was why Israel needed to be in Lebanon, in the first place—a question Israelis would soon be asking themselves as casualties in the security zone mounted.

In one piece of good news for Israel, the Shiites initially blocked the Palestinian efforts to return to their old haunts in southern Lebanon, and to the extent that they fought off the Palestinians, it eased the pressure on Israel. Israel's relief turned almost to exhilaration in the late 1980s when the Shiites took to fighting among themselves. As the radicals of Hezbollah continued to gain strength in the Shiite communities of Beirut and south Lebanon, they threatened Amal's political leadership, and the rivalry came to armed conflict, one of the last in Lebanon's fifteen-year civil war. The civil war ended in 1990 and reforms were adopted that provided for more equitable power sharing among the diverse factions.

Once the Shiites had set aside their internal disputes, Hezbollah underwent a remarkable political metamorphosis. Most of the clerics—not all—discarded the revolutionary rhetoric of "the oppressed vs. the oppressor" and the valid criticism of Lebanese politics as "rotten to the core." Instead of fighting for Khomeini's principle of *wilayat al-faqih,* the clergy's judicial supremacy, they opted to participate in Lebanon's secular, multisectarian parliamentary system. Hezbollah began running candidates in the 1992 election. The party won eight seats that year, and became the largest single bloc in the National Assembly. The Hezbollah legislators soon earned respect for their integrity, political savvy, and ability to form pragmatic legislative alliances.[54]

At the same time, Hezbollah went back to fighting the Israelis in their security zone—or their "(in)security zone," as Professor Norton dubbed it.[55] There, too, Hezbollah modified its tactics: fewer suicide bombers and more professionally prepared ambushes and camouflaged, remote-controlled roadside bombs—what became IEDs in Iraq (improvised explosive devices)—and its fighters exacted a steady toll on the Israeli troops. Their own casualties, measured by the ratio of Hezbollah-to-Israeli losses, actually declined from 5:1 in the 1980s to 2:1 in the 1990s.[56]

What it boiled down to, perhaps, was a drift away from the Iranian formula for holy war in pursuit of an Islamist world, toward the nationalistic goal of driving the Israeli occupiers out of Lebanon. It was a goal that all Lebanese of any persuasion could understand, and the more Israel tried to punish noncombatants for the perceived offenses of Hezbollah, the more it strengthened Hezbollah's standing with the Lebanese people. In that sense, Israel created Hezbollah.[57]

In 1993, after eight IDF soldiers were killed in a Hezbollah attack, Israel opened a fierce air and artillery bombardment of southern Lebanon called "Operation Accountability." Its stated purpose was to wipe out terrorist bases. The large-scale Israeli attacks from land, air, and sea actually hit about fifty villages, destroying whole neighborhoods, killing more than 130 people, and creating more than 200,000 refugees who fled north in fear. Only a handful of guerrillas were killed. Israel said it hoped by its initiative to put pressure on the Lebanese government to deploy the Lebanese Army in the south to clean out the Hezbollah guerrillas. But the government refused to restrain the Shiites as long as Israel occupied Lebanese territory.

With the help of American mediation, the two sides finally agreed that Israel would no longer target civilians and Hezbollah would confine its attacks to the IDF and the SLA in the security zone and not fire its rockets at northern Israel. The understanding, although it lasted three years, was honored more in the breech. Hezbollah alleged that Israel fired on civilian targets in southern Lebanon 231 times in that period, while it admitted to retaliating with rocket attacks on northern Israel thirteen times.[58] Fewer suicide attacks did not mean they were out of the question. Salah Ghandour, married and the father of two, all four uprooted from southern Lebanon, pleaded with his Hezbollah superiors for the opportunity to be a martyr. Reluctantly, because he was a family man, they finally granted his wish. On May 25, 1995, he drove a car into an Israeli convoy and set off a powerful explosive. He died and took twelve Israeli soldiers with him. Hezbollah gave his widow a crude videotape of the event, and the children played it over and over again to watch with pride how they lost their father.[59] In the early months of 1996, the attacks accelerated in the security zone, and the casualties mounted. Both sides knew that another storm was brewing.

In April, Israel struck again in a land and air assault code named "Operation Grapes of Wrath." The stated goal was to silence Hezbollah rocket attacks against northern Israel, and to undermine popular and political support for the militants. Even more powerful than the earlier operation, "Grapes of Wrath" included air strikes against military and civilian targets as far north as Beirut. Israel vowed to destroy Hezbollah strongholds, but its guns also pounded civilian targets, destroying homes, roads, water tanks, and even bombing a power station to disrupt electricity to homes, stores, factories, and offices. By striking at targets of economic significance, Israel gave the impression that they were waging a war against the Lebanese infrastructure. As in 1993, refugees streamed north toward Beirut, and some fell victim to Israeli attacks. By striking at civilians, the Israelis seemed bent on creating an unmanageable number of refugees. Nor did the death toll reflect the stated Israeli objective to eliminate Hezbollah. About thirteen civilians were killed for every one guerrilla—about 165 noncombatants to only thirteen Hezbollah fighters.[60] Israel laid siege to Lebanese ports and broadcast a warning for Lebanese civilians to vacate their homes in the south, or risk being identified and attacked as Hezbollah. Israel always claimed that their overriding goal was to halt terrorism, but attacking civilian targets to achieve a political purpose is one way to define terrorism—in this case, IDF terrorism.

Lebanon appealed to the UN Security Council, but its plea went nowhere in the face of a threatened American veto. Ignoring the fact that Israel was occupying Lebanese soil in violation of UN Resolution 425, America refused to consider another resolution condemning Israel that did not include a condemnation of Hezbollah for its alleged terrorist activities. The logic of the American position was to broaden the definition of terrorism to include the defense of one's homeland.

On the eighth day of the Israeli offensive, Hezbollah launched an early morning rocket barrage against northern Israel. The IDF responded with a helicopter gunship attack against Nabatiyeh. One "smart" bomb hit a three-story building where a Lebanese family of eleven had taken refuge. Nine members were killed, including a four-day old baby, her mother, three brothers, three sisters and one sister's fiancé. Later in the day, an armored Israeli column shelled a UN compound in Qana (site of the marriage ceremony at which the Bible says Jesus changed water into wine), where 850 Lebanese civilians had taken refuge. The seventeen-minute barrage killed 109 people, including four Fijian UN soldiers, and wounded another 150 refugees.

That massacre finally caught the world's attention. President Clinton called for an immediate cease-fire, and dispatched Secretary of State Warren Christopher to the Middle East. Christopher and French Foreign Minister Herve de Cherrette took the better part of a week to hammer out another agreement like the one that ended the 1993 conflict. Israel was willing to give up the security zone, but wanted concessions from the other side. It insisted on the withdrawal of Syrian troops from the Bekaa Valley, as well as Lebanese guarantees against Hezbollah attacks on Israeli territory. Both Syria and Lebanon refused, so the agreement came down to a truce in place. Israel remained in the security zone and Hezbollah was left free to attack Israeli military targets. A commission without enforcement power, which consisted of representatives from the United States, France, Syria, Israel, and Lebanon, would report cross-border attacks by either party.

In effect, the sixteen-day Israeli offensive came to nothing. It was a net minus for Israel, because it made Hezbollah the toast of Lebanon for standing up to the invaders. On one visit to a Christian neighborhood, two Hezbollah press officials were taken by surprise when an old man recognized them and waved in greeting. "Hezbollah, Hezbollah," he shouted as the two Shiites cringed in fear at being recognized by a Christian crowd. "We are all Hezbollah. We are all behind you. God be with you. You have made us proud." Relieved and gratified by the friendly smiles of passersby, the two men waved back and went on about their business.[61] Never before had the Party of God enjoyed such popularity. People of all factions, even Christians, celebrated their resistance and contributed funds to their cause.

In the south, Hezbollah kept up the pressure. The pattern of Hezbollah attack and Israeli retaliation persisted, and the 1996 agreement was repeatedly violated. Again in 1997 and twice in 2000, Israeli planes bombed power-generating plants near Beirut, at least once in response to Hezbollah Katyusha rocket attacks on the upper

Galilee that killed two civilians and injured nine. The IDF in the security zone continued to take casualties: 23 dead and 110 wounded in 1998, 13 dead and 57 wounded in 1999.[62] The Q-word, "quagmire," found its way into the Israeli vocabulary, as the nation glumly contemplated Israel's Vietnam. To minimize losses, the IDF and SLA cut back on patrols and hunkered down in fortified guard posts. In response, Hezbollah obtained TOW wire-guided antitank missiles from Iran to blast through the Israeli bunkers. Reportedly, these were the same TOW missiles supplied in the 1980s by the United States, through Israel, in the arms-for-hostages swap. Of the seven Israeli soldiers killed in the first two months of 2000, most were casualties of TOW missile attacks.[63]

On May 24, 2000, Israel withdrew unilaterally from its security zone in Lebanon. By that time, the mighty IDF was a beaten army. It had dazzled the world with lightening victories over its Arab enemies in 1967 and 1973. Even in 2000 and beyond, no Arab army or combination of armies could, or would even dare stand up to it. In conventional combat, the IDF was supreme within its sphere; in occupation, it was defeated. The long grind, the daily attacks, the unremitting pressure, the steady casualties, the inability to retaliate effectively, the futility of failed negotiations, all contributed to a serious breakdown in morale, both in the security zone and on the home front. While Israel failed to drive a wedge between Hezbollah and the Lebanese people, Hezbollah succeeded in turning Israeli public opinion against the occupation. A new Labor government headed by Ehud Barak surveyed the facts on the ground and decided that the costs of the occupation outweighed the benefits.

CHAPTER 7

PALESTINE: OCCUPATION AND INTIFADAS

No number of atrocities however horrible can deprive a nation of its right to independence, nor justify its being put under the heel of its worst enemies and persecutors.

—Louis Namier (1971)

In 1967, Israel transformed itself from a besieged fledgling into an occupying power. Taking preemptive action to ward off its imminent destruction, it needed only six electrifying days to defeat three Arab armies and seize all the land west of the Jordan River and the Gulf of Aqaba from the Golan Heights to the Suez Canal, a stunning feat of arms, and the beginning of a long nightmare about the West Bank and Gaza Strip that continues in the West Bank as this is written, successfully extending the occupation for four decades of intermittent death and terror. Can it be said that Israel has defied the odds of history?

Israel's Labor government immediately proposed in 1967 to give the Sinai Peninsula back to Egypt, the Golan to Syria, and most of the West Bank (except East Jerusalem) to Jordan in exchange for diplomatic recognition and the right to live in peace. Within days both Egypt and Syria rejected the offer, and at a conference in Khartoum in the late summer of 1967 eight Arab nations renewed their vow to destroy Israel, for which they came to be identified as the "rejectionist states." In 1979 at Camp David, after Anwar Sadat had succeeded Gamal Abdul Nasser as president and gained credibility in the 1973 Yom Kippur War, Egypt finally made peace with Israel. Jordan followed in 1994 after renouncing any claims to the West Bank. But Syria never budged from its rejectionist position, and the Golan Heights remained in Israeli hands, an unresolved issue.

Initially, Israelis argued among themselves over the West Bank and Gaza. Some within the Labor government, including ex-premier David Ben Gurion, wanted to apply the land-for-peace formula; others on the political right argued for annexing the entire West Bank; one proposal by Labor Minister Yigal Allon would have cut the baby in half by keeping a strip of land along the Jordan River for security reasons and returning the rest to Jordan. Israel did annex East Jerusalem, but kept its appetite for the rest of the West Bank under control. Successive Israeli governments, both Labor and Likud, adopted a more subtle approach in its policy toward Palestinian lands that some have called "creeping annexation." The Knesset enacted housing subsidies, and encouraged settlement. By 2004, roughly 235,000 Jews had made their homes in the West Bank and Gaza in approximately 160 settlements. Another 180,000 had moved to East Jerusalem where Jewish settlements surrounded the Arab section.[1] In 2004, Israel began building a barrier against terrorist incursions that encroached on some of the Palestinian land that the Israelis had illegally settled. A year later, the Israeli army disbanded the settlements in Gaza and ended its occupation there.

At the extremes of the political spectrum, where powerful forces pull the Israeli government and the PA (Palestinian Authority) in opposite directions, the Arab–Israeli dispute plays out as religious warfare inspired by fundamentalist interpretations of the Koran and Torah. On one issue, rejection of the so-called two-state solution, the interests of radical Islam and radical Judaism are in complete harmony. Otherwise, they are at polar opposites: the Islamists want a Palestine without Jews; the ultraright Jews want an Israel without Arabs. In the real world, the side in control has usually accepted the other as second-class citizens. Military power tilts strongly to the Israeli side roughly in proportion to the British military advantage over the Kikuyu in Kenya's Mau Mau war.

Nothing could more clearly illustrate their great rift than words spoken by two men representing Jewish and Palestinian extremes to *New Yorker* reporter Jeffrey Goldberg in 2004. Rabbi Moshe Levinger, an early leader among Jewish religious settlers, advocated the expulsion of all Arabs from Israel and the West Bank. "Foreign residents [Arabs] will be allowed to stay in [Greater] Israel if they follow our laws and don't demand [voting] privileges," Levinger told Goldberg.[2] But he did not believe the Arabs would agree to that, so he favored their forcible removal. At the other extreme, the late Sheikh Ahmed Yassin, a founder and spiritual leader of Hamas, vowed "to raise the banner of Allah over every inch of Palestine [including Israel]." He added with a glint of compassion, "There were some Jews who lived in Palestine before Zionism. The children of these Jews will be allowed to stay under the protection of Islam. But the rest of the Jews must be defeated, or they must leave."[3] Their posturing seems to leave little room for compromise, although Yassin was quoted in 2002 as offering a truce if Israel would withdraw completely from the West Bank and Gaza.[4]

The turnover of the West Bank and Gaza to Palestinian control has long been the basis for a proposed two-state resolution of the Israeli–Palestinian conflict. Following the 1967 war, the United Nations passed Resolution 242 calling on Israel to withdraw from the occupied territories, which raised Palestinian hopes that the remaining 22 percent of pre-1948 Palestine outside of Israel might become available to them as a small but viable nation. Alas, the proliferation of the settlements has long outdated Resolution 242.

The religious right has hamstrung Israeli policy in the occupied territories. Minutes after the Israeli army conquered the Old City of Jerusalem from the Arabs on June 7, 1967, members of the B'nai Akiva youth movement, identifiable in their colored knit skullcaps, hustled their beloved Rabbi Zvi Yehuda Hacohen Kook to the sacred Western Wall of the Temple Mount, where he declared, "We hereby inform the people of Israel and the entire world that under heavenly command we have just returned home.... We shall never move out."[5]

The next year his followers established the first religious settlement at Kiryat Arba outside Hebron. Levinger led the movement. He rented rooms in a Hebron hotel to hold a Seder for his family and a small group of followers. Afterward he refused to leave until the government gave him permission to build Kiryat Arba on a hill outside the city. It might be considered the first Jewish colony in Greater Israel. In three-and-a-half decades, it grew to several thousand of the most obdurate messianic settlers.

In the years that followed, idealistic youth spread out on scouting missions in Judea and Samaria looking for settlement sites. Their interest went well beyond the less provocative former Jewish or sparsely populated areas to predominantly Arab neighborhoods where Jewish incursions were certain to stir up political turmoil. Except for the successful establishment of Kiryat Arba, however, not much happened until after the Yom Kippur War in October 1973 when the Egyptian army caught the IDF napping in the Sinai Desert and diminished its stature. Then, out of a new-found mistrust of the Labor government, the religious settler movement gained momentum. In 1974, the followers of Rabbi Zvi Kook came together as the Gush Emunim (Bloc of the Faithful) with a fully developed politico-religious ideology that called for the extension of Israeli sovereignty over the occupied territories to redeem god's promise of a Jewish kingdom. They opposed any territorial concessions, including the return of the Sinai to Egypt. They also staged public demonstrations to underscore their attachment to what they considered to be the holy lands of Judea and Samaria, and carried out illicit settlement activities.

Under Levinger's activist leadership, Gush Emunim established other settlements in Arab-populated communities of the West Bank, facing off against the IDF and outmaneuvering the Labor government in the process. Levinger, a tenacious fighter for his cause, followed the nonviolent pattern of his triumph at Kiryat Arba. He would set up temporary residence at a desired location for a religious celebration, and refuse to leave on religious grounds, making sure his resulting standoff with the army was well publicized. Then he would negotiate an agreement in which the settlers would leave in return for the establishment of a small yeshiva on the site. Over time when the hubbub had died down, the faithful would gradually return to make the settlement permanent while the government looked the other way.[6]

The Yom Kippur War also stirred the secular Labor government to embark on an aggressive policy of land acquisition, which, it told the world, was motivated by security concerns. It authorized settlements outside of Arab population centers, strung out in the Jordan Valley north and east of Jerusalem and in the Judean desert to the south. They were supposedly a first line of defense, as proposed in the 1967 Allon Plan for peace with Jordan.

Israeli land policy took a giant leap in 1977 when Likud came to power. The new right-wing government legalized the Gush Emunim settlements, and gave the religious colonizers allowance for more land seizures—as much as international pressure would tolerate. But Likud went even further. Relying on pre-1948 laws from the British Mandate and the Ottoman Empire, the Israeli army seized undeveloped, unregistered lands (sometimes confiscating property owned outright by Palestinians), and built settlements near Arab population centers within easy commuting distance to Tel Aviv and Jerusalem. Most of the new settlers were typical suburbanites, middle to upper-middle class, secular to moderately religious in outlook, raising families, building communities, with service and high-tech jobs in Israel's growing economy.

It became a land rush of major proportions. Under Labor Party rule prior to 1977, the number of Jewish settlers in the occupied territories grew by an average of 770 per year; under Likud from 1978 to 1987, the average annual growth multiplied almost eightfold to 5,960 per year. Likud also doubled yearly government expenditures for settlement activity. The underlying purpose, according to Middle East specialist F. Robert Hunter, was "to create a domestic lobby that would support the retention of the occupied territories by Israel."[7] If Likud exercised Israeli land policy more vigorously than Labor, there was nothing intrinsically new about either. Taken together, it amounted to an extension of land acquisition that began with the arrival of the earliest European Jews in the late nineteenth century.

As Housing and Construction Minister in 1991, Ariel Sharon led the renewed expansion of settlements in the occupied territories. He started 1,300 new residential units close to Jerusalem and along the Israeli border, and filled them with immigrants from the former Soviet Union.[8] This was consistent with Sharon's personal plan for the West Bank. He was determined never to withdraw from unified Jerusalem, Israel's capital; to keep permanent control of the Jordan Depression; to permit no settlement dismantlement; and to bar the return to Israel of Palestinian refugees. Once Sharon had restarted settlement expansion, succeeding Israeli governments kept it going. During the Oslo period from 1993 to 2000, the Jewish population of the West Bank doubled from 100,000 to 200,000,[9] and continued to grow into the new century

After the 1967 Six Day War, Yasser Arafat traveled incognito inside the West Bank trying to stir the Palestinian people to revolt against the occupation, but they gave him and the PLO a cold shoulder. At that time, they had little stomach for revolution. In their life span, outsiders had always ruled them, most recently Jordan, before that Britain, and before World War I the Ottoman Empire. In a sense, Israel was just another occupier.

Israel's ruling Labor Party, eager to show a benevolent face, opened up its economy. About a third of the Palestinian population took jobs generated by Israel's Western-style engine of growth. For the most part, these were dead-end, low-level jobs, the kind of physical, servile work the Israelis did not want to do themselves. Ultimately, in the depth of their humiliation, whether they realized it or not, many Palestinian laborers worked against their own political interests to expand and solidify Jewish control by helping to build Jewish housing in Arab neighborhoods.

But even the lowest paid Palestinians gained a modicum of purchasing power. They could put bread on the table. Many families enjoyed a level of prosperity they had not known before, and the Israeli government permitted schools to flourish, helped to build hospitals and clinics, and allowed Arab newspapers and journals to publish—under a regime of censorship.

Soon enough, the Palestinians discovered that the jobs did not give them control over their own lives or guarantee their human rights. Contrary to the impression conveyed in the American media, the Israeli occupation of the West Bank and Gaza has been very harsh, sometimes even brutal. Despite its benevolent policies in the beginning, Israel has exercised what can best be described as a military dictatorship that includes the ubiquitous Big Brother presence of the Israeli domestic intelligence agency, Shin Bet, or GSS (General Security Services). Eventually, it would grip Palestine with an iron fist and hold down the Arab people with a tight bureaucratic system of permits for virtually any routine activity or need, from drivers' licenses, to travel documents, to water quotas.

Palestinians began to feel the collar tighten in the mid-1970s after the Yom Kippur War. Arab newspapers found themselves being closely scrutinized. The freedom to publish did not mean that the editors were free to speak ill of the occupiers. Anyone critical of Israeli policies could be put under house arrest, or imprisoned without being charged for up to six months.

If expression was restricted, anti-Israeli activity was crushed. Individuals merely suspected of committing anti-Israeli acts could expect Israeli law to come down hard. The IDF had, and still has, the authority to destroy Palestinian family homes without compensation. As a last resort, terrorist suspects could be, and were deported, even though that extreme measure is contrary to the Geneva Convention.

Israeli restrictions intruded into everyday life. Palestinian families needed permits just to unite with relatives who lived outside the territory, and the permits were usually issued to those families who cooperated with occupation authorities and denied to those who did not. Men who married women from communist or Arab countries could bring their wives back to Palestine only to visit, not to live. If the occupied lands were a prison, such spousal visitation would be a generous regulation. But no such privileges were extended to real Palestinian prisoners in Israeli jails, who in nearly four decades of occupation have been routinely degraded, tortured, and often beaten.[10]

Travel has been very difficult for Palestinians. The IDF maintained checkpoints at the borders and within the territories. Outsiders are told that the Israelis must guard against subversion and terrorism to maintain their occupation. But that sort of rationale does not convey the direct person-to-person experience of occupier and occupied, or how that experience can demean them both. One Palestinian woman (identified as Samia), a Christian who has held important educational and religious positions within her society, described to American author Wendy Pearlman what she went through on professional trips to Amman, Jordan:

> We were treated like dirt when we used to cross the border. We were stripped and searched so thoroughly that it just made you sick. You know, they have these handheld machines that they could just wave in front and back of you, and they serve the same function. But they chose to strip you, simply in order to humiliate you. One day the security policewomen even removed my sanitary napkin. Can you imagine? She said, "I'm Sorry. I have to do this." I said, "I'm sorry for you." I think that [the Israelis] are more dehumanized in the process of occupying us than we are.[11]

It is impossible to verify the part about removing the sanitary napkin, but the argument Samia makes, that the occupation dehumanizes the occupiers, has ample backup. Some Israeli soldiers who manned the checkpoints made this identical point in interviews with the *Washington Post.* "When we do [physical and verbal abuse], we are not doing it only to the Palestinians, but to ourselves, too..." said Michael Aman, a former staff sergeant in the IDF's 202nd Paratroop Battalion. "These [checkpoint] duties corrupt [the guards]." He acknowledged that Israeli authorities warn the soldiers not to behave badly toward Palestinian civilians. But the soldiers do not always hold up under the pressures of a "dreadful mission," such as the fear that an innocent-looking Palestinian might be carrying a bomb or some other weapon. An IDF tribunal convicted one of Aman's friends of repeatedly beating Palestinians at the busy Hawara checkpoint near Nablus, sentenced him to six months in prison, and reduced him in rank from sergeant to private. The convicted paratrooper's identity was withheld for fear of reprisals against him or his family.[12]

Water was another source of animosity. Control of the land gave Israel jurisdiction over the water supply to the detriment of the Palestinians who needed permits just to sink wells. These were granted grudgingly and only for drinking, while Jewish usage was not similarly restricted. The water quota for Jewish settlers was two to three times the allotment for Palestinians. As to actual consumption, an Israeli ex-administrator estimated that for every gallon of water pumped for a Palestinian, twelve gallons were pumped for an Israeli settler. In 1982, then Defense Minister Sharon ordered that management of the West Bank water system be turned over to the Israeli water company, Mekorot, which, primarily, supplied water to the Jewish settlers. On one occasion, Mekorot expropriated land from an Arab without compensation to drill a well for a nearby Jewish settlement. It never bothered to obtain the necessary approval from the Civil Administration, the Israeli agency that handles nonmilitary affairs in the territories.[13]

The tight controls of the occupation exacerbated mutual hostilities. The level of violence began to rise. On the Jewish side, while Gush Emunim forcefully renounced terrorism, some of Gush's most militant adherents embraced it in an underground movement. One terrorist incident in 1980 was touched off when Arab gunmen murdered six yeshiva students in Hebron. The Jewish underground responded by planting bombs in the cars of five Palestinian mayors. The plotters intended not to kill the mayors, but to let them live with painful injuries to remind them of the cost of taking Jewish blood, even if they did not personally commit the atrocity. Only two bombs were successfully detonated, and two Arab mayors suffered serious injury. Two other bombs failed to go off. The fifth blew up as an Israeli demolition expert tried to disarm it, inadvertently but no less effectively leaving him with painful reminders of the cost of terrorism. Another terrorist act in 1983 again followed the murder of a Hebron yeshiva student. Jewish activists raided the Islamic College of Hebron, killing three Arab students and wounding thirty-three. The conspirators plotted for two years to blow up the Dome of the Rock, the Muslim holy site where Muhammad claimed to have ascended into heaven for an audience with God and the prophets. The plot was never carried out because the terrorists could not obtain rabbinical approval for such a far-reaching act. It came to light only after the police broke up the underground by arresting members for other terrorist activities.[14]

During the life of the Jewish underground from the late 1970s to the early 1980s, Rabbi Meyer Kahane delivered an even more pernicious anti-Arab message. Kahane was familiar to Americans in the 1960s as the fanatical Brooklyn rabbi who founded the Jewish Defense League. At a time when the black inner cities were exploding across America, Kahane and his small following demonstrated against crime in the streets and black anti-Semitism. Kahane spoke out against American anti-Semitism in all its manifestations, and condemned the liberal Jewish establishment for not doing enough about it. He also took up the cause of Soviet Jews barred from immigrating to Israel by the Kremlin's communist government.

In 1971, Kahane and his most loyal followers moved from Brooklyn to Jerusalem. Two years later, he founded Kach (Defiance) and relocated with his followers to the hotbed of radical expansionism, Kiryat Arba. God would ultimately redeem the Jews, he preached, but they could hasten the day by seizing the initiative. He would tolerate no compromise with the Arabs. Those Arabs who still lived in Israel, he wanted evicted. Those who lived in the occupied territories were to be terrorized and driven out.

While Kahane preached hatred, he played no part in acting it out. But his followers did, in a manner reminiscent of Nazi Brown Shirts who victimized German

Jews in the 1930s. They attacked Arab families that moved into Jewish neighbor-hoods, chased Arab workers for the fun of it, and held anti-Arab "victory parades." A follower, Craig Leitner, tells of cruising with friends one night in a rented car. When they spotted a lone Arab walking along the road, Leitner got out of the car and attacked him, hitting and kicking him until he fled into the darkness. Later they set Arab cars ablaze, and then fired on an Arab bus, wounding several innocent pas-sengers. Kahane expressed his approval. In the late 1980s, Kach organized vigilante groups against the Arabs, openly intending to "shoot to kill."[15]

Kahane gained a small but devoted following in the expansionist movement. In 1984, he shocked Israel by winning a seat in the Knesset. The Knesset promptly tightened the election law, and Kahane failed in his bid for reelection. In 1990, Islamic extremists assassinated him in New York. His followers in the West Bank continued to embrace his message of hatred and violence, some who remained in Kach, and others who formed a group called Kahane Chai (Kahane Lives).

The First Intifada

Tensions from the occupation of the West Bank and Gaza mounted in the 1980s. Arab violence against Jews occurred more frequently with Palestinian youth in the vanguard. Higher birth rates and lower infant mortality had made Palestine a young society. By 1984, almost half the Arab population of the West Bank and Gaza was fourteen or younger.[16] Schools of all kinds had opened—universities, two-year colleges, trade schools, and teacher training schools. Tuitions were relatively afford-able, and parents put a high priority on their children's education. Whatever course of studies the students might have signed up for they were inevitably exposed to the political realities of their unpalatable subordination to the Israelis. The schools became hotbeds of political ferment. Various groups within the PLO as well as the Communist Party and the Islamic Association (Muslim Brotherhood) competed for their loyalties. A generation gap developed, as students came home from their involvement in school politics critical of their parents for not doing enough to resist the occupiers.

Islamist influence grew at the expense of the more secular PLO. In 1968, Yassin took over the Muslim Brotherhood in Gaza and guided its steady expansion over the ensuing two decades. Paralyzed from the neck down as a result of a teenage sports accident in 1952, Yassin steered clear of inciting anti-Israeli resistance through the 1970s and Israeli intelligence left him alone, even thought of him as a welcome counterweight to the PLO. He gained control of Gaza's Islamic University and most of the Gaza mosques, oversaw the doubling of Muslim worshippers, and built schools, libraries, day-care centers, clinics, sports clubs, and more mosques for his followers. He preached in Gaza, and spoke at mosques in the West Bank and Israel, delivering the Brotherhood's message of Islam as a total way of life, just as its Egyptian founder, Hassan al-Banna, had spread the same word a few decades earlier.

Before long, outside events combined with the pent-up frustrations of the Palestinian predicament to further radicalize Palestinian youth. The Iranian revolution in 1979 inspired them with the hope that they, too, might throw off their oppressors. As the new decade approached, Israel's economy tanked, magnifying all the deprivations and indignities of the impoverished Palestinian existence. In 1982, the IDF deflated the PLO in Southern Lebanon, and forced Arafat to relocate his headquarters to faraway Tunisia. In the years that followed, fortunes subtly changed as Hezbollah deflated the IDF, employing suicide bombers against the occupation army. These events intensified the pressure inside the territories and emboldened the Palestinians to act against the Israelis in the West Bank and Gaza.

The beginnings of a liberation movement came from the more militant side of the Islamist movement. A faction of Gaza intellectuals, led by Fathi Shkaki and Abd al-Aziz Odeh, graduates of the radical Muslim Zakazik University in Egypt, rejected Yassin's go-slow approach. Shkaki, a physician, and Odeh, a cleric who lectured in Muslim law at Gaza's Islamic University, praised the Khomeini revolution in Iran and preached a fiery message of violent rebellion against the Israeli occupation. Their pantheon of heroes began with Hassan al-Banna, the Egyptian founder of the Muslim Brotherhood, and included the Brotherhood's radical Egyptian theoreticians, Sayyid Qutb and Muhammad Abd al-Salam Faraj, and the Syrian revolutionary, Sheikh Izz al-Din al Qassam, who led an Arab rebellion against British rule in Palestine in the 1930s.[17] Shkaki and Odeh established an underground organization, eventually called "Islamic Jihad of Palestine," drawing recruits from local mosques and the Islamic University, and finding compatibility with hard-core Fatah terrorists in Israeli prisons. Similar to the NLF in Algiers three decades earlier, members of the Islamic Jihad were organized into tight cells of five to seven men. They were few in numbers and highly disciplined, but their total strength was unknown because of their tight secrecy. They chose obscurity to better blend in with Palestinian crowds, purposely rejecting the beards and long robes that distinguished the Brotherhood.

Islamic Jihad conducted a series of low-level attacks against the Israelis in the mid-1980s, often coordinating with Fatah activists loyal to Arafat whom they got to know in prison. One product of their alliance—with the PLO supplying the planning and Islamic Jihad, the manpower—was a grenade attack in October 1986 on the cadets of the IDF's Givati Brigade during a swearing-in ceremony at the Western Wall in Jerusalem. The father of a cadet was killed and a dozen other persons were wounded.

The Israelis arrested Shkaki in 1986 for smuggling arms and inciting violence. At his trial, he lectured the court on the fundamentals of Islamic law, drawing crowds of Arab youth who listened in rapt attention. His defiant pamphlet, *Khomeini: The Islamic Solution and the Alternative,* became a hot item in Gaza bookstalls. He was convicted on both counts and, in 1988, deported to Syria, after which he ran Islamic Jihad from the outside until he was assassinated in Malta in 1996.

In May 1987, six members of the Islamic Jihad pulled off a daring escape from the Gaza Central Prison. There had been many earlier attempts to break out of the high-security prison, but this was the first to succeed. The prisoners sawed off the bars to their cell window, dropped down to the inner courtyard, cut through barbed wire, and climbed over the outer wall into the early morning bustle of Gaza City. One escapee was quickly recaptured, but the other five holed up in a building within sight of the IDF's Gaza headquarters while Israeli security forces looked high and low for them. The escape earned Islamic Jihad high marks of approval from the Palestinian populace that had all but ignored it until then.

Yassin had already taken a tentative step toward political belligerency in 1983 when he set up a militant wing within the Muslim Brotherhood that began to stockpile weapons in Yassin's mosque. Israeli intelligence soon got wind of it from Arab sources and raided the mosque. Yassin was arrested, tried, convicted, and sentenced to thirteen years in prison, but released a year later in a prisoner exchange. After that, Yassin preached nonviolence until 1987 when the beginning of the first Intifada and pressure from his restive followers got the better of his caution.

Civil disturbances in Gaza—including demonstrations, riots, tire burning, rock throwing, roadblocks, and even attacks on Israeli patrols—rose dramatically during 1987. Arabs stabbed fifteen Jews that year. A Jewish salesman was stabbed to death. Hostile Arab crowds jeered and stoned IDF patrols and civilian administrators. In Jerusalem, Islamic Jihad contemplated its first suicide bomb attack, but Shin Bet uncovered the plot before it could be carried out. From their hideout in Gaza City, the "Jihad five" conducted a series of "terrorist" attacks. In August, they shot and killed an Israeli officer on a Gaza street in broad daylight. They threw grenades at the IDF Gaza headquarters, ambushed a vehicle belonging to the Israeli intelligence service, and killed two Arab collaborators. On the first day of October, three Jihad gunmen, including one of the escapees, were killed in a shoot-out at an Israeli checkpoint. Five days later, on October 6, Israeli agents and border police ambushed two cars in downtown Gaza City and, in a furious chase, killed four gunmen, including two more escapees. An Israeli agent was also killed. The final two escapees fled to Egypt.

In sermons and handbills throughout the territories, the Jihad blew that incident up as an example of valor and self-sacrifice. Islamic Jihad marks it as the beginning of the first Intifada. Most historians cite an incident two months later, on December 8. The immediate trigger was a traffic accident in Jebalya, a refugee camp of sixty thousand residents near Gaza City. An Israeli truck plowed into a van carrying Arab laborers, killing four and wounding seven. Rumor swept the Arab street that it was a deliberate act of revenge by the relative of an Israeli stabbed to death two days earlier in the Gaza market. Returning from the funerals that evening, thousands of mourners approached the barbed-wire fence surrounding an IDF outpost where a company of Israeli reservists was stationed to keep the peace in Jebalya. The demonstrators threw stones, shouted curses, and chanted, "*Jihad ! Jihad!*" The soldiers fired shots in the air, consistent with their rules of engagements, but to no avail. A patrol ventured out to disperse the crowd, but the crowd surged back. Rioting spread throughout the camp, and continued until almost midnight.

Overnight, barricades of heavy rocks, broken furniture, and sewer pipes were thrown up to block the narrow roads and alleyways of Jebalya. By 6:00 a.m. the next morning, the angry crowd was already reforming, egged on by students of Islamic University. When Israeli patrols ventured out from their compound, the frenzied Palestinians jeered and taunted the soldiers, and hurled stones and homemade Molotov cocktails. The soldiers responded with tear gas and fired shots in the air, and discovered to their surprise that these had no effect. The Palestinians stood their ground. Some bared their breasts and dared the Israelis to fire on them. One of the patrols arrested a stone-throwing youth who displayed a particularly good aim. With the crowd on the verge of rushing to his rescue, the patrol commander ordered the soldiers to fire at their legs. Three Palestinians were hit, and one bled to death from his wounds. The Arabs recoiled from the fusillade, while the soldiers, reinforced by another patrol, made off with the arrested youth, and pulled back into their beleaguered outpost.[18]

In the days that followed, the uprising spread to the camps, towns, and cities of southern Gaza and the West Bank. Rioting continued for twelve straight days. Violence or commercial strikes were reported in Rafah, Ramallah, Jenin, Bethlehem, East Jerusalem, al-Bireh, Nablus, Tulkarm, and other locales. Recognizing that to use firearms would ignite the wrath of the IDF and create a bloodbath, the Arabs made rock-throwing the symbol of resistance.[19] On occasions when a youth would be shot and killed, his funeral would inspire more demonstrations to keep the momentum going.

Only Islamic Jihad was in touch with the angry mood of the demonstrators. Other major players were slow to catch on. To Israeli leaders, it was *déjà vu,* the same old ho-hum disorder that would run its course. Then-Defense Minister Yitzhak Rabin went through with a preplanned trip to the United States, leaving a leadership vacuum when an early deployment of troop reinforcements to key cities might have nipped the intifada in the bud.[20]

It took Arafat at his PLO headquarters in Tunisia several days to understand the deeper significance of the uprising. Then, seeing the danger of being left behind, he tried to get out front and lead it.[21]

Yassin and six of his key followers reportedly met at Yassin's home the night of December 9–10, 1987, to found Hamas (courage, an acronym for *Harakat al-Mukawma al-Islamiya,* Islamic Resistance Movement). They drew its warriors from the military wing of the Brotherhood, and this time added a covert branch to hunt down and murder Arab collaborators and "moral deviants." For Yassin, the wraps were finally off. A few days later, the six-man steering committee put out a handbill vowing to wage holy war against the Zionists. The first leaflet with the Hamas name on it did not come out until January. It would take still a few more weeks before Hamas became fully engaged in the intifada.[22]

The intifada, therefore, was a genuine people's revolution from the ground up, kindled by the oppressive Israeli occupation. Popular committees sprang up locally to direct individual protests. Handbills urged the "heroes of the stone and firebomb war" to set up roadblocks to deny the Israeli army access to the cities and refugee camps, to unfurl the Palestinian flag from minarets, churches, rooftops and light poles, and, above all, to keep throwing stones. "We must set the ground alight under the feet of the occupiers," they said.[23]

From these committees emerged a loose umbrella organization known as the UNC (Unified National Command), led by people who were not household names in the Palestinian society and who did their best to keep their identities secret, but the Shin Bet soon learned their names. The UNC was hardly unified, however. In the West Bank, it included member factions of the PLO and the Communist Party. Arafat, although late for the party, refused to allow UNC upstarts to take over leadership of the struggle for Palestine, and eventually won out by taking over the leadership of UNC. Islamic Jihad talked to the UNC, but never agreed to abide by its decisions. Hamas went its own way. In any case, Israeli intelligence, intent on stopping the distribution of the fiery handbills, tracked down the original UNC leadership within a few months and put it out of action. Twice more it regenerated, and each time the Shin Bet erased it. Arresting leaders, however, did not stop the flow of handbills, because new leaders would step up.

Nor did it translate to suppressing the intifada, which ebbed and flowed for six years. If one day might be calm, it only meant that angry demonstrations were imminent, and the crowds would soon reappear, throwing stones and firebombs, and unfurling Palestinian flags. Then Israeli troops would retaliate with tear gas and rubber bullets, and sometimes, with live ammunition when the crowds became too unruly. Hardly a day passed when a Jewish commuter or businessman did not get stoned driving through an Arab population center. Some motorists retaliated by shooting into the crowds, causing death or injury. But despite its fury, the first intifada was child's play compared to the second that would follow at the turn of the millennium. In between, the belligerents gave peace a chance, but the effort failed.

Oslo and the Second Intifada

By and large, the American public gets a one-sided view of the Arab–Israeli conflict—the Israeli side. The Arab atrocities are real enough, but the context that arouses the Arab anger is often missing. For example, Israel's road map of the West Bank is a seldom-mentioned roadblock on the American diplomatic road map for peace. The Israeli map shows a network of roads connecting West Bank Jewish settlements with Israel and with each other, roads that bind Jewish control of the West Bank like so many straps of asphalt, encapsulating more than three decades of often vigorous housing and infrastructure development. The "by-pass" roads, as they are commonly known, built on land confiscated from Arab farmers to facilitate the safe travel of Jewish settlers, and off-limits to Palestinians, offer one more reason among several for the failure of peace between Israel and Palestine.

Many of the by-pass roads were laid down during the early 1990s at a time when the Labor Government of the late Premier Yitzhak Rabin and then-Foreign Minister Shimon Peres was talking peace with Palestinian leaders under the Oslo initiative. Rabin and Peres, who shared the 1994 Nobel Peace Prize with PLO Chairman Arafat, negotiated at cross-purposes. They truly wanted peace—especially in the form of relief from the youthful Arab stone throwers of the first intifada, but they had no intention of giving Arafat anything more than a token Palestinian nation perpetually under Israel's thumb. Israeli designs on the so-called occupied territories are the unspoken context for terrorism that American presidents have consistently tried to finesse, even before a new generation of Palestinians brought it to the world's attention.

Beyond building roads, Rabin and Peres increased the number of Jewish settlers in the West Bank by 40 percent (from 100,000 to 140,000 people) over four years, oversaw a large-scale program of housing development on existing settlements, and acquired new Arab land for future expansion.[24] In 2001, the Mitchell Report on the causes of the second (al-Aqsa) intifada recommended a freeze on settlements, which are illegal under international law.[25] It is a recommendation that the Israeli government, no matter who's in charge, has heard ad nauseam, and seems always to greet "in-your-face" by announcing plans to build more settlements.[26] Rabin was more nuanced. He halted the expansion of settlements on new land even while continuing to acquire new land, but authorized more construction in existing settlements to accommodate "natural growth."

While thus changing the "facts on the ground," to borrow the Israeli parlance, and solidifying Israel's "creeping annexation" of the West Bank, Rabin managed to convince the world that his heart was pure simply by negotiating with Arafat who really had little to offer. The Israelis asked only that he to put a stop to the violence or in the words of Hanan Ashrawi in a slightly different context, "that the occupied people . . . protect the occupation army."[27] The political left in Israel, Arafat, and President Clinton (in the role of "honest broker") all saw the buildup, and said nothing. A few years later, when the Oslo dream crashed, Arafat seemed to regret his timidity, prompting the late Palestinian–American scholar, Edward Said, to wish while Arafat lived that "his nightmares are made up of unending rides on the [Jewish] roads."[28]

Rabin and Peres contributed at least as much as any previous Israeli government to the consolidation of the West Bank into the Greater Israel of Biblical promise. Confirmation of that comes from no less of an authority than Finance Minister Dan Meridor in the Likud government that followed them. Rabin and Peres said Meridor, "deserve the highest praise" for their settlement policy. He told a *Ha'aretz* correspondent in 1996 as Likud was taking power under Binyamin Netanyahu that he had reassured the American ambassador that Likud "will not change the Labor government's real policy of massive settlement."[29] "Real policy" is the operative term for Meridor, highlighting the difference between perception and reality. Rabin and especially Peres were widely viewed as "doves," but when it came to settlement policy, which is at the heart of the Israeli–Palestinian conflict, the hawks in Likud and the doves in Labor were on the same track.

After Rabin and Peres, successive Israeli governments headed by Likud's Netanyahu and Labor's Ehud Barak negotiated further concessions under Oslo, always retaining slices of the Palestinian pie for Israeli settlements and security. Sharon came to power in 2001, but never got around to negotiating with Arafat. If he had, he would have kept a bigger slice than Barak. What remains constant amid all the shuffling of personalities, when Israeli leaders sit down at the table, they play their cards with Palestinian chips. Arafat's death in 2004 did not change that. In essence, Israeli settlers have been the de facto "white minority" dominating the majority Palestinians under an iron-fisted military dictatorship. From that dismal condition, akin to "apartheid," as former U.S. President Jimmy Carter has described it, have come two violent expressions of Palestinian grief, the intifada (uprisings). The first was a genuine popular revolt sparked by a harsh Israeli occupation and spearheaded by youthful stone-throwers. The second brought armed conflict of the most brutal kind in which Islamic terrorists targeted innocent civilians and the Israeli military fought back with rockets, tanks, and bulldozers, flattening Palestinian homes and killing innocent civilians along with the terrorists.

It must have been fatigue after four years of rioting that induced Israel and the Palestinians to enter into peace negotiations in 1991. The Oslo talks were to be carried out in three stages: (1) a Declaration of Principles, (2) an interim agreement, and (3) permanent status. The first stage negotiations got underway in Madrid with a Palestinian delegation—composed of prominent Palestinians from educational and charitable organizations—demanding the full withdrawal of Israeli troops from the occupied territories as a first step. Their position was consistent with the provisions of UN Resolution 242 and other declarations of the world body. But Israel had no intention of withdrawing. While the talks dragged on in Madrid, the Israelis, backed by the United States, entered into secret negotiations with the PLO in Oslo and Washington.

The first fruits of the Oslo talks in 1994 called for Palestinian control of the West Bank town of Jericho and 65 percent of the Gaza Strip. The following year, the interim agreement (Oslo II) divided the West Bank into three zones: Zone A, the cities and towns, less than 3 percent of the land; Zone B, the rural villages, about 23 percent; and Zone C, farmland, water tables, and land confiscated for Israeli settlements and roads, about 74 percent. Israel turned over Zone A (except part of Hebron) to the PA. In Zone B, the Palestinians took responsibility for civil affairs, while the IDF retained control of security. Zone C was left totally in Israeli hands pending negotiations on a permanent status.[30] Oslo II was signed on September 28, 1995, in a sun-drenched ceremony behind the White House. President Clinton smiled benignly as an ebullient Arafat shook hands with Rabin and Peres. Optimism reigned supreme for completion of the final stage negotiations within two years. But the facts on the ground—principally the mutual hatreds—soon caught up with the hopes in the air.

In an outlandish twist of fate, Rabin paid for his compromise with his life. On the night of November 4, 1995, after a peace rally in Tel Aviv's Kings of Israel Square, Yigal Amir, a yeshiva student with ties to the religious right, shot and killed him for his role in creating what little there was of a Palestinian state (65 percent of the tiny Gaza Strip and 3 percent of the West Bank—the Jewish far right would not give a square inch). It came as a great shock to most of the outside world that a Jew had killed the Jewish prime minister. The assassin, incited by inflammatory rabbinical rhetoric against the Oslo agreement, obviously did not recognize how skillfully Rabin had advanced the expansionist cause that the right wing embraced by building by-pass roads and more housing and confiscating new land for future development.

Hamas and Islamic Jihad had opposed the Oslo initiative from the beginning with suicide missions like one in October 1993 when a bomb-laden car crashed into an Israeli bus, leaving thirty people wounded. Hamas claimed credit for the incident. Through the 1990s, suicide missions were an occasional, but unambiguous menace.

Right-wing Jewish settlers had also bestirred themselves that year—partly to protest the Oslo negotiations and partly in reprisal against Arab attacks—by committing random assaults against Palestinians that resulted in at least one death and several injuries. Then, on February 25, 1994, during the Muslim holy period of Ramadan, a devout Orthodox Jew and respected physician, Dr. Baruch Goldstein, tried to outdo the Muslim terrorists. Dressed as an officer of the IDF and armed with an automatic Glilon rifle, Goldstein slipped into the al-Ibrahimi Mosque in Hebron very early in the morning and opened fire on about five hundred unsuspecting Muslim worshippers. He emptied four clips containing 111 bullets each, killing twenty-nine Muslims and wounding more than two hundred before the weapon jammed, which gave surviving worshippers the opportunity to jump him and beat him to death. A state investigation concluded that Goldstein, a member of the late Meir Kahane's Kach movement, had planned the atrocity well in advance, but had acted alone out of a self-imposed religious duty without giving notice to anyone, including his wife and four children and his co-extremists in Kach.[31] In March. the Israeli Cabinet outlawed Kach and Kahane Chai, declaring them to be terrorist organizations.

In the Arab culture, such gruesome acts are sure to trigger the unwritten law of the vendetta. Hamas reacted by stepping up its terrorist campaign. In April, it carried out two bus bombings inside Israel, which together killed fourteen Israelis and wounded more than seventy. In October, a suicide bomber killed twenty-two people by blowing up a commuter bus in Tel Aviv. A Hamas spokesman justified it as part of its *jihad* against the "Israeli occupation of all of Palestine" and retaliation for Gold-stein's Hebron massacre. While Arafat was in talks with the Israelis, Islamic Jihad joined in the slaughter. Between the two Islamist groups, they carried out at least eight suicide bombings in Israel in 1995. Americans visiting or living in Israel were among those killed.

After the signing of Oslo II in the fall of 1995, Arafat took over the PA in an atmosphere poisoned by extremists on both sides. It was strange to see Arafat positioned in the political middle. As promised in Oslo II, he moved quickly to reign in terrorist activities, and learned that his authority went nowhere with radical Palestinians, even those in his own ranks. Two PLO member groups, the PFLP, founded by George Habash, and the DFLP (Democratic Front for the Liberation of Palestine), the Naif Hawatmeh faction, bolted the umbrella organization to continue their campaigns of violence. Islamic Jihad simply ignored him. Hamas temporarily suspended its terrorist activities and entered into talks with the PA about participating in elections scheduled for January 1996. Hopes were dashed in early January when the Shin Bet assassinated Hamas' chief bomb-maker, Yahya Ayyash, by booby-trapping his cell phone. Hamas exacted revenge on February 25 when a suicide bomber blew up a commuter bus in Jerusalem, killing twenty-six and injur-ing eighty. Hamas announced afterward that this bombing settled the score for the Ayyash assassination, but that did not keep the blood from flowing. On March 3, another bus bombing in Jerusalem killed nineteen and injured six, and the next day a suicide bomber struck outside a Tel Aviv shopping mall, killing twenty and wounding seventy-five, including children celebrating the Jewish Purim holiday. A Hamas splinter group claimed responsibility.

These devastating hits came as Peres was filling out Rabin's term. Facing election on May 29, he spoke of waging war against the terrorists, and ordered a raid on the home village of the suicide bombers. At the same time, he promised to continue the peace talks. Skeptical Israelis weighed his words against the realities and thought he was promising more than he could deliver. His substantial lead in the polls was reduced to a dead heat. Then in an apparent effort to toughen his dovish image, he ordered a disastrous IDF incursion into southern Lebanon in April that resulted in the displacement of thousands of Shiite peasants and the death of two hundred refugees, half of them from the deliberate shelling of the UN compound in Qana. In May, after less than seven months as prime minister, Peres was voted out of office.

His Likud successor was thought to be the real hawk. American-educated Binya-min Netanyahu, whose brother, Jonathan, died a hero in the famous hostage rescue operation at Entebbe, had campaigned on a promise of "peace with security." He was expected to take a hard line against further Oslo negotiations. But he surprised every-one by vowing to move the peace talks forward. At the Wye River (Maryland) plan-tation in 1998, he agreed to tweak the West Bank zones in Palestine's favor. Zone A grew from 2.8 percent to 18.2 percent under full Palestinian control. Zone B receded slightly from 23.2 percent to 21.8 percent under shared control, while Zone C shrank from 74 percent to 60 percent under full Israeli control. It was a shuffle of the deck that made no practical difference because the IDF still ranged over 81.8 percent of the West Bank. All the thorny issues of IDF withdrawal, Palestinian statehood, settlements, Jerusalem, and refugees remained for final stage negotiations in 1999.

If the miniscule Wye concessions were meant to appease the Palestinians, Netanyahu had already done quite enough to anger them. In September 1996, he threw a bone to his religious right supporters by carving a new entrance to a tunnel for tourists alongside the Temple Mount (Haram al-Sharif to the Muslims), a site sacred to Islam and Judaism alike. It was significant because it seemed to flout Jewish sovereignty over the Temple Mount, which the Muslims also claimed. So it was certain to ignite Muslim protests. Pitched battles between Arab demonstrators and Israeli troops erupted throughout the West Bank as Arafat's Palestinian police vacillated between quelling and protecting the rioters. The death toll came to more than sixty Palestinians and twelve Israeli soldiers.

In January 1997, Netanyahu agreed to a partial redeployment of the IDF in the West Bank, but left a settler group of four hundred devout Jews amidst 120,000 Arabs in the heart of Hebron with a military guard to protect them. The Palestinians inferred that Netanyahu was not serious about reversing the Israeli settlement policy. He reinforced that impression in March by approving a huge new housing project in East Jerusalem called Har Homa at a site overlooking Bethlehem, which closed the circle of new Jewish homes around the old Arab section. Ground was broken on March 18. Five days later a Hamas "martyr" exploded a suicide bomb in a Tel Aviv cafe, killing three Israelis and wounding forty-eight.

Before the year was out, still another housing development sprouted up in Ras el-Amud, an Arab section of East Jerusalem, on land purchased by an American businessman, Irving Moscowitz. This one, Netanyahu publicly opposed, but did not stop. Hamas launched two more major strikes in Jerusalem. On July 30, two suicide bombers slipped into a crowded market, killing sixteen and wounding 178, and on September 4 three more "martyrs" blew themselves up in a pedestrian mall, killing five and wounding nearly 200. The horrid suicide bombings, reminiscent of Zionist terrorism in the 1930s, and Algerian terrorism in the 1950s were duly reported in the American media while the context was largely ignored.

In 1999, Netanyahu stood for reelection, but lost to Labor's Barak, a decorated soldier who made peace with Israel's neighbors his first priority. He kept his promise about Lebanon by unilaterally quitting Israel's counterproductive occupation. He reached out to Syrian President Hafez al-Assad to negotiate the Golan issue, but could not close the deal. Then turning to the Palestine issue, he sat down with the man he had once set out to kill on an Israeli commando raid in Beirut. Barak staked his presidency—and lost it—on striking an agreement with Arafat to finalize the Oslo Accords.

The series of negotiations between Barak and Arafat, including meetings at Camp David with President Clinton as mediator, aroused great expectations, but ended with shattered dreams. Significantly, the Jewish Virtual Library, which lists 127 "major" Palestinian terrorist incidents from the first Oslo agreement in 1993 to early 2004, recorded none from November 7, 1999 to October 26, 2000, a period of nearly one year of intense bargaining for peace.[32]

The talks focused on the 22 percent of Palestine that remained after the 1948 war. Arafat had conceded in the earlier Oslo talks the extension of Israel into the West Bank to cover the heaviest concentrations of Israeli settlements. The land actually mattered less to him than the status of Jerusalem. He wanted East Jerusalem as the Palestinian capital, and he wanted sovereignty over Haram al-Sharif (Temple Mount). These things Barak could not give if he wanted to survive in Israel's rough-and-tumble political atmosphere, yet under tremendous pressure from President Clinton he offered Arafat the Muslim and Christian sections of the Old City, but not Haram. In this and other ways, he went further than any other Israeli leader. He would also return all of Gaza and 90 percent of the West Bank to Palestinian control. Although the West Bank would still have been divided into three parts and Arafat would not get all he wanted in Jerusalem, it was the best offer the Palestinians had ever had. He turned it down without making a counter offer. Clinton proposed a settlement that would have given Palestine sovereignty over the sacred-to-them Dome of the Rock and Israel, control of the Western Wall beneath which ancient Jewish temples are believed buried. Both parties rejected it. The talks broke up in failure. Barak returned home to withering criticism from Sharon for even discussing the partition of Jerusalem.

—

On September 28, 2000, Sharon visited the Haram al-Sharif (Temple Mount), accompanied by more than a thousand police. Both Palestinian and American officials warned Prime Minister Barak that Sharon's presence at this sensitive site could trigger violence. Dennis Ross, America's Middle East envoy, was quoted as saying, "I can think of a lot of bad ideas, but I can't think of worse one."[33] Barak, however, refused to prevent it, insisting that Sharon was playing domestic politics aimed at him, and did not mean to provoke an Arab insurrection. At Haram, Sharon declared, "I came here with a message of peace. I believe that we can live together with the Palestinians. I came here to the holiest place of the Jewish people in order to see what happens here."[34]

What happened was mayhem. The next day, Palestinian demonstrators throwing stones confronted Israeli police firing rubber-coated bullets and live ammunition. Four Palestinians were killed, and about two hundred injured. Fourteen Israeli police were also injured. A day later, with television news cameras rolling, twelve-year-old Muhammad al Durra was killed in a cross-fire between Israelis and Palestinians as he huddled against a wall behind his father who tried in vain to protect him. Nongovernment sources inside Israel argued that the fatal bullets did not come from the IDF.[35] Demonstrations continued for several days. On October 12, an Arab mob lynched two Israeli military reservists. The Mitchell Report on the causes of the second Intifada called Sharon's visit to the Temple Mount ill considered and badly timed—diplomatic language to obfuscate a provocative act, but reserved blame for the renewed Intifada on the decision of Israeli police to use lethal force and on the failure of leaders on both sides to restrain the antagonists.[36]

Stone-throwers soon played a secondary role to terrorists. The Palestinian Islamists seemed to take heart from Israel's total withdrawal from Lebanon to end the persistent Hezbollah attacks against the IDF. Now, they thought, they would bring the war home to Israel and the settlements in the West Bank and Gaza. Within those spheres it was a war without boundaries, geographical or ethical. Hamas, Islamic Jihad, Fatah's al-Aqsa Martyrs' Brigade, and other armed, nongovernment groups or individuals might strike anywhere without distinguishing between military and civilian targets. They used homemade bombs for "martyrdom operations" and crude homemade mortars to attack settlements and other targets. They ambushed civilian and military vehicles on the road, or poured in sniper fire on Jewish settlements from concealed positions with pistols, rifles, semiautomatic weapons, and ammunition they acquired illegally from Palestinian security services, stole from Israeli armories, or purchased from rogue Israeli merchants. Some of these weapons were smuggled in from Lebanon through Jordan and Egypt, courtesy of Hezbollah and the PFLP.[37] Israel would retaliate with precision bombs and rockets to kill militants and giant bulldozers to level homes and offices. Civilian bystanders inevitably got in the way and paid the ultimate price. American military aid and Israel's state-of-the-art defense industry supplied the IDF with its devastating firepower.

The peace movement collapsed in 2001, and not just Arab militants contributed to a pronounced change in mood. When President Bush took power, he said at the first meeting of his NSC on January 30 that Clinton had overreached in his efforts to resolve the Arab–Israeli dispute, and it was time for America to disengage. A startled Secretary of State Colin Powell protested that a hands-off approach might encourage Sharon, expected to be the next Israeli prime minister, to unleash the powerful IDF against the Palestinians with dire consequences. The president's reply revealed a hard edge to his thinking, "Maybe that's the best way to get things back in balance. Sometimes a show of strength by one side can really clarify things."[38] Throughout his first four-year term in office, the president remained firmly on Sharon's side, putting the burden for peace on Arafat to halt the terrorism.

In February, Barak was voted out of office. Sharon, who had promised during the election campaign to bring peace, led Israel through the fires of hell during his first fifteen months in office. When he formally took power on March 7 with a coalition cabinet that prominently included Peres as his foreign minister, a Hamas leader said suicide bombers were "lined up to greet" him.[39] The first to step forward on March 27 in Jerusalem wounded twenty-eight people. The same day Islamic Jihad planted a car bomb in Jerusalem that wounded seven. The next day a suicide bomber from Hamas struck at a school bus stop near Kfar Sava, killing two and wounding four.

Sharon rejected the Mitchell Report's call in May for a total freeze on settlement construction, ordering instead a unilateral cease-fire against the Palestinian terrorists.

Hamas responded on the night of June 1 by raising the level of violence. A suicide bomber struck outside a disco at the Tel Aviv shore, where young Russian immigrants were lined up waiting to get in. Twenty-one people were killed, including the bomber, and 120 injured. Sharon held to the cease-fire, except for the continued covert assassination of known Palestinian terrorists. His restraint proved to be a public relations success that gained him a spate of international support. But at best, it was a tenuous cease-fire, with terrorist attacks escalating through the spring and into the summer. In August, a Palestinian detonated bombs packed with nails and shrapnel in a crowded Jerusalem pizzeria. Nineteen people were killed, six of them children, and more than a hundred wounded.

That moved Sharon to retaliate. After an urgent meeting of a divided cabinet, he sent a large police force to Orient House, the Palestinian political headquarters in East Jerusalem. The police removed a large stash of documents and replaced the Palestinian flag flying from the roof with the Star of David. Sharon explained the flag exchange as a symbolic gesture that struck the Palestinians "in their soft underbelly" where it would disturb them the most. Orient House, he vowed, would never reopen.[40] More Palestinian attacks and more Israeli retaliations followed. On September 9, an Israeli Arab became a suicide bomber for the first time. Mohammed Shaqir Habishi blew himself up at a train station in northern Israel, killing three and wounding ninety.

On October 17, the assassination of a prominent politician removed all Israeli restraint. Rehavam Zeevi, who had resigned two days earlier as minister of tourism in the Sharon cabinet, was found dead in a pool of blood outside his room in Jerusalem's Hyatt Hotel, shot three times in the head and face. The PFLP said it had dispatched hit men to hunt him down for the killing two months earlier of PFLP leader Mustafa Zibri (Abu Ali Mustafa), when two missiles fired from helicopters struck his office in Ramallah. He was one of about fifty Palestinians killed over the years in targeted Israeli assassinations, a death toll that sometimes included innocent bystanders.

Sharon reacted forcefully, telling his cabinet, "Everything has changed." He restored travel curbs in the West Bank and Gaza that he had lifted only three days earlier. He sent tanks and armored cars to seal off Nablus, Jenin, and Ramallah, where tanks stopped a half-mile from Arafat's headquarters. The isolated Palestinian leader expressed regret for Zeevi's assassination, but refused to turn over the suspects. The situation lapsed into an even more dangerous cycle of violence. More angry Palestinian demonstrations inspired more shootings and terrorist attacks. Israel broadened its military incursions, sending troops into several Palestinian towns.

The Bush Administration, under pressure to do something about the Arab–Israeli conflict as it sought Arab support for its plan to invade Iraq, sent retired Marine General Anthony Zinni to the trouble spot as special envoy to the Middle East. Zinni did his best to bring the parties to the negotiating table, but the mission was really a fiasco from start to unresolved finish. It began with Zinni on a four-hour helicopter tour of Israel and the West Bank on November 27, during which two

Arab gunmen from Jenin fired on passersby at a bus station in Afula in northern Israel, killing two and wounding dozens before police shot them dead. It was another vengeance attack sponsored in this case by Islamic Jihad and Fatah's al-Aqsa Martyrs Brigade. Zinni watched the cleanup and the evacuation of the wounded from a helicopter that hovered overhead. That night a Hamas gunman killed an Israeli woman and wounded three other people near a Gaza settlement.

Zinni said that he had learned a lot that day, and that it proved the importance of gaining a cease-fire. Two days later, a suicide bomber sent by Islamic Jihad boarded a bus near Hadera, and set off an explosion that left three dead and nine wounded. Two days after that, on December 1, two Hamas suicide bombers standing about thirty yards apart touched off simultaneous massive explosions a half-hour before midnight at the Ben Yahudda shopping promenade in Jerusalem. Ten Israelis were killed and about 180 wounded. Zinni said these efforts to sabotage his mission would not succeed. At rush hour the next morning, another Hamas bomber blew himself up inside an Israeli bus in Haifa, killing fifteen passengers and wounding forty-six.

Responding to pressure on Arafat to rein in the militants, the PA security forces arrested about a hundred Islamic militants. But Arafat had made so many such gestures, which had all turned up empty, that the Israelis simply belittled it as a charade. Sharon sent the army into the West Bank to bottle up Palestinian towns, and the Israeli Air Force launched heavy strikes against Jenin and other targets. Apache helicopters destroyed two of Arafat's three personal Russian-made helicopters at his Gaza headquarters, and badly damaged the third. Bulldozers plowed up the runways at the PA's international airport. Within days helicopter gunships took out a security post at the entrance to the Ramallah government compound. The idea was to immobilize Arafat, and then they tried to shut him up by destroying his 100-foot radio transmission tower.

Arafat, one of the great survivors of the twentieth century, acquired a siege mentality. Fearing that the Israelis were going to kill him, he actually took tentative steps to rein in the radicals. PA police approached the home of Yassin in Gaza to put him under house arrest, but stone-throwing youth came to his defense, reinforced by about 1,500 adult men, some of them armed with rifles. The Palestinian police fought the Palestinian demonstrators with tear gas, rubber bullets, and riot sticks. One man was killed and three others were wounded in the melee, which ended when Yassin agreed to house arrest. The police then stationed themselves a mile from his home, which left the paralyzed holy man confined to his house with room to spare. The PA also conducted raids against Hamas militants in the West Bank, but announced their intentions in advance, giving their targets time to disappear.

Zinni called for a two-day cease-fire, and Hamas responded with more attacks. Israeli ground and air forces retaliated with strikes against Palestinian targets in the West Bank and Gaza. Zinni departed two days later to fly home for the Christmas holidays. He returned on January 3, 2002, but hopes for renewed talks, almost nonexistent to begin with, were torpedoed by the Israeli seizure of a ship in the Red Sea, which Israel said was destined for Gaza and loaded with arms from Iran.

The arms seizure and subsequent display for the media yielded a bounty of propaganda for the Sharon government. Sharon said it proved that Arafat was a terrorist. Zinni was less severe in his judgment, but he conceded that Arafat was caught "with his hand in the cookie jar." Arafat denied that he or his government had anything to do with it, but he failed to convince the Americans. Six months later, with less fanfare, the Israeli government announced the arrest of five Israelis for allegedly selling 60,000 rounds of ammunition to the militant Palestinian group Tanzim. The five men were not part of the religious right, although four of them lived in two small settlements near Hebron. All but one belonged to the IDF. It was strongly suggested that the sale involved much more than ammunition, that it may have included weapons, uniforms, and other military equipment, and was part of a long-term pattern.[41] Tanzim, the military wing of Fatah headed by Marwan Bargouti, is best known for carrying out guerrilla attacks against Israeli settlements, buses, and military targets. That Israelis should traffic in arms with militant Palestinians is comparable on the scale of lunacy to a Jew assassinating an Israeli prime minister.

Twenty-eight-year-old Wafa Idris made history on January 27. She became the first female suicide bomber. She killed an old man and wounded more than a hundred passersby on the Jaffa road in Jerusalem. Fatah sponsored her, but Yassin said it was contrary to Islamic law for a woman to commit such acts when men were available to do them. That did not stop more Muslim women from joining the ranks of martyrs. In fact, martyrdom became an obscene fad in the youthful Palestinian society. Later that spring, three boys in their mid-teens, armed with knives and crude homemade bombs, crept up on a tightly guarded settlement in Gaza and were shot dead before they reached the wall. One boy had left a note saying he wanted his grave to be like Muhammad's, and asked his family to "visit my grave if you have time." The boys' parents demanded an investigation to determine if any radical group had recruited them. Hamas and Islamic Jihad denied responsibility, and promised to speak out in local mosques against children going on suicide missions.[42]

Zinni doggedly pursued his efforts to forge a cease-fire. In March, he called Israeli and Palestinian negotiators to a meeting. To his surprise, they greeted each other like old friends, shaking hands, embracing, back slapping, and chatting amiably. But when they got down to business at the bargaining table, positions hardened and they began screaming back and forth. Zinni pounded his fist on the table and screamed back at them to stop. Then he presented his proposal for a cease-fire: the Palestinians must first put a stop to the terrorism; then the Israelis were to pull back its army from Palestinian territory. For the PA, the plan had two basic flaws. First, Arafat could not control Hamas or Islamic Jihad, and, second, it left the first step up to the Palestinians. The negotiating teams returned to present the plan to their respective leaders. It was fine for the Israelis because it put Arafat on the spot. They called the Americans to indicate their formal acceptance. But the Palestinians turned it down because it was "sequential" rather than "parallel." They argued that the Palestinian crackdown on terrorism and the Israeli pullback should take place simultaneously.

On March 27, while the two sides were mulling the Zinni Plan, Hamas made the discussion moot by sending twenty-three-year-old Abdel-Basset Odeh to a Passover Seder at the Park Hotel in Natanya dressed like a girl, clean shaven and wearing a curly wig, with a bomb belt under his outer garments. He walked past security at the front door, and slipped into a dining room where 250 people were celebrating the delivery of the ancient Jews from slavery in Egypt. The blast killed twenty-nine and injured 140. In a fit of outrage, Israel launched a full-scale military response called Operation Defensive Shield, which proved to be the "clarification" that President Bush had anticipated more than a year earlier. Armored columns attacked Ramallah, Qalquilya, and Bethlehem, and in succeeding days entered Beit Jala, Tulkarm, Jenin, Salfit, Nablus, the largest city in the West Bank, and, finally, Hebron. In effect, it was an Israeli reoccupation of the entire West Bank, which began with some notable battles.

Sharon vowed that the siege of Ramallah would last for weeks; it actually stretched out for months. Troops sacked the offices of the PA, found documents confirming Arafat's complicity in terrorist activity, and seized weapons barred under terms of the Oslo Accords. They made no effort to arrest Arafat who remained confined to his office suite. About this time, Zinni and his negotiating team paid Arafat a visit at his compound, the Muqata. In the midst of all the destruction and foul stench, he found Arafat looking more alive than he had ever seen him. The old revolutionary, he thought, was in his element.[43] Sharon promised Arafat safe passage to leave, but said that if he did, he would not be allowed to return. Arafat opted to stay, and even after the IDF finally withdrew in November, he spent almost the entire last two-and-a-half years of his life inside his ruined compound.

Bethlehem witnessed a five-week standoff between the IDF and 123 Palestinian gunmen holed up in the Church of the Nativity at the site of the manger where Jesus was born. The militants mingled with more than a hundred policemen, clerics, school children, and peace activists who also took refuge inside the church. As historian Penny Young wrote, "The sight of the huge Israeli tanks lumbering through Bethlehem's narrow stone streets around what is one of the oldest and holiest churches in Christendom was almost apocalyptic."[44] Eight people died in the siege. Although Israeli bombs and missiles pulverized surrounding buildings, the church was unscathed. The hostilities were resolved through negotiations, with the thirteen most dangerous militants agreeing to exile.

In Jenin, the source of many Islamist recruits for suicide missions, the IDF met its stiffest resistance and suffered its highest casualties, twenty-three dead, fourteen in one bad day, and seventy-five wounded. What the IDF planned as a three-day mission required twelve days to execute, as a hundred-or-so well-prepared urban guerrillas faced off against a thousand Israeli troops. The Israelis' most effective weapon was a huge, fifty-ton armored bulldozer that could turn a narrow passageway into a wide avenue as it crushed flimsy cinderblock houses and touched off hidden bombs. The IDF left the refugee camp in ruins, redolent with the stench of death, and hounded by Palestinian claims of hundreds of civilians massacred that proved to be unfounded. A UN investigating team counted fifty-four killed, including several noncombatants, and another forty-nine missing. That was lower than the death toll in Nablus where seventy-eight Palestinians died in a parallel Israeli attack.[45]

AI (Amnesty International) took stock of the damage in its annual report covering 2002, the worst year of the al-Aqsa intifada. It reported, in round numbers, the death of a thousand Palestinians at the hands of the IDF, including 150 children. Israeli assassinations of terrorist leaders accounted for thirty-five deaths, including some innocent bystanders. AI also documented the destruction of two thousand Palestinian homes, and charged the IDF with abuses that amounted to war crimes, namely the obstruction of medical assistance, the targeting of medical personnel, unlawful confinement, the torture of prisoners, and the use of "human shields." On the Palestinian side, Hamas, Islamic Jihad, Fatah's al-Aqsa Martyrs Brigade, and other militant groups killed more than 420 Israelis. The dead included 265 civilians, forty-seven of whom were children. Twenty foreign nationals, several of them Americans, were also among the dead. The deliberate targeting of civilians, said AI, "constituted crimes against humanity."[46] The two-year death toll of children, going back to September 2000, was more than three hundred, about 250 Palestinians and seventy-two Israelis. AI was particularly critical of the IDF for killing Palestinian children throwing stones at Israeli tanks when the lives of Israeli troops were not at risk.[47]

The Saudi monarchy pressured the White House to put the squeeze on Israel to withdraw its strike force from the West Bank. President Bush paid attention because he thought he might need Saudi help for the invasion of Iraq, then in the planning stage. So he spoke to Sharon, who agreed to end the West Bank incursion if the United States would quash a full-blown UN inquiry into the Israeli destruction of Jenin. It all came to pass, and Israel pulled its strike force out of the West Bank, leaving behind its occupation force.

Palestine's Arab neighbors, the Europeans, and the United States pressed forward with initiatives to end the intifada. A British undercover agent persuaded the pro-Arafat Tanzim to stop killing innocent women and children. Then the PA prevailed on Yassin for Hamas to do the same. It helped that Saudi Arabia threw its weight behind the PA. But it all went for naught when on July 23, 2002, Israel dropped a one-ton precision bomb on the residence of Salah Shahadeh, the military leader of Hamas. Shahadeh and thirteen others, who lived in the same apartment building, including nine children, were killed—along with the peace effort.

King Abdullah of Jordan talked President Bush into drawing up a "road map" for peace. But the President refused to deal with Arafat, demanding that he turn over the reins of government to a prime minister. Arafat appointed a long-time ally, Mahmoud Abbas (Abu Mazen), but retained control of security, which left the new prime minister without the power to enforce his decisions. Then Bush announced a "road map" similar to the Clinton proposal that Arafat had rejected—with the notable exception that the Bush plan called on each of the parties to act simultaneously on its part of the bargain. "Sequential" was out; "parallel" was in. Israel would have to halt settlement activity and withdraw its army from Palestinian territory, and simultaneously trust the Palestinians to put an end to terrorism. This time Israel balked.

Nevertheless, the Americans, having just crushed the Iraqi army in March and April 2003, now sought to leverage their victory with a summit conference in Jordan to tackle the Arab–Israeli dispute. The American neoconservatives had been saying that the road to Jerusalem goes through Baghdad, and the Americans had just gone through Baghdad. Bush, a Texas politician shrewdly guided in electioneering, lacked experience in international affairs. That did not deter him. When he came to the summit at a Jordanian resort on the Gulf of Aqaba on June 4, 2003, he let it be known that he was divinely inspired. The then Palestinian foreign minister, Nabil Shaath, explained it thus in a BBC documentary in 2005:

> President Bush said to all of us, "I'm driven with a mission from God. God would tell me, 'George, go and fight those terrorists in Afghanistan,' and I did. And God would tell me, 'George, go and end the tyranny in Iraq,' and I did. Now, again, I feel God's words coming to me, 'Go and get the Palestinians their state, and the Israelis their security, and get peace in the Middle East,' and, by God, I'm gonna do it."[48]

A somewhat different version of the Bush soliloquy was reported in the respected Israeli newspaper *Ha'aretz,* based on minutes of the meeting obtained a week after the June 2003 summit. In this case, Abu Mazen was relating it: "Bush said, 'God told me to strike at al Qaida, and I struck them. And then he instructed me to strike at Saddam, which I did. And now I am determined to solve the problems of the Middle East. If you help me, I will act, and if not, the elections will come and I will have to focus on them.'"[49] Abbas would not repeat his story for BBC. He recalled only hearing Bush say, "I have a moral and religious obligation. So I will get you a Palestinian state."[50] In any case, neither Shaath nor Abu Mazen took the president's words literally, but saw them as a manifestation of his deep religious faith. But Bush reportedly expressed similar thoughts to Canadian Prime Minister Paul Martin at a later meeting between the two. The White House spokesman Scott McClellan denied that President Bush ever said any such thing, although it is consistent with other statements from Bush indicating that he sees his destiny tied to God's will. For example, he told the sympathetic Christian author Stephen Mansfield, "I feel like God wants me to run for president." To say the least, it was an unusual way to conduct foreign policy.

The public part of that high-flown get-together was shamelessly staged in the now-familiar slick style of the White House productions. The four leaders in attendance—Bush, Abbas, Sharon, and Abdullah—walked side-by-side in the sweltering Red Sea heat to a platform built at the seaside for their encounter with the international media. The stand was air-cooled from beneath the floor to keep them from sweating and streaking their makeup powder in front of the cameras. Abbas read a statement dictated by the Americans, saying that the terrorism must end. He expected Sharon to announce a simultaneous end to settlement expansion and a total Israeli withdrawal from the West Bank and Gaza. After all, the road map called for parallel movement. Sharon said none of that. He only reiterated his determination to fight terrorism until he had wiped it out. Watching on television, Hamas and the other terrorist groups were hanging on every word. Peace died another death.

On August 19, 2003, a Hamas suicide bomber disguised as an Orthodox Jew blew up a crowded bus in Jerusalem, killing twenty-three people, including seven children. Abu Mazen appealed to Arafat to turn security over to him so he could track down those responsible and bring them to justice. Arafat refused, and Abu Mazen resigned. When the Palestinians do not act against terrorism, the Israelis tend to take matters in their own hands—in a much harsher manner. In the late winter of 2004, they assassinated the top two Hamas leaders from the air, Yassin and Sheikh Abdel Aziz Rantissi. The Bush Administration lost interest in Arab–Israeli peace, and shelved the road map. As promised, the president turned his attention to his reelection.

Late in 2003, Sharon announced a plan to withdraw unilaterally from all of Gaza and four isolated settlements of the West Bank. Eight thousand Jewish settlers would have to move back to Israel. In the summer of 2005, Sharon carried out the withdrawal in the face of opposition from Israel's religious right, which voiced condemnation of him, their erstwhile hero, similar to what they heaped on Rabin after he signed the Oslo Accords. Settler resistance failed to materialize in Gaza on the expected scale. Most settlers left of their own accord as the government marshaled thirty thousand troops to physically remove the last diehards.

Operation Defensive Shield, in which hundreds of active terrorists were killed or captured, clearly blunted Palestinian terrorism. The raw figures tell the story. In the first three months of 2002, the Palestinians carried out forty major terrorist attacks, an average of three a week. The IDF's onslaught began at the end of March after the Seder bombing in Natanya. In the next three months, the Palestinians mounted nine attacks inside Israel, an average of three a month. Another in the West Bank on April 27 was notable for its depravity. Three armed Palestinian men attacked the small settlement of Andora, near Hebron. One of them shot and killed a five-year-old girl hiding in terror under her bed, and wounded her mother and two younger brothers. Three adults were killed elsewhere in the settlement. Both Hamas and the PFLP claimed responsibility.[51] From mid-June until the end of the year, the attacks ceased altogether. In all of 2003, there were only five incidents. But they were bloody affairs, suicide attacks that collectively produced seventy-nine killed and nearly four hundred injured. One incident in Haifa that resulted in nineteen killed and sixty wounded took place on October 4 in a restaurant owned and frequented by Jews and Israeli Arabs, as if to signal denunciation of any form of fraternization between them. Islamic Jihad claimed credit.[52]

If Oslo failed, the rampant violence of the second intifada made the Palestinian predicament even worse. For the Zionists, Algerians, Vietnamese, mujahidin in Afghanistan, and Hezbollah in Lebanon, guerrilla warfare and/or terrorism helped to drive out occupiers. But it did not work for the PLO in the 1970s and 1980s, and so far it has backfired on the Palestinian Islamists. In 2002, Abu Mazen called the second Intifada a "disaster," and chastised leaders of the Fatah movement for pursuing it. "What happened in these two years," he told them, "is a complete destruction of everything we built."[53] Unfortunately, Fatah and the Islamists ignored him, at least until Arafat's death in November 2004.

A trickle of deadly terrorist attacks that continued in 2004 meant that Sharon had failed to carry out his promise to eliminate terrorism. He had only doused the flames while the fire smoldered beneath the surface, sometimes to flare up in more death and destruction. Recognizing the ultimate inadequacy of his iron fist, Sharon tried the concrete-and-barbed-wire shield. In June 2002, Israel began the construction of a barrier to keep terrorists out of Israel, but it seemed also to have another, more devious purpose of annexing Palestinian land. In several places, the wall veered off the "green line," which delineated the pre-1967 border, into the West Bank to encompass densely populated Israeli settlements. A UN investigator from South Africa, John Dugard, charged in an official report that this amounted to "de facto annexation."[54] Israeli officials called the report biased. The invasive wall would enclose about 200,000 Israeli settlers, and leave many Arab farmers stranded on the Israeli side. To build it, the Israelis had to expropriate fertile Arab farmland and uproot olive trees hundreds of years old. In one instance, the wall (at a point where it is actually an electrified fence and patrol road) separated Johnny Atik's home near Jerusalem from his eight acres of olive trees. The land from which Israel shut him out was then confiscated under a 1950 law, which allowed the Custodian of Absentee Property to seize property left behind by refugees from the 1948 war.[55] Of no minor significance on the broad issue of the wall's impact, the 22 percent remaining of the original Palestine would be further reduced, adding more complications to future negotiations over West Bank territory.

Arafat's death in November 2004 created a more hopeful atmosphere for peace negotiations. But as this was written, all the old issues that frustrated the Oslo Accords remained unresolved: the settlements, land and water rights, the by-pass roads, refugees, and the status of Jerusalem. Any peace agreement that does not put them to rest will leave a festering wound in this ancient land of hope and sorrow. Perhaps the Palestinians will come to accept their place on the reservation, as did the Native Americans who were outnumbered and subdued by white settlers from Europe in the eighteenth and nineteenth centuries. Or perhaps, as the Arab numbers grow faster than those of the Jewish settlers, the struggle that began more than a century ago will continue for another century, or more, and draw the world into its ruinous vortex.

Abbas proved no more capable than Arafat of controlling Hamas and Islamic Jihad. It did not help the peace movement, at least in the short term, that Sharon was incapacitated with a stroke and Hamas, whose charter calls for the destruction of Israel, won a free and fair election in January 2006 and took control of the Palestinian government. That resulted in a divided government, with Abbas, the Fatah leader, retaining the presidency and Hamas trying to form and administrate a government. Political bickering between the two factions turned to fighting in the streets, culminating in June 2007 in a total Hamas victory in Gaza and the Fatah takeover of government in the West Bank, and further complicating the road map to peace.

Israel represents a permanent Western presence in the Middle East that Arabs widely resent. From a Western viewpoint, it would be insensitive to begrudge the Jewish people their desire to reclaim their ancient homeland, especially in light of European anti-Semitism that produced malicious pogroms and the genocidal Holocaust. But the European Jews came to Palestine with full knowledge that the Arabs claimed it too. The Jewish victims of Europe prevailed in the Middle East, and the Arabs became the victims of the victims. How, or if the conflict will end is anybody's guess. The Israelis occupation of the West Bank has lasted four decades. The Crusades lasted two centuries before the Christians were finally driven out. While rejectionist Arabs with their new terrorist weapons see the Crusades as their guiding star, the elimination of Israel is nowhere on the visible horizon. As for the two-state solution, if history is any guide, the odds are against it. But any effort to mediate an agreement merits enthusiastic applause.

CHAPTER **8**

AFGHANISTAN: THE SOVIET VIETNAM

Now, it is not good for the Christian's health to hustle the Aryan brown,
For the Christian riles, and the Aryan smiles, and he weareth the Christian down;
And the end of the fight is a tombstone white, with the name of the late deceased,
And the epitaph drear: "A fool lies here who tried to hustle the East."
                                                                    —Rudyard Kipling (1892)

By substituting the word "communist" for "Christian," a few well-chosen words from Rudyard Kipling, put to verse in 1892, present the Soviet occupation of Afghanistan, 1979–89, in a readily understood context. The rest of this Afghanistan story is detail. Kipling's advice, of course, still applies to Christians. However, it came too late for the British army that twice invaded Afghanistan from Colonial India in the nineteenth century. The Soviet army in 1979 had no such excuse.

Afghanistan was the last war the Soviet Union ever fought and a precipitous come-down from its heroic victory over Nazi Germany, 1941–45, when its troops were defending their beloved homeland. The Soviets in Afghanistan, like the Americans in Vietnam, actually won most of the battles. They had the superior army, but they lost the war. That can happen to occupiers who waste their blood trying to "hustle" people who want to determine their own fate.

Variations on the "Great Game"

Britain and Russia played the "Great Game" in the nineteenth century. The Brits, pushing northwest from India, and the Russians, south toward the warm waters of the Indian Ocean, never met in Afghanistan, but had their hands full fighting the local tribes. The first British invasion of Afghanistan ended in disaster. The "Army of the Indus" entered the country from the southeast with twenty thousand troops in December 1839, an ill-considered move to counter Russian influence. Accoutered with all the comforts of a colonial expedition looking for a new playground, the British brought 38,000 camp followers and servants, 30,000 camels to carry personal effects, a large herd of cattle, and a pack of foxhounds.[1] Many of the provisions were lost to raids by local tribesmen as the troops fought through to Kandahar. Then, after a two-month layover, they left a brigade behind and continued on to Kabul. On the way north they subdued Kalat. The march took seven months in all. When word of their triumph reached the British resident in Baluchistan, he jubilantly informed Mehrab Khan of Kalat, "The British army has entered Kabul without firing a bullet." Before replying, the old Khan gazed reflectively at the sky, until the diplomat prompted him for a response. "Yes, I am thinking," he said. "You people have entered the country, but how will you get out?"[2]

Two winters later, the Kabul garrison, down to 4,500 troops and 12,000 camp followers and hemmed in by rebel tribes, negotiated what they thought was safe passage to Jalalabad. Of the 16,500 men, women, and children who set out from Kabul through the high pass in early January, only one wounded and starving man reached Jalalabad. More than fourteen thousand died. Many succumbed to the cold, but many more died at the hands of the Afghan tribesmen who ignored the agreement and poured down a murderous fire from commanding positions overlooking the pass. More than a hundred soldiers and up to two thousand camp followers were taken prisoner. The British sent an expedition back the following summer to retrieve prisoners and punish the Pashtun tribes, and then withdrew.[3]

When, in 1878, they returned to Kabul with another invasion force, concern about Russia again entered into their calculations. Through the 1860s and 1870s, the Tsar's forces had steadily consolidated their hold on the Muslim lands bordering Afghanistan north of the Amu Darya and east of the Caspian Sea. As a counterweight, the British wanted to establish a military mission in Afghanistan, but the Afghan ruler, Sher Ali, politely refused. So the British launched another futile war, in which they fought, not Russians, but Afghans. The result was not quite as ruinous as the earlier invasion. They won some battles and lost some. Casualties were high on both sides. Yet, it proved to be no less a fool's quest.

Russia, as wary of the British as the British were of it, experienced its own nineteenth-century misadventure in Afghanistan. In the winter of 1839–40, the Tsar sent an expedition of five thousand troops across the Amu Darya to repel the British invasion. But the Russian column turned back without engaging the British, losing a thousand men to the extreme cold and tribal harassment. Given that turbulent history of British and Russian intervention, whatever possessed the Soviet Union in the next century to occupy that graveyard of modern great powers?

Since antiquity some of history's greatest conquerors have marched on the soil of today's Afghanistan. Alexander the Great appeared with a Greek army in the fourth century BC, but his empire collapsed soon after he died in Baghdad at the age of thirty-three. The Arabs first arrived in the seventh century, and gradually pressed east to Kabul in the ninth century. When they retreated they left an enduring legacy, Islam. Genghis Khan and his Mongol hordes descended from the north in the thirteenth century. Tamerlane followed a century-and-a-half later.

The Afghans saw the conquerors come and go, and whoever stayed behind became part of the local mosaic and engaged in fierce tribal rivalries. Rural Afghans always valued their tribal heritage above their national identity. Today they range in ethnic diversity from the dominant Pashtun located across the breadth of Afghanistan and eastward into the western mountains of Pakistan; to the Tajiks, Turks, and Uzbeks in the north; to the Hazaras with unmistakable traces of Mongol ancestry in the center, and many smaller groups. They speak mainly Pashto (also called Afghani) and Dari (a version of Farsi, the Persian language). The Pashtun, Tajiks, and Hazaras together comprise about 82 percent of the population.

Within Afghanistan, the Pashtun are identified as Afghan, in contrast to the other tribes who reside within the geographical boundaries but live by their particular ethnic identities. Therefore, it can be said that the Pashtun are the only true Afghans, but even they are divided between two major tribes, the Popalzai (ruling class) and Ghilzai (rebel class), who fight each other as bitterly as they fight other tribes or European intruders. If anything can be said to unify all these tribes, it is Islam, except that the Muslims of Afghanistan are divided among the Sunni (84 percent) and Shia (15 percent).[4]

As a land of tribal and ethnic diversity, led by warlords, and riven with internal strife, Afghanistan surely qualifies as one of the most difficult places in the world to govern. During the nineteenth century and more than half of the twentieth, a succession of emirs (kings) reigned in a line that followed the last of the great conquerors, Ahmad Shah. Autocratic rule may have come naturally to some, but it was also a favored survival tool. Assassination was always a threat. Ferment prevailed over the land, and rulers were ever cracking down on dissenters.

Yakub Khan chose a different way in the fall of 1879 after sitting shakily on the throne for only a few months. In September, his brother Ayub Khan led a demonstration in Kabul of Afghan soldiers seeking back pay. When the demonstrators threatened the British residency, the defenders opened fire. The soldiers retreated to their quarters, recovered their weapons, and returned to slaughter the guards and residents almost to a man, including the head of mission, Louis Cavagnari. A few weeks later, as a British column of 7,500 troops advanced on Kabul to mete out punishment for the massacre, they ran into Yakub Khan going in the opposite direction. The reluctant emir abdicated his throne and was exiled to India. He lived a long life, until 1923, and was quoted as saying that he "would rather be a grass-cutter in the English camp than be the ruler of Afghanistan."[5]

Modern Times

Despite its isolation on a high shoulder of the world, Afghanistan was not immune to the influence of modernization, an evolution that created tensions with religious elders who preached the immutable word of God transmitted by Muhammad. Gradually, but inevitably, the economy advanced, as Afghanistan built a rudimentary industry and infrastructure.

The pace of development quickened early in the Cold War as the dominant world powers played another version of the "Great Game." The Soviet Union extended credit and sent advisors to construct a road from Kabul through the mountains to the Soviet border. In the same way, the Soviets paved the streets of Kabul, built an air base at Bagram north of the capital, and made other moves to boost the Afghan economy. It also provided funds for the purchase of tanks, planes, and helicopters, and opened military training in the USSR to Afghan officers. America, then well regarded in that part of the world because it carried no colonial baggage, initially spurned Afghan pleas for economic and military aid. But it changed course when it saw its Cold War adversary gaining influence. It took responsibility for other road projects, jump-started the Afghan national airline, Ariana, encouraged American educators to teach at Kabul University, and opened American schools to Afghan students.

Mohammed Daoud was president of Afghanistan at the time. His cousin, brother-in-law, and college classmate, Zahir Shah Mohammed, was king. Daoud was a strong leader, not only in foreign affairs, but also in his despotic rule domestically. After the American rejection, in the late 1940s and early 1950s, he did not hesitate to deal with the Soviets. In that way, he pressured the Americans, and when the United States came around, he played the Soviets off against them.

He made the mistake, however, of reviving an issue left behind by the British, the demarcation of Afghanistan's eastern boundary that cut through Pashtun territory, which, with the partition of the Indian subcontinent, left many Pashtun formally subjects of Pakistan, although the government in Islamabad has never exercised much control over them. In 1960 and, again, in 1961, he tried to stir up the natives by sending Afghan troops into the mountainous tribal area of western Pakistan. To Daoud's surprise, the tribesmen repulsed both incursions, with help the second time from the Pakistani air force. But forays continued, until Pakistan suspended diplomatic relations and closed the frontier, cutting off trade and blocking annual tribal migrations. An impasse developed in which Afghanistan was the big loser, partly because the shutdown obstructed American aid that had flowed through Pakistan.

Another issue that plagued Daoud was constitutional reform. Monarchies were tumbling all around the Muslim world, and King Zahir wanted to stave off a similar fate by introducing democratic reforms. Daoud proposed a one-party state, which fit his own predilection for autocratic control, and when this was rejected he resigned the presidency in March 1963. The king accepted the resignation, and appointed Dr. Mohammed Yousuf, a Ph.D. in physics from Goettingen University, as Daoud's successor.

With Daoud out of the way, Yousuf oversaw the passage of a new constitution, which ushered in a season of freedom. But freedom proved to be a double-edged sword. Leftist study groups at Kabul University took advantage of it in 1965, by creating the PDPA (People's Democratic Party of Afghanistan), which that year would jump into the fires of political activism. Students demonstrated on October 25 over their poor prospects for employment and the low pay of the few jobs available once they graduated. When the demonstration got out of hand, the army was called in and the soldiers opened fire. Two students and a bystander were killed. In leftist circles, October 25 became "Martyrs' Day." Yousuf resigned, and a succession of obscure presidents followed in his footsteps, until 1973, when Daoud seized a moment with the king abroad to stage a bloodless coup and return to power.

Among the leaders of the student demonstrations in 1965 were three committed Marxists and future presidents of Afghanistan, Nur Mohammed Taraki, Babrak Karmal, and Hafizullah Amin. Although all three were communists, they were markedly different in background and temperament. Taraki was born into a humble, semi-nomadic family. He was bright, but with scant educational opportunities, and rather weak of character. Karmal was upper middle class with a first-rate education and a polish that made him acceptable in high social circles. His father had been a major general and military governor of Paktia Province. Amin was trained as an educator, and earned a Ph.D. in America. Of the three, he was the most ideologically driven and dictator-prone. Taraki was about twelve years older than the other two. All had close ties to the Soviet Union. Taraki and Karmal had a falling out in 1966, and founded separate left-wing parties, Khalq (The People) by Taraki, with a hard-line rural and lower class orientation and a deep interest in the plight of the Pashtun, and Parcham (The Banner) by Karmal, which was more inclined to accommodation with the broader segment of society. Amin sided with Taraki, and soon gained influence within Khalq.

In his second term, Daoud picked up essentially where he left off. With the king in exile, he rewrote the constitution to incorporate a one-party system, and purged extremists left and right from government service—that is, extremists other than himself. He pursued a policy of neutrality between east and west, and drew closer to India and some Arab states, much to the consternation of his Soviet neighbors.

His undoing had actually been in the works since his first regime when he began accepting Soviet military aid. By the time of his second term, several thousand Afghan military officers had been trained in the Soviet Union. Many of them were receptive in the seventies to overtures from Parcham, which having been shut out of sharing power with Daoud, undertook a stealth campaign to recruit active duty officers to its cause.

The immediate trigger for an uprising was the murder of a Parcham ideologue, Mir Akbar Khyber, accompanied by a rumor that the CIA was behind it. Although the rumor was not supported by any proof, it set off an anti-American demonstration at the funeral. Daoud, alarmed by this show of support for the communists, imprisoned the Parcham and Khalq leaders, and while they were behind bars, the new communist recruits in the army mounted an assault on the Daoud regime with a few hundred men and a few dozen tanks. Early on April 27, 1978, the tanks rumbled out onto the Kabul streets amid morning traffic. The Daoud loyalists' efforts to rouse other Afghan ground and air forces to its defense were ineffective. The rebels, led by Major Mohammed Aslam Watanjar, laid siege to the royal palace where Daoud, his family, and the presidential guard had holed up, and overcame the defenders. Daoud and most of his family died in the fighting.

The communists organized an interim government, the Revolutionary Council of the Democratic Republic of Afghanistan, with Taraki as president and prime minister, and put together a cabinet with the portfolios more or less evenly divided between the Khalq and Parcham factions. Karmal, Amin, and Watanjar served as deputy prime ministers under Taraki. But the honeymoon did not last long. A power struggle ensued in which Amin's considerable organizing skills turned the tide in Khalq's favor. Within a few months the Khalq, like the pigs in Orwell's *Animal Farm,* were "more equal" than all the others. Karmal was banished to Czechoslovakia as ambassador, and then, when recalled to Kabul during a purge of Parcham disciples, disappeared, later to turn up during the Soviet invasion. Amin remained as the sole deputy prime minister and, such was the force of his personality, he soon dropped the "deputy" and became the de facto ruler of Afghanistan. Taraki's role as president became increasingly symbolic.

Khalq embarked on a rigorous program of communist reform: redistribution of the land, the abolition of usury, cancellation of or reduced payments on indebtedness, provision for the establishment of cooperatives, the prohibition of bride selling, and universal education for both sexes based on a Marxist curriculum. Because most of these measures, including the ban on bride selling, flew in the face of tradition, they met with widespread resistance in the countryside. Khalq countered with a brutal put-down, incarcerating thousands of political prisoners without trial and executing hundreds of them out of public sight behind prison walls. The army attacked one defiant village called Kerala, destroyed it, and killed more than a thousand inhabitants.[6] In March, the city of Herat rebelled and most of its army garrison went over to the rebels. The government lost control for several days as the rebels hunted down and murdered government officials and Soviet advisors. Then it launched an all-out retaliation with tanks, planes, and helicopter gun ships. Thousands died and much of the city was reduced to rubble. The rebels who survived slipped away and formed a guerrilla army under Ismail Khan. As Amin's repression continued, the insurgency spread.

The Kremlin watched this reign of terror with growing dismay. After the Herat affair, calls for intervention were raised in Moscow. Successive Soviet delegations flew to Kabul in 1979 trying to persuade Amin to soften his approach. But he refused to alter course. Fearing that Amin might cozy up to the Americans—some observers have linked him to the CIA—the Soviet leaders decided to take him out. First they conspired with Taraki to lure him into an ambush at the presidential palace. Amin survived a shoot-out (his bodyguard was killed), after which he mustered a force that captured the palace and killed Taraki. That cleared the way for Amin to become president with dictatorial powers. Unwilling to leave Afghanistan to its own fate, high Soviet officials narrowed their options to one: invade Afghanistan, dispose of Amin, and bring Karmal out of cold storage.

The Soviet Intervention

The buildup to invasion began as early as September. By October 9, four thousand Soviet troops were believed to be guarding the Bagram air base north of Kabul. About eight hundred Soviet tanks and eight hundred armored personnel carriers were prepositioned in Afghanistan for troops to come later. In early December, up to two thousand more troops were flown in. A detachment moved north to secure the Salang Pass through the Hindu Kush. From the 20th to the 22nd, an airborne regiment was deployed to Kabul airport, and the detachment at Salang Pass was reinforced. The buildup went into high gear on December 24. Airborne troops were shuttled into the Kabul airport round the clock. Three days later, they occupied Kabul, while a unit of elite Spetsnaz (equivalent to the American Special Forces) headed for Darulaman Palace in Kabul where Amin had taken refuge. After encountering a spirited resistance, reinforced Spetsnaz troops captured the palace and killed Amin. The next day two motorized divisions began crossing the Amu Darya, followed in a matter of days by two more divisions until 58,000 Soviet troops with 1,000 armored vehicles occupied Afghanistan's major cities. Within weeks, according to U.S. State Department estimates, the Soviet military strength reached 85,000 men, 1,750 tanks, 2,100 armored personnel carriers, 500 combat aircraft, and 200 helicopters.[7]

Why the Soviet Union invaded Afghanistan has been the subject of much speculation. At the time, America was suffering through the humiliating Iran hostage crisis and still reeling from its defeat in Vietnam. To the Marxist ideologues in the Kremlin, those reverses were evidence of the inevitable decline of capitalism, while the PDPA ascent to power in Kabul the year before, they believed, was another milestone on the road to global communism. They watched with deepening gloom as the Afghan resistance gained momentum. To them, the idea that the Kabul regime might go down in flames and reverse the course of Marxist history was unacceptable. As the Russian scholar Svetlana Savronskaya puts it, KGB chief Yuri Andropov and Defense Minister Dmitriy Ustinov were too wrapped up in Marxist ideology to appreciate the influence of Islam. "Afghanistan," she said, "did not fit into the mental maps and ideological constructs of the Soviet leaders. Their analysis of internal social processes in Afghanistan was done through the conceptual lens of Marxist–Leninist doctrine, which blinded the leadership to the realities of traditional tribal society."[8] With respect to ideological blinders, the Soviet leaders were not so different from American neoconservatives who in 2001 believed that the 9/11 attacks on America could not have been carried out without state sponsorship from a rogue nation like

Saddam Hussein's Iraq. The neoconservatives professed a different ideology, of course,

Alarmist KGB reports from inside Afghanistan helped shape the controversial decision to invade. A narrow circle of Kremlin leaders debated the issue behind closed doors, with Andropov and Ustinov arguing persuasively for intervention against Ustinov's top generals who opposed it on grounds that too few troops were being committed to the mission (a complaint that would have an eerie echo in the Pentagon in 2003 as America prepared for war in Iraq).[9] Once the decision was made, the leaders did their best to keep the nature of the conflict secret. Soldiers deployed to Afghanistan were told they were being sent to "defend the southern frontiers of the motherland."[10]

The nearly decade-long war that followed cost the Soviet Union up to 15,000 military personnel killed and 37,000 wounded.[11] After withdrawal in 1988–89, the Soviet empire collapsed and the Soviet Union itself broke up into its constituent parts. So much for the inevitable course of history!

After securing Kabul, the Soviets immediately installed Karmal as president of the DRA (Democratic Republic of Afghanistan), but his control in the countryside was virtually nonexistent. Civil servants defected in large numbers from the Karmal government. The Soviet-controlled Afghan army experienced heavy casualties during the war, 34,000 to 42,000 men killed or wounded, and it suffered even more damage from the desertion of 52,000 to 60,000 troops, many of whom joined the rebels.[12]

Logistics were central to this war without front lines. The Soviet army had the training and modern equipment to fight NATO on European battlefields, but much of that was ill suited for guerrilla warfare. Heavy equipment was particularly difficult to haul in the rugged mountains and the massive Soviet firepower ineffectual where the elusive rebels could easily slip away. The mechanized Soviet soldier never ventured far from his armored personnel carrier, for good reason. The standard Soviet flak jacket weighed about thirty five pounds. Add to that the weight of his ammunition belt and weapons (the heavy machine gun weighed another seventy pounds), and one can easily see how difficult it was for plodding Soviet soldiers to catch up to lightly armed Afghans. A few months into the war, the Soviets began making effective use of helicopters, both for attack and the tactical transport of troops. Helicopter gun ships in close support of the Soviet troops took a heavy toll of the Afghan fighters, the mujahidin.[13]

Initially, the Soviet ranks were filled with conscripts from the central Asian republics north of the Amu Darya on the theory that their ethnic and Muslim identity would impress the Afghans in the hearts-and-minds struggle. But they proved to be woefully inadequate to the task of fighting insurgents, and were soon replaced by better-trained soldiers from the European republics.

The Magnificent "Muj"

The mujahidin, on the other hand, were largely unpaid volunteers defending their tribal lands. When attacked, they resisted fiercely. Where Soviet supply lines crossed their territory, they went on the offensive. The depth of their commitment to fighting the communist occupiers was beyond question, but part of their fervor sprang from the prospect of capturing arms that could be sold in Pakistan and Iran for money to feed their families. Their favorite targets were convoys loaded with supplies. Raiding Soviet/DRA outposts or ambushing columns for the weapons of dead enemy soldiers was another attractive form of engagement. In one fortuitous raid, the guerrillas captured a truck filled with money, which they split among themselves. A normal division of spoils was 20 percent for the leader and the remainder evenly divided among the rest. Additionally, the leader took possession of captured heavy weapons.[14]

One thing that stood out about the mujahidin was their disunity of command. They broke down into seven main factions, each with its own commander, plus smaller factions within factions, all jealous of their territorial prerogatives, and generally unwilling to coordinate activities on a large scale.[15] In late January 1980 across the border at their sanctuary in Peshawar, the mujahidin announced the formation of an Alliance for the Liberation of Afghanistan, but it broke up almost immediately into rival factions competing for arms and support from Pakistan.[16] An exception to this pattern of disunity persisted in the region around Kandahar where local rebels achieved a measure of lasting cooperation.

Yet, individually and in small groups, they were gallant men, superb light infantry, particularly adept at ambush and commando-style fighting. In the early days, their arms consisted of World War I-vintage bolt-action rifles, Kalashnikov automatic weapons, RPGs (rocket-propelled grenades), and a simple faith in God, eloquently expressed on the field of battle by Abdul Baqi Balots who commanded a group of thirty-five men in the village of Sama Garay in the fertile Kunar Valley northeast of Jalalabad. Several such villages dotted the valley, all with their own separate, uncoordinated fighters. On February 15, 1983, the Soviets launched a cordon and search operation, deploying a large blocking force to the south and flying in airborne to the north and east. As waves of helicopters ferried troops to their drop zones, one of Balots' guards approached him and nervously observed that things looked different that morning. "Don't worry," Balots replied, "our lives are in the hands of God, not the Russians. We are destined to die on the day that is destined for us. It will not be pushed backward or forward."[17] His men fought bravely when they had to against a vastly superior force before they could make their escape into the hills, and for some, it was destiny's day.

Often, when the mujahidin would hear the roar of combat nearby, they would come running to join the fight. Once a battle was finished, win or lose, they would return home to their families until the next battle loomed. Because they fought in this manner, one battle at a time, they could not take advantage of a victory or sustain an offensive. On the other hand, their general disunity made it impossible for Soviet and government forces to decapitate their central command and control, because these did not really exist.

The mujahidin also benefited from their nearly universal support outside the cities. It is said that an army travels on its stomach. In the hills and valleys of Afghanistan in the early stages of the war, food and shelter were always available at the next farmhouse. The peasantry, moreover, kept them well informed about enemy activities in their neighborhood.

Ambushes large and small, mostly small, occurred almost daily. One in May 1981 fifty miles south of Kabul on the road to Gardez showed the mujahidin at their most effective. A band of eleven men armed with one RPG, seven Kalashnikovs, and two bolt-action Enfield rifles set themselves up at a narrow gorge where the Logar River flows next to the highway. After establishing their firing positions in the early morning, they retired to neighborhood homes for a leisurely breakfast. They expected reconnaissance helicopters to pass as usual ahead of the convoy. That would be the signal to return to their positions. But this day, the choppers did not appear. The guerrillas were still eating when the convoy with 150 to 200 vehicles fairly bulging with supplies reached the gorge at about 10:00 a.m. They rushed to battle to find that the lead tank had already passed beyond the kill zone. The RPG gunner, Mulla Latif, was breathing so hard from his run that it affected his aim. He fired twice at the second tank and missed both times. Then he reloaded, ran down to the highway, sat cross-legged to steady himself, and blasted away from point-blank range. The tank exploded, and brought the convoy to a complete stop, strung out along the highway. Hundreds of mujahidin poured out of the mountains to join the attack and share in the loot. Victory was complete. Supplies that they could not carry off, they burned.[18]

The Soviets launched nine offensives into the Panjshir Valley north of Kabul near the Salang Tunnel. This was Tajik territory where Ahmad Shah Massoud, perhaps the rebels' best military tactician, knew how to use the mountain terrain to advantage. When he caught on to the Soviet tactic of sending Afghan government troops out ahead as they advanced into the valley, his men would dynamite the mountainside and send boulders crashing down between the enemy units. The Afghans, many of whom sympathized with the rebels, would often simply join them. The fifth Panjshir operation, one of the biggest of the entire war involving eleven thousand Soviet and four thousand DRA troops began in May 1982 with two days of heavy air strikes. Then helicopter-borne troops were deposited at the center of the valley while one armored Soviet column advanced from one end, and another armored column from the opposite end. Massoud's men watched from the high ground, and when opportunities arose they counterattacked and laid ambushes. They knocked out heavy tanks where the valley narrowed, slowing the advance, or sometimes spread out the enemy by luring units into side hollows. Still, the superior Soviet/DRA troops got the better of it, killing about a thousand mujahidin against three hundred to four hundred of their own losses.[19] Over time the steady pounding took a toll on the Tajiks. Massoud, who had established contact with the Soviets even while fighting them, finally negotiated a deal in the spring of 1983. The Soviets would operate a base at the southern end of the Panjshir, but no longer attack in the valley. It came as a shock to other mujahidin warlords who considered it a sellout.[20]

The Soviets soon employed scorched-earth tactics to deprive the guerrillas of their vital civilian support in the countryside. They bombed villages, destroyed farms, scattered mines, poisoned wells, ruined irrigation systems, killed sheep and cattle, and forced the peasants to flee—terrorism on a massive scale. In all, the Soviets created six million Afghan refugees. About half of them wound up in Pakistan for the duration of the war; the rest landed in Iran or Afghan cities.[21] It made logistics more difficult for the mujahidin, but they coped. Those from the eastern mountains took sanctuary in Pakistan, and carried weapons and provisions back over the steep trails to take their revenge on the Soviets.

After the flight of the peasants, the sanctuaries in Pakistan and Iran became crucial to the war effort. There, the guerrillas were afforded rest, medical treatment for the wounded, rudimentary training, and resupply. The CIA set up shop in Pakistan and worked under a presidential "finding" signed early in 1980 by President Carter that authorized covert action to aid the mujahidin. In the early years of the conflict, the CIA bought surplus light arms such as Enfield rifles, grenade launchers, mines, and SA-7 antiaircraft weapons, much of it from China and Egypt, which it funneled through Pakistan's "black-ops" agency, the ISI (Inter-Service Intelligence Directorate). The CIA took care to buy only foreign-made weapons available on the black market. That kept the agency's fingerprints off the goods when, unavoidably, the Soviets would capture guerrilla weapons on the battlefield.

For most of his presidency, Carter had worked hard to improve ties with the Soviet Union, but he perceived the Afghan invasion as a stab in back, and took a u-turn in his Soviet policy. At this stage, however, the Americans gave no thought to defeating the modern Soviet army, only to bleeding it in thousands of minor engagements, skeptical that the mujahidin were capable of doing more. In one sense, they were already doing more—more bleeding. Rebel casualties over the nine years, one-and-a-half months of war were estimated at 180,000 to 290,000 killed and wounded, against approximately 50,000 Soviet casualties.[22]

In 1984, the Soviets stepped up the pressure by committing the elite Spetsnaz to a campaign of helicopter-borne attacks against mujahidin supply lines. Well trained and highly motivated, the Spetsnaz used sophisticated communications technology to pick up rebel conversations and pinpoint locations, and then followed up with aggressive raids supported from the air by helicopter gun ships and fixed wing fighters. Sometimes, they carried out raids at night. With casualties mounting, the rebels became demoralized, so much so that their backers feared a total collapse of the resistance.

The Tide Turns

The Reagan Administration responded in March 1985 with a new presidential directive authorizing an escalation of aid for the rebels with the bold new purpose of "defeating," not just "harassing" the Soviets. The Americans supplied the mujahidin with light and heavy machine-guns, recoilless rifles, and mortars, and that was perhaps the least of it. To offset the Soviet advantage in communications, the Americans provided equipment to secure Afghan rebel conversations. To throw the Soviets off the rebels' trail, they studied satellite photos to scout out different infiltration routes. To knock out the deadly helicopters and fighters, they procured surface-to-air missile launchers. First, they tried Soviet heat-seeking SA-7 surface-to-air models, which had only modest success, and then the Swiss Oerlikon, which proved too heavy to pack around the mountains, and the British Blowpipe, a rather complicated device to operate in the field. Finally, they deployed the American Stinger with an infrared seeker. When the guerrillas learned to use the Stingers, they scored 269 hits out of 340 Stinger firings, according to U.S. Army estimates. More significantly, the Soviets lost control of the skies, and were forced to back off from their close air support of ground troops.[23]

Behind the scenes, Charles Wilson, a Democratic Congressman from East Texas, played a key role in this dramatic turnaround. Wilson sat on the House Appropriations Committee and two of its subcommittees, Foreign Operations and Defense, which control funding for the Departments of State and Defense and the CIA. Depending on the personal dynamics of the individual occupying those seats, they offered (and still offer) an enormous opportunity to influence American foreign policy. Wilson was a very dynamic man. From a Congressional district dominated by Bible-thumping Christian conservatives, he was a New Deal liberal. A white man from the boondocks, he mixed well with urban Jewish and black Congressmen. Tall, good-looking, unmarried, and outgoing, he was a notorious womanizer and an alcoholic. He would travel to Muslim lands with a gorgeous doll at his side and a supply of booze in his luggage. He once brought along a Texas belly dancer to perform for an appreciative Egyptian minister of defense. An inveterate hedonist, he created a hot tub scandal in a Las Vegas pleasure dome with leggy hotel call girls bearing cocaine.

Above all, Wilson was a patriot, proud of his Texas heritage and, especially, of the Texans' brave last stand at the Alamo. He romanticized about courageous people not afraid to die fighting for freedom. He idolized the Israelis after their stirring victory in the Six Day War, and when he went to Congress in 1973 he became their steadfast and influential friend. In the summer of 1980, he read a news dispatch about the defiant "muj" resistance, and from that time forward, he championed their cause. Although only one of twelve members of the Appropriations Defense Subcommittee, and not the chairman, he knew how to manipulate the levers of power. In his first act on behalf of the Afghan resistance and without firsthand knowledge of the struggle, he called a subcommittee staffer and told him to double CIA funding from a measly $5 million to a slightly less measly $10 million. Eventually, the mujahidin appropriation grew into the hundreds of millions of dollars, and Saudi Arabia pledged to match every American dollar spent on the Afghan rebels. Wilson, working backdoor through a nonconformist, blue-collar CIA operative, Gust Avrakotos, was a prime mover in the acquisition of more and better arms for the mujahidin, especially the ground-to-air missiles. He traveled often to Pakistan, befriended Prime Minister Mohammed Zia ul-Haq, and visited the refugee camps, where without fail he donated his own blood for his heroes, the "muj."[24]

The deeper American commitment made a huge difference. Arguably, Reagan's new presidential directive was the decisive action that reversed the tide of war. CIA and Pentagon specialists came in droves to Pakistan. They tutored the ISI, and the ISI, in turn, trained the Afghans in secure communications, guerrilla warfare, urban sabotage, the use of heavy weapons, and sophisticated demolition with chemical and electronic timing devises and remote control switches. The CIA helped the rebel teams prepare for battle, mapping operations with satellite photographs that showed experts the best approach to a target and the best way to withdraw. ISI advisors often traveled with rebel units into Afghanistan to supervise attacks on such targets as airports, railroads, bridges, roads, and fuel depots. As effective as the Stingers were at shooting helicopters and fighter planes out of the air, the Soviets lost even more aircraft on the ground to nighttime mortar raids on Bagram and other air bases.[25]

By 1986, the battles had escalated in frequency, size, and intensity throughout the country. In one indication of the mujahidin's increased ability to hold their own in large battles, Soviet and DRA forces spent three weeks in futile attacks against guerrilla base camps in the mountains of Paktia province near the Pakistan border. The camps were heavily fortified with deep underground bunkers, ammunition storage depots, air raid shelters, and hospitals connected by tunnels dug into the mountainside. The Soviets failed to dislodge the rebel fighters with their latest heavy artillery, tanks, and aircraft. Elite Spetsnaz troops were beaten back in face-to-face combat, and Soviet tactical bombers were kept at a safe distance with Stinger missiles.[26] According to one well-informed American, this was the first battle in which Arabs trained in camps established by Osama bin Laden fought as a single unit. Previously, Arab volunteers had been dispersed among Afghan units.[27]

The next year, the Soviets began withdrawing. As the Soviet units pulled out, they turned their bases over to the government forces and left most of their heavy equipment behind. Like the Americans in Vietnam, the Soviet troops had won most of the battles and inflicted more casualties, but lost the war, in no small measure because pressures against it mounted at home.

The Soviet adventure in Afghanistan coincided with the last gasp of the old guard in the Kremlin. The ailing Leonid Brezhnev was holding on as the titular head of government, while his comrades tended to the issues of the time. His death on November 10, 1982, brought the KGB chief, Andropov, to power for fifteen months before he too died on February 4, 1984, to be succeeded by Brezhnev's faithful protégé, Konstantin Chernenko, a complete nonentity who lasted thirteen months until his death on March 10, 1985. Then Mikhail Gorbachev took over with dreams of remaking the Soviet Union into an open society, and, to his great disappointment, actually witnessed the disintegration of the Soviet empire on his watch.

When Gorbachev stepped into the job, he wanted first to put the Afghan affair behind him so he could move on to weightier issues, such as internal reform and East–West detente. He gave his military leaders one year to clean up the mess. Meantime, he sacked Karmal and replaced him with Mohammed Najibullah, a cofounder of Parcham and well regarded in the Kremlin for his performance as intelligence chief in the Karmal government. After a year, when the Soviet military had not produced a victory, Gorbachev turned to diplomacy. Since 1982, the United Nations had been trying to negotiate a peace settlement, shuttling among Kabul, Islamabad, Tehran, and Moscow with very little to show for the effort. To spur the talks, Gorbachev announced in July 1986 the withdrawal of eight thousand troops, and indicated that all Soviet troops would come out when a satisfactory settlement had been reached. But the talks—and the fighting—dragged on through 1987 until February 1988 when Gorbachev announced a total unilateral withdrawal in stages beginning on May 15, 1988. The last Soviet troops rolled back across the Amu Darya on February 15, 1989.

The Americans rejoiced in the Soviet defeat to which they had made a significant contribution. They did not know at the time that they had helped also to set in motion the rise of militant Islam and a challenge to American world hegemony.

CHAPTER 9

IRAQ: A THOUSAND CUTS

Human blunders, usually, do more to shape history than human wickedness.
—A. J. P. Taylor (1961)

The Bush Administration's idea for Iraq was a quick war, a smooth turnover from dictatorship to democracy, and a fast exit. Before the invasion, Vice President Cheney famously predicted that the people would greet us as liberators (and some did, especially the Kurds and some Shia in the south, but certainly not the Sunnis). Neoconservative sources from deep within the Pentagon were estimating troop withdrawals in sixty to ninety days from the start of war; more realistically, five to six months. "The plan is to get it done as quickly as possible, and get out," said Lieutenant Colonel Michael Humm, spokesman for Undersecretary Douglas Feith. Other neoconservatives were even more sanguine. Kenneth Adelman, an advisor at the White House, predicted a "cakewalk." (Adelman said later he was referring to the invasion itself, not the occupation.) Richard Perle, then chairman of the Defense Policy Board who never fought in war, brazenly predicted that the Iraqi military would "collapse after the first whiff of gunpowder." (Perle would say later that he favored removing Saddam Hussein by political means, but he was still a cheerleader for the invasion.) Defense Secretary Rumsfeld also expressed optimism: The Iraq war, he said, "could last six days, six weeks. I doubt six months."[1]

L. Paul Bremer III arrived in Baghdad in early May 2003 to head the occupation government, known as the CPA (Coalition Provisional Authority), and promptly outlawed the Baath Party and disbanded the Iraqi army. Next to the initial decision to invade, those acts amounted collectively to the biggest mistake of the Iraq adventure. Gone were the central unifying forces that might have transcended Iraq's ethnic and sectarian differences. Gone, too, were the Iraqi security forces that might have helped put-down the insurgency. And, perversely, from this huge new pool of unemployed came many underground fighters who knew the tactics and weapons of warfare. Having dismissed the professionals, the CPA hired amateurs to keep the peace, and these army and police recruits became targets of the insurgency alongside the Americans.

It was definitely no cakewalk. In more than two-and-a-half years of occupation from April 9, 2003 through 2005, a total of 996 days, U.S. troops sustained 1,615 killed by hostile fire,[2] about 600 troops a year, leaving behind bereaved families in hundreds of mournful communities around the United States. Not every day did a casualty occur, but on average, the enemy killed roughly five U.S. soldiers every three days. By the end of 2007, the deaths of American military personnel from both combat and noncombat causes approached four thousand. The number of wounded was in the range of sixty thousand, about half of them very serious. America's coalition partners lost two hundred dead through 2006, but innocent Iraqis suffered by far the worst death toll of the war: 47.668 dead by actual body count and up to 655,000 by sample survey through June 2006.[3] The World Health Organization estimated 151,000 Iraqi dead in the same time frame in a broader sampling under war conditions that limited its scope.[4]

Although the human cost was more important, the price to America of the Iraq war also included the outlay in dollars. As of March 2007, Congress had appropriated $378 billion for the wars in Iraq and Afghanistan, according to the Congressional Research Service.[5] It estimated the cost would rise to $800 billion through 2008, surpassing the cost of the Vietnam War. Democrats in Congress later factored in the "hidden costs" of Iraq and Afghanistan—higher oil prices, care for the war wounded, and interest on borrowing—and came up with a figure of $1.5 trillion.[6]

Despite the high cost, America generally has not felt the financial impact of Iraq as much as in past wars because the economy now generates so much more wealth. Bush has also made it easier for the current war generation to swallow by lowering taxes and borrowing, thus shifting the burden to future generations. To put it in its most ironic context, Americans spent twice as much shopping at Wal-Mart than funding the Iraq war. Total defense spending of $437 billion in 2004 was only about 4 percent of the gross domestic product, compared to 9 percent during the Vietnam War, and 14 percent at the height of the Korean War.[7] By the turn of the year 2008, however, the economy began to falter as unemployment grew, incomes declined, and the shopping spree suddenly dried up.

In absolute terms, Iraq was the most expensive war in sixty years. What has it bought the taxpayers in the "war against terror"? The answer is a more dangerous world if you judge it by the U.S. State Department's finding that the number of "significant" terrorist attacks worldwide more than tripled from 175 in 2003 to 655 in 2004.[8] After that, the U.S. government broadened its definition of terrorism to include incidents with no or few deaths, causing the number to jump to 11,000 in

2005 and fuzzing over real comparisons to 2004. The National Counterterrorism Center did report, using different criteria from previous surveys, that "high fatality" incidents more than doubled in Iraq, from about 65 in 2004 to about 150 in 2005, and remained at about the same level, 70, in the rest of the world.[9]

From August 2002 to January 2003, while General Tommy Franks was writing up the plan that guided the American blitzkrieg from Kuwait to Baghdad, Saddam ordered Iraqi troops to remove small arms and ammunition from army bases and hide them in the countryside.[10] During the initial charge, as the conventional coalition forces drove up the river valleys in the cradle of civilization, Baathist Party loyalists slipped across the border to Syria with money to support underground fighters.[11] When Baghdad fell, the former Baathist rulers were ready for a classic guerrilla struggle. They could not have foreseen it, but they did not need to secrete arms in advance. Opportunities arose in the early days of the occupation to loot munitions from Iraqi army storage depots.

Before long, Islamists entered the fray, the majority of them Saudi nationals. Some joined Jama'at al-Tawhid wal-Jihad (Unification and Holy War Group), the terrorist organization of Abu Musab al-Zarqawi who carried out a number of high-profile murders until his death in June 2006. His was only the best known Islamist group in Iraq. There were others, equally ready to snap up new recruits lured through the Internet. Although no reliable breakdown of the insurgents exists, one estimate puts the ratio at 90 percent secular Sunni Baathist, and 10 percent Sunni Islamist.[12] But the forces kept shifting as the Islamist strength ebbed and flowed with losses offset by new recruits and outside money.

Born Ahmad Fadeel al-Nazal al-Khalayeh in 1966, Zarqawi grew up a petty criminal in a slum of Zarqa, Jordan. His adopted name, Zarqawi, means "man of Zarqa." A school dropout at age seventeen, he first traveled to Afghanistan in 1989 and joined Islamists in training. It is reported that he met and befriended bin Laden there and later became his rival. In 1992, he was arrested in Jordan for conspiring against the monarchy and spent seven years in prison where he gained a reputation as a bully with leadership skills. After his release, he was accused of plotting to blow up the Radisson Hotel in Amman, and later convicted in absentia and sentenced to death for conspiracy in the 2002 assassination of an American diplomat. At some point in the 1990s, he formed his own organization, which merged with al Qaeda in 2004 and became known as al Qaeda in Iraq. That put him on the receiving end of the pipeline from the flow of money available to bin Laden, and made him the most powerful Islamist insurgent leader in Iraq. He soon became America's number one Islamist enemy with a $25 million bounty on his head. He was reportedly behind several suicide bombings both inside and outside of Iraq.

Criminal activity has also entered into the mix of Iraqi resistance. Not long before the invasion, Saddam released about two thousand prison inmates who returned to their old lifestyles. Kidnapping for ransom became an especially lucrative enterprise. The *Washington Post* reported near the end of 2005 that 425 foreigners had been kidnapped since the American troops arrived, of which about one in five were killed. Sometimes the abductors would sell their captives to Islamist groups, and sometimes the Islamists would do their own kidnapping.[13]

The insurgency began gradually after President Bush's May 1, 2003, speech when he stood before a banner that said "Mission Accomplished" on the deck of the aircraft carrier USS *Abraham Lincoln* and declared an end to major combat operations. "[T]he United States and our allies have prevailed," he said. The looting that immediately followed the fall of Baghdad, as American troops stood idly by, must have encouraged the Iraqi insurgents waiting in the wings. Chaos had to be more to their liking. Here and there, individually and in small groups, the insurgents challenged American troops in a variety of situations, mostly with small arms and grenades, or by ambush and sniper fire. Six American soldiers died in May, but in June the number quadrupled to twenty-four. It began to look as if the war was not over. When a reporter asked about the growing insurgency in early July, the president said, "There are some who feel like that, you know, the conditions are such that they can attack us there. My answer is, bring 'em on"—words he came to regret.[14] And well he should. From the time he spoke until early 2008, the U.S. military toll reached four thousand dead and many thousands more severely wounded.

IEDs

Experience taught the insurgents that roadside bombs, called IEDs in Pentagon speak (improvised explosive devices), were their most effective weapon and could be employed at least risk to themselves. The IED is the insurgents' low-tech answer to stealth technology. Old Iraqi ordnance was planted in roadside wreckage or dead animals in the dark of night and touched off by remote control when military vehicles passed in daylight.

As of November 21, 2005, the Brookings Institution, which tracks Pentagon releases, reported 2,095 military deaths from all causes since the invasion in March 2003. Of that total, 614 were caused by IEDs, slightly less than 30 percent of the total.[15] But if the invasion and nonhostile deaths are factored out, beginning in July 2003 when the first IED death was recorded, the ratio of IED deaths to total hostile military deaths rises to two-out-of-five, or 40 percent, and that ratio kept going up year by year as this static war dragged on. By the first half of 2007 it reached 80 percent.

As early as October 2003, the IED had become such a threat to coalition forces that the Pentagon established teams to carry out forensic investigations of blast scenes. They took note of Iraqi innovations and devised techniques for avoiding IEDs or reducing their effects. IEDs, according to *Jane's Intelligence Review,* are not the product of a single manufacturer, but are cobbled together in a variety of ways "by largely independent IED-making cells spread across Iraq."[16] Later, when Shia militia began retaliating against Sunni atrocities, American military investigators found evidence of Shiite IEDs made in Iran.

Efforts to protect the U.S. troops with better armor have not been entirely successful. In 2004 and 2005, Congress appropriated $4.74 billion for new body armor, better armored Humvees, heavier plating for trucks, electronic jamming devices to impede remote control, and improved training. These measures undoubtedly helped soldiers survive, but the IEDs continued to take a grim toll in American dead and wounded, with most of the IED casualties affecting men and women inside allegedly armored vehicles.[17] The insurgents have countered improved U.S. armor by building more powerful IEDs, using stacked land mines or several artillery shells wired together, with the charges shaped to concentrate the power of the explosions. These shaped charges became ever more powerful and sophisticated—so advanced that they earned a slick new name in Pentagon-speak: EFPs (explosively formed projectiles)—and by 2007 caused more death and injury to American troops than any other single factor. According to U.S. military sources, they were made in Iran for use by radical Shia militia in Iraq.

Perhaps the deadliest IED of the war was exploded near Haditha on August 3, 2005, when a huge roadside bomb flipped a twenty-five-ton amphibious troop carrier onto its top, sealing the escape hatch. Then it caught fire. Fourteen of fifteen Marines inside were killed, along with their Iraqi interpreter.[18] The IED had been buried underground and detonated as the troop carrier passed over it. Spurred by this success, insurgent bomb makers increased the production of "underbelly" bombs, to the dismay of U.S. troops.[19]

"It's a losing game," said Daniel Goure of the Lexington Institute, a defense think tank in Arlington, Virginia, "because they can always build a bigger bomb."[20] It was a losing game, too, because body armor fell short of expectations. A Marine Corps forensic study released in late 2005 estimated that about 42 percent of Marine deaths could have been avoided with fuller bulletproof plating around the torso. If this figure were extrapolated to include Army deaths, perhaps hundreds of soldiers might have been saved with better body armor. Many of the fatal wounds penetrated the sides and necks of the victims where the armor did not reach. The Pentagon began addressing the problem by ordering side plate attachments to the protective vests even before the study was declassified and the information made public by a group of combat veterans known as Soldiers for the Truth. The troops were to be outfitted as the plates arrived in the field, but it took months for full delivery.[21]

Those who survived IED explosions were often left with devastating injuries. They received the best medical care available, from rescue corpsmen to field hospitals to U.S. military hospitals in Germany to rehabilitation centers in the United States. Many men and women as severely wounded as these would have died in past wars. Not only were arms and legs blown off, but head injuries causing blindness and brain damage afflicted young people in the prime of life. Their medical care and rehabilitation were superb, but once completed, they might be left to vegetate with prosthetic limbs, wheel chairs, seeing-eye dogs, brain malfunctions, or posttraumatic stress disorder. In a major scandal, reporters Dana Priest and Anne Hull of the *Washington Post* wrote articles about the neglectful bureaucratic treatment of crippled Iraq veterans undergoing outpatient care and being housed adjacent to the Army's Walter Reed Medical Center near Washington.[22] Congress began investigations that also uncovered the substandard treatment of Iraq veterans at Veterans Administration hospitals.

In conventional wars, soldiers face death in relatively short bursts of combat. It was different in Iraq. The simple everyday act of riding in a convoy outside the base was death defying. A life could be shattered by remote control without notice. The victims never see the enemy, never use their weapons, and in cases of instant death, never know what hit them.

Suicide Bombers

Early on, the international media actually paid less attention to IEDs than suicide bombs. The latter have killed fewer American troops, but they often kill more people in a single setting. The suicide bomb can be as accurate as a laser-guided missile, and just as deadly. Initially, the victims were usually Shiites or Iraqi police or military recruits or foreign workers in nongovernment organizations—and perpetrators made little, if any effort to spare Iraqi civilians. The modes of attack, remote bombs versus suicide bombs, could sometimes identify the type of bombers, secular Sunni Baathist who preferred to live, versus Sunni Islamists who welcomed martyrdom. That observation is somewhat more than speculation because the Islamists often announced their atrocities. The more heinous the acts, the more pride they seemed to take in them.

In the first major suicide attack on August 7, 2003, one of Zarqawi's followers set off a truck bomb at the Jordanian embassy, killing nineteen and wounding sixty-five. Just twelve days later, on the 19th, a suicide driver wheeled a cement truck up to the wall of a converted three-story hotel building being used as U.N. headquarters, and blew it up. The blast killed twenty-two people, including fifteen U.N. staffers, and wounded more than a hundred. Among the dead was Sergio Vieira de Mello, the respected Brazilian diplomat chosen to head the U.N.'s post-invasion reconstruction effort.[23] An Islamist group calling itself the Brigades of the Martyr Abu Hafz al-Masri—believed to be linked to Zarqawi—later claimed responsibility for the attack. Undoubtedly, it hoped to drive the United Nations out, and was largely successful. U.N. Secretary General Kofi Annan vowed not to withdraw, but the staff in Baghdad was drastically reduced temporarily.

Two months later, insurgents went after the Red Cross and the Baghdad police. Five suicide bombers struck International Red Cross headquarters and four police stations on October 27 in a forty-five-minute coordinated assault that killed 36 people and wounded more than 200. No one stepped forward to claim credit, but the attacks, carried out at a rather high level of sophistication, bore the earmarks of an Islamist operation. At least one of the bomb-laden vehicles aimed at the police was a patrol car, and another, a pickup truck like many in police use. At the Red Cross, the bomber drove an ambulance through a protective barrier, and then detonated his payload. That blast killed one Red Cross employee and fourteen residents of nearby buildings.

Shiites were another insurgent target. The most radical Sunni Islamists have always looked down on them as "infidels" and "polytheists." On August 29, ten days after the attack on the United Nations, a car bomb exploded outside the Imam Ali Mosque in Najaf, Iraq's holiest Shia shrine. At least 120 people were killed, the most prominent being Ayatollah Muhammad Bakr al-Hakim, a leading cleric who preached cooperation with the American authorities. No one took responsibility for this attack either. But *Newsday* reported in February 2005 that Zarqawi's father-in-law, Yassin Jarad, carried it out in a bomb-laden ambulance. The information published in the Long Island daily was derived from two unnamed Kurdish intelligence officials involved in the interrogation of captured Islamists from the Zarqawi organization.[24] If Zarqawi was trying to foment civil war, the Shia did not rise immediately to the bait. Their leading cleric, Ayatollah Ali al-Sistani, urged his followers to be patient because the majority Shiites, so long outside the ring of power, had much to gain from the promised constitutional democracy based on the principle of majority rule. Sistani is a spiritual man who knows how to count.

What happened in the last half of 2003 was only the beginning. Suicide attacks rose from twenty in 2003 to forty-eight in 2004, and the number continued to climb in 2005.[25] Up to July 2005, about 400 suicide attacks were reported in Iraq since the American invasion, 90 of those in May of that year. On March 3, 2004, suicide bombers in Baghdad and Karbala attacked Shia worshippers as they celebrated the feast of Ashura. One hundred and eighty-one people were killed in the two bombings about fifty miles apart. The deadliest single suicide attack through 2005 occurred on February 28, 2005, in Hilla, about sixty miles south of Baghdad. The bomber struck near a government office where police recruits were lined up to get physicals. One hundred and twenty-five people died. One of the most heartrending bombings came on September 29, 2004, during a ribbon-cutting ceremony for a U.S.-built sewage-treatment plant in southern Baghdad. Soldiers were passing out candy to children when a remote-controlled bomb in a pickup truck exploded in their midst. As people rushed to gather up the dead and wounded, a suicide bomber edged a car into the crowd and touched off a second explosion. At least forty-one people were killed, including thirty-four children and one U.S. soldier.[26]

Whether by roadside bomb, ambush, suicide attack, or fire fight with small arms and grenades, the unsparing violence went on continually through peaks and valleys and, here and there, a descent into barbarism. City streets were unsafe, and people ventured out of their homes only when necessary. Insurgents planted IEDs on busy roads. For a time, the highway from Baghdad to the international airport was a death trap for soldiers and travelers. The insurgents sabotaged power plants, leaving homes and businesses without electricity, and blew up oil pipelines, disrupting a prime revenue source counted on for reconstruction. They roamed the countryside attacking truck drivers who delivered goods to the occupation forces and foreign contractors. Despite the risks, job seekers from neighboring Muslim countries, Europe, and the United States flocked to Iraq in pursuit of high wages in the war zone. A fair number did not live to enjoy their new-found affluence.

Kidnapping

Kidnapping became the rage in 2004. Truck drivers were especially vulnerable. They might be killed on the road or in captivity, or they might be released. One Turkish driver was released on a promise not to return. He broke his promise, and when caught again, he was killed.

Much of this was happening under the radar, so to speak, of the international media. At least the kidnappings carried out against lone victims or small groups were not generating big headlines until an American from Pennsylvania named Nick Berg fell into Zarqawi's hands in May 2004. Berg, supposedly in Iraq looking for work as a builder of communications towers, was apparently abducted by a small Iraqi gang and sold to Zarqawi. Later he appeared on videotape sitting on a floor bound hand and foot with five masked men standing behind him. One of the captors read a proclamation, and then pulled out a sword and beheaded him. Allegedly, the executioner was Zarqawi, and his motive, revenge for the American torture of Iraqi prisoners at Abu Ghraib prison. In the videotape, Berg was dressed in an orange jumpsuit like those worn by American detainees.[27]

The next month, the Zarqawi group held a South Korean translator, Kim Sun Il, and showed him on videotape pleading for his life. Zarqawi offered to spare Kim's life if the South Korean government would withdraw its 660 troops from Iraq and cancel the deployment of three thousand more. The demand was refused, and a few days later police found Kim's body, the head severed, on the road between Baghdad and Fallujah.[28] In September, the now familiar scene of a kidnap victim in an orange jumpsuit kneeling in front of five masked men and pleading for his life was repeated three times. One of the captors, presumably Zarqawi, beheaded two other Americans, Jack Hensley and Eugene Armstrong, and a Briton, Kenneth Bigley. The three worked on a reconstruction project for Gulf Supplies and Commercial Services, a company from the United Arab Emirates.[29]

In July, the abduction of a Filipino truck driver, Angelo de la Cruz, resulted in a win for the terrorists. He was one of about four thousand Filipinos working in Iraq and seven million around the world earning a collective $10 billion annually to support impoverished families at home. His abductors threatened to decapitate him if the Philippines did not withdraw its token force of about one hundred soldiers. Under pressure at home to do everything possible to free him, Philippines President Gloria Macapagal Arroyo promptly pulled her troops out, and de la Cruz was released.

The autumn brought the most senseless of all the abductions. Margaret Hassan, born Margaret Fitzsimmons in Ireland, finished her education in London where her family had moved. She fell in love with and married Tahseen Ali Hassan, an Iraqi studying engineering. She moved with him to Iraq, learned Arabic, and became an Iraqi citizen to go with her Irish and British citizenships. She served at the British Council during the early years of Saddam's dictatorship and worked her way up to director. In 1990, the year Saddam's army overran Kuwait, the British Council suspended its work in Iraq, and she took a job at Care International as director of the Baghdad office where she became a popular figure working with children and distributing relief to the poor. On October 19, 2004, gunmen dressed in police uniforms stopped her car and took her away. In captivity she appeared in three videos. The last reportedly showed her pleading for her life and urging Britain to pull its troops out of Iraq when suddenly she fainted. As she lay still on the floor, one of her captors poured water on her head. She came to, and again appealed to the British government to save her. Adding emphasis to her pleas, her abductors, who did not identify themselves, threatened to turn her over to Zarqawi. Then she disappeared from sight and was presumed dead, but her body had not been found as of early 2008.[30]

Combat and Politics

By the year 2004, the insurgency was in high gear. In early April a year into the occupation, the first of several full-scale urban uprisings drew in American troops. The rebels, in this case, were Shia followers of Sheikh Muqtada al-Sadr. He had been critical of the occupation, but remained quiescent until the Coalition Authority shut down his newspaper, *Al-Hawza*. His Mahdi Army with a force of up to ten thousand fighters at the time seized public buildings and police stations in several communities and the Baghdad neighborhood called Sadr City, and clashed with coalition forces in Nasiriyah, Amara, and Basra. U.S. troops soon regained control in Sadr City, but not without losing seven soldiers killed in a Mahdi ambush. By April 16, after only a few days of combat, the Mahdi forces retained firm control only of Karbala and the twin cities of Najaf and Kufa. U.S. troops launched attacks in both areas, and the fighting continued over the next several weeks. On May 24, the militia withdrew from Karbala, but held out in Najaf/Kufa with heavy losses until Muqtada al-Sadr called a halt on June 6. Except for a flare-up in August, that ended the Mahdi uprising for the time being. His army having been soundly beaten, Sadr became more active in politics and recruited a larger militia.

The coalition effort to put down the Sunni insurgencies was far less decisive. Fallujah stood out as a hotbed of resistance. At about the time the Mahdi flexed their muscles in the south, four American civilian contract workers were killed in an ambush as they drove through the predominantly Sunni city of 300,000 inhabitants about forty miles west of Baghdad. Three of the four, Steve Helvenston, Mike Teague, and Jerry Zovko, were former Navy SEALs, and the fourth, Wesley Batalona, an ex-Army Ranger. They worked as guards for Blackwater Security Consulting of Moyock, North Carolina, and were providing security for food delivery in the

Fallujah area. New to Iraq, driving two sport utility vehicles two-to-a-car, each without a machine gunner to cover the rear, they got lost in downtown Fallujah. Suddenly they came under a torrent of small arms fire that killed them almost instantly. As a triumphant crowd gathered, a youth poured gasoline on the wreckage and set it afire. A man held up a sign that said, "Fallujah, cemetery of the Americans." As soon as the wreckage cooled, some demented onlookers dragged the charred bodies through the streets in a show of subhuman disrespect of the dead reminiscent of Mogadishu in 1993. Two of the charred corpses were strung up like grotesque trophies on the girders of a bridge spanning the Euphrates River.[31]

After the death of the four Blackwater guards, the order came from higher levels of command (some say the White House) to attack. The 1st Marine Expeditionary Force had just taken over the Fallujah occupation and its commander, Lieutenant General James T. Conway, had wanted to accelerate reconstruction projects to win the support of local people. Instead, he followed the orders from on high, and did so with too few troops to accomplish the mission and with limits on the rules of engagement to avoid excessive civilian casualties. In heavy fighting that began on April 5, 2004, the Marines overran the outlying sections of the city, but did not try to penetrate the downtown area. Instead, they were abruptly ordered to withdraw and leave the battleground in the enemy's hands. The insurgents considered it an American defeat. The United States settled for a political solution, the formation of the so-called "Fallujah Brigade," a force of more than a thousand former Iraqi soldiers who promised to provide security and fight the insurgents. The Marines gave them eight hundred AK-47 automatic rifles, twenty-seven pickup trucks, and fifty radios to carry out their mission. But the Fallujah Brigade, whose members were largely from the local area, did very little enforcement over the ensuing months. Many, if not all of them tacitly supported the insurgency. Some in the Fallujah Brigade even joined the insurgents in skirmishes with the Americans. Eventually, all the donated equipment ended up the hands of the enemy.[32]

That April, 135 U.S. troops Iraq-wide were killed at the hands of the insurgents, the second deadliest month of the occupation up to that time. Unable to make headway in battle during a presidential election year, the Bush Administration struck a blow with political symbolism. On June 28, in a secret ceremony in the heavily guarded Green Zone of Baghdad, America returned "sovereignty" to Iraq. The "turnover" had been moved up two days from June 30 and taken from the public arena to avoid disruption by insurgents. The gesture had only symbolic significance because, by definition, sovereignty means "supreme authority," and the compliant Iraqi government could hardly claim supreme authority under the weight of the American-led occupation.

The transfer of sovereignty, however, did nothing to improve security. In the capital of Anbar Province, Ramadi, a city of about 450,000 people forty miles up the Euphrates River from Fallujah, a thousand U.S. Marines belonging to the 2nd Battalion of the 4th Marine Regiment tried to keep a low profile and leave security up to the Iraqi police. But insurgents often targeted them, and when the Marines would engage the enemy, which was frequent, the Iraqi police and National Guard seemed suddenly to vanish, unless they stayed to fire on the Marines. In four months of urban warfare, the U.S. garrison suffered 31 killed and 175 wounded.[33] In Haditha, farther upstream from Ramadi, insurgents assaulted a police station in early November, captured twenty-one Iraqi policemen, tied their hands behind their backs, and shot them all dead.[34]

But the U.S. command, obsessed over Fallujah, could not allow the April debacle to stand. This time a much larger force was committed to achieve overwhelming superiority. It consisted of about six thousand Marine and Army troops bolstered by two thousand Iraqi government troops. Several thousand more troops ringed the city as a blocking force, but not before an estimated three thousand out of five thousand insurgents slipped away to fight another day. Noncombatants had been warned to leave, and most of them had evacuated. The attack began from the north on November 8, and the troops quickly swept into the downtown district. By the 12th, the Americans controlled 80 percent of the city. By the 20th, the American victory was complete. Much of the fighting had been house to house, and despite the overwhelming American firepower, the U.S. troops had sustained significant casualties: 51 killed and 425 seriously wounded. "The [second] battle of Fallujah was not a defeat [in contrast to the first one in April]," said Jonathan F. Keiler in the *Proceedings* of the Naval Institute, "but we cannot afford many more victories like it."[35]

If the Marines won the battle of Fallujah, what did they actually win? General Muhammad Abd Allah Shahwani, director of the Iraqi intelligence service who before the invasion headed a CIA unit of Iraqi exiles that trained for undercover missions inside Saddam's Iraq, flatly denied that retaking Fallujah was a significant military triumph. "What we have now," he said six weeks after the fighting there ended, "is a city almost destroyed and most of the insurgents are free. They have gone either to Mosul or to Baghdad or other areas."[36]

The fighting was heavy that fall throughout the Sunni Triangle. Insurgents attacked police in Baghdad, Tikrit, Baquba, Buhriz, and Mosul. In Baghdad at opposite ends of the city on December 3, the insurgents killed at least thirty people (many of them police), freed dozens of prisoners, and lifted armaments from a police arsenal. Zarqawi claimed credit for the attacks.[37] Near Mosul on December 21, a suicide bomber infiltrated a U.S. military mess tent during lunch hour and touched off an explosion that killed twenty-two people, including fourteen American soldiers and four American civilian contract workers.[38] Al-Jazeera reported on December 28 that at least twenty-seven Iraqi police were killed in attacks on police stations and checkpoints in several locations.[39]

At the turn of the year 2005, Shahwani, the Iraqi intelligence chief, told reporters that the insurgents actually outnumbered American forces in Iraq. He estimated 40,000 full-time fighters and another 200,000 fighting part-time and providing support services. Pentagon estimates of the insurgents topped out at 20,000. The number of U.S. troops in Iraq fluctuated roughly between 130,000 and 160,000.

Shahwani reasoned that the insurgents enjoyed wide support in the Sunni areas because of tribal bonds and close ties to the 400,000-man Iraqi army, which the Coalition Authority had dissolved in May 2003. He said several towns and even some neighborhoods of Baghdad were virtually under the control of the insurgents. He stopped short of saying they were winning, but added, "I would say they aren't losing."

January 30, 2005, was "purple finger day" in Iraq. People went to the polls amid heavy security to elect provincial parliaments and a 275-member national assembly to form a transitional government and write a new constitution. At the polling places, they dipped a finger in purple ink to keep them from voting twice. Some of them proudly held up ink-stained fingers to demonstrate for cameras their eagerness to participate in the new democracy. The downside was their tendency to vote along ethnic and sectarian lines, which did nothing for Iraqi unity. Given insurgent threats of violence, the turnout was larger than expected, especially in Shia and Kurdish areas. Sunnis voted in lower numbers after their leaders had urged them to boycott the election. The promised violence left forty-four dead on that day, a lower number than expected.[40] President Bush hailed the Iraqi vote as "the voice of freedom from the center of the Middle East."

After a lull in the fighting, the insurgency erupted five days after the election with attacks from one end of Iraq to the other. In the deadliest incident south of Kirkuk, an Islamist group calling itself Takfir wa Hijra, which originated in Egypt, stopped a minibus carrying fourteen Iraqi army recruits, ordered them off the vehicle, and shot twelve of them dead. The other two were allowed to return to their base to warn fellow recruits against fighting on the American side.

The Marine force that had taken Fallujah the previous November pushed upriver in late February toward the Syrian border in an operation called "River Blitz." This was hardly a blitz like the great offensives of World War II or even the rapid drive to Baghdad in 2003. It consisted initially of imposing curfews and travel restrictions as scattered gun battles broke out. The guerrillas either faded away or offered only light but sometimes deadly resistance to the American advance. After the troops withdrew, the insurgents returned. At some localities, the Marines established fortified bases and would send out patrols, which were vulnerable to roadside bombs and sniping attacks.

Operation River Blitz was followed by Operation New Market at Haditha, by Operation Matador against al-Qaim near the Syrian border, by Operation Desert Scorpion, which began against insurgents who had re-infiltrated Fallujah and spread out from there. In terms of casualties, there was give and take between the two sides. If the United States with their air support and superior firepower inflicted more casualties than they took, they did not come out unscathed.

The January election was followed by three months of haggling before the National Assembly could agree on April 28 to form a new transition government headed by the Shiite, Ibrahim al-Jaafari. The next day insurgents responded to this American political success with a dozen car bombs in Baghdad and a series of attacks on military targets throughout Iraq, killing at least forty people and wounding more than a hundred.[41]

In late May, the new transition government announced a military initiative, "Operation Lightning," to drive the insurgents out of Baghdad. Beginning on May 29, an Iraqi police and military force of forty thousand, backed by ten thousand American troops, set up checkpoints to monitor traffic in and out of the city, and entered several insurgent-dominated neighborhoods, searching vehicles and homes and arresting suspects. Insurgents struck back with attacks on two police stations, an Iraqi army barracks, and a checkpoint. A senior U.S. intelligence official summed up the day with the comment, "We have not seen any indication that the insurgents are packing up their bags."[42] But in Washington, Vice President Cheney pounced on this show of Iraqi resolve. He went on television and declared that the insurgency was "in its last throes."[43] A year later, the insurgency was still going strong.

Good News and Bad

The National Assembly gave itself until August 15, 2005, to draw up a constitution. Even though the Sunnis had held back in the January vote, they were included in the negotiations, which bogged down over such issues as religion, power, and the distribution of wealth from oil. The Iraqi oil fields lie in provinces inhabited predominantly by the Shia and Kurds. So the Sunnis demanded that the oil revenues go through Baghdad to assure distribution on an equitable basis. August 15 came and the issues were not resolved. The parties added another week, and then another three days, and on August 26, an unfinished draft was submitted for the Assembly's consideration. The unhappy Sunnis decided that they would try to defeat the constitution when it came up for ratification on October 15. But it passed, and in the December 15 parliamentary elections amid heavy security and negligible violence the voting was heavy, even among the Sunnis. It took more than a month to certify the results, but to nobody's surprise the United Iraqi Alliance, a bloc of Shia religious parties came out on top. It won 128 of the 275 seats in the Assembly, and pushed through the Assembly the election of Shiite Nouri al-Maliki as prime minister with the backing of perhaps the most powerful Shiite militia leader, Muktada al-Sadr. Since the United Iraqi Alliance remained ten seats short of an outright majority, it would have to negotiate with another party to form a coalition government.

While mainline troops bore the brunt of the fighting, elite Special Operations forces went looking for prominent players in Saddam's Baathist Party regime. Most of them were captured or voluntarily surrendered; some were killed. Saddam's notorious sons, Uday and Qusay, chose to die in a shoot-out. Hussein was found hiding in a spider hole, and later hanged for his war crimes. Abu Musab al-Zarqawi, the Islamist behind some of the worst atrocities of the insurgency, was the object of an intense manhunt that dragged on for three years. Finally, Task Force 145 cornered him in a safe house north of Baghdad, and took him out with a precision air strike.

Like the political milestones that the White House trumpeted as building blocks of an emerging democracy, the demise of these rogues raised expectations of ultimate triumph. The Bush people thought Hussein's capture in December 2004 would break the back of the resistance. But the insurgency actually picked up speed. IED attacks nearly doubled in 2005 and another 680 U.S. troops died that year from hostile fire, the majority from IEDs. In July alone, IEDs caused thirty-six of forty-five hostile deaths (80 percent).[44]

A similar optimism arose from Zarqawi's death in June 2006. That event coincided with the formation of a permanent Iraqi government after six months of negotiations. The Shiite Prime Minister Nouri al-Maliki had formed a cabinet that would include a Sunni defense minister. President Bush was so elated that he took a victory lap of sorts. He slipped away from a meeting of his top security officials at Camp David for a five-hour visit in Baghdad to meet Maliki and his cabinet. Back at the White House the next day, he warned opponents of the Iraq war that any premature withdrawal of American troops would "endanger our country."[45]

The "lethality" of the insurgency created a "reconstruction gap," according to a January 2006 report by Stuart Bowen, a special inspector general for Iraq reconstruction. Money allocated for infrastructure repairs had been shifted to the training of security forces. Beyond that, the insurgents continued their assaults on infrastructure targets, new and old. Consequently, only about 25 percent of planned oil plant repairs, 36 percent of planned water and sewer projects, and 61 percent of planned electricity projects were on schedule. Services in these areas were below prewar levels under Saddam.[46]

Civil War

The following month north of Baghdad, about a dozen masked men stole into the Askariya Shrine in Samara, one of the holiest sites of Shia Islam, and blew up the mosque's golden dome. There, the twelfth Imam in Shia legend is said to have disappeared into a suspended state of "occultation" in the tenth century AD. As a matter of Shia faith, he will rise again for Judgment Day to bring justice to an iniquitous world. The bombing caused no casualties, but inflicted grievous injury to Shia sensitivities. Next day throughout Iraq, Shiites in the thousands took to the streets to vent their frustrations over this insult to their faith. In the days that followed, innocents died as Shia militia attacked Sunnis and Sunni hit squads attacked Shiites. The Shia had finally responded to Sunni provocations, plunging Iraq into sectarian violence that rose to such a fever pitch that General John P. Abizaid, the overall American commander in the Middle East, said after testimony in Congress in early March that, for the moment, it had surpassed the insurgency as the major security concern for the U.S. command.[47]

As the year wore on, all Iraq slipped ever closer to chaos in the wake of the Samara bombing. In the neighborhoods and suburbs of Baghdad, Shiite and Sunni gangs roamed the streets at night killing members of the other sect. The American-trained

Iraqi security forces could not handle them. In July, fifteen thousand U.S. troops had to be called in to quell the bloodshed, and even the American reinforcements were not enough. The *Washington Post,* citing morgue officials, reported in October that 90 percent of the killings were execution style, with many of the victims blindfolded, bound hand and foot, horribly tortured (often with electric drills penetrating the skull, torso, or limbs), and shot repeatedly in the head and body.

The Torn Social Fabric

Behind the scenes, Ambassador Zalmay Khalilzad, the neoconservative who had lobbied for the American attack to remove Saddam, painted a grim picture of a broken Iraq. In a confidential message to Secretary of State Rice obtained by the *Washington Post,* he laid out the negative effects of everyday life in Baghdad on Iraqis employed at the embassy. From the green zone where American and Iraqi officials breathe in relative comfort, he told of deep strains on families, neighborhoods, and communities that were pulling the nation apart.

Khalilzad described Baghdad neighborhoods as emerging ethnic or sectarian enclaves in which Islamists and/or sectarian militia, the shock troops of the de facto civil war, exercised intimidating influence. Increasingly, public opinion was turning against the American and coalition presence. Barricades were going up in predominantly Sunni or Shiite areas to deny access to outsiders, and informers were patrolling the streets just in case any outsiders slipped through. Neighborhoods were going to seed. One embassy employee called the once-upscale Mansur neighborhood "an unrecognizable ghost town." A Shiite employee told of attending a funeral in his neighborhood almost every night.

Ethnic cleansing was a hidden subtext of the civil war. A Sunni Kurd employee complained that her landlord had evicted her from her home of several years under a decades-old law that had not been previously enforced. A tent city was under consideration in the Kurdish city of Irbil to handle the influx of Kurds from Arab cities throughout Iraq. One Sunni Kurd whose life was threatened left the country altogether.

In formerly style-tolerant Baghdad, it was no longer considered safe for men and boys to wear shorts in the stifling heat of temperatures up to 115 degrees or for women to go outside without their heads covered. Electricity to run air conditioners was unevenly distributed, available for as little as four hours in some neighborhoods. Despite the fact that Iraq has the second largest crude reserves in the world, long lines to fill gas tanks were a daily occurrence. The fortunate few with the means to pay could find their gas on the black market at 400 percent of the controlled price.

The general malaise was creeping closer to the fortified green zone. American-trained Iraqi police guarding the entrances were acting more like militias, Khalilzad wrote. An employee asked the embassy for press credentials because a guard checking her identity one morning had held up her embassy badge and yelled, "Embassy," a virtual death warrant if heard by the wrong person. To protect Iraqi staff, the embassy was careful to keep them from appearing on videotaped news events and to shred documents showing the surnames of Iraqi personnel.

Khalilzad ventured the comment that "[the staff's] personal fears are reinforcing divisive sectarian or ethnic channels, despite talk of reconciliation by officials.... Objectivity, civility, and logic that make for a functional workplace may falter if social pressures outside the green zone don't abate."[48] Not to mention that the whole misguided venture to democratize the Middle East might crumble in failure.

"Iraqification"

In the Vietnam War, President Nixon ballyhooed his "Vietnamization" program as the key to American withdrawal. As Nixon explained it, America would turn the defense of South Vietnam over to the South Vietnamese army, and would depart confident that its intervention had not been in vain. It was all smoke and mirrors. Within three years of the American departure, the communists had overrun the entire country.

The training of Iraqi security forces—one might call it the "Iraqification" program—has much the same odor. The early performance of the new Iraqi police and military left much to be desired. In April 2004, Major General Martin Dempsey complained that 40 percent of newly trained Iraqi security forces attached to the Army's 1st Armored Division in operations at Najaf and Fallujah refused to fight against fellow Iraqis. Another 10 percent, he said, actually "worked against" the American troops.[49] Later that year in Mosul, most of the city's five thousand U.S.-trained police either withered away or joined the insurgents who temporarily took over eight of ten police stations. Before retreating, the insurgents looted the stations for Kalashnikov rifles, bulletproof vests, police cars and uniforms, and set fire to three of the stations.[50]

At the time late in 2004, Iraqi military and police forces numbered about 170,000, but only about 6,000 were combat ready. Anthony Cordesman of the Center for Strategic and International Studies estimated in a report on Iraq's security problems that it would take at least a year to train and equip the rest of them to the point where they could succeed against the insurgency.[51] Fourteen months later the situation had improved. Training had continued, and the United States had turned security for two sectors of the city over to two battalions of Iraqi troops. The U.S. command hoped that by November 2006, the whole city of 1.5 million could be put in the hands of 24,000 Iraqi police and guardsmen. But early in 2006, Mosul "still teeter[ed] on the edge of chaos."[52]

New signs of weakness in the Iraqification program emerged more than three years later. In September 2007, after British troops pulled out of Basra, Iraq's southern-most city near the Persian Gulf, security was handled not by the Iraqi government, but by Shia militia loyal to Muqtada al-Sadr. Six months later, Prime Minister Maliki dispatched about thirteen thousand troops to establish government control, but in pitched battles, not only did the government troops fail to dislodge the militia, but at least a thousand of them refused to fight or ran from the battle-field, leaving serious doubt about the ability of the Maliki regime to take control of Iraq.

The escalation of violence in Iraq raised political pressures in the United States leading up to midterm elections in 2006. Even though the president himself was not up for reelection, the Bush Administration's stewardship of the war became the central issue. The American electorate turned emphatically against the war—fitting a pattern of other great-power occupations covered in these pages—and stripped Republicans of their control of Congress. As the Democrats prepared to take over, they tried to pressure Bush to begin drawing down the U.S. troops in Iraq. But instead, Bush ordered the deployment of 21,500 additional troops to Baghdad and Anbar Province, where the ethnic violence and insurgency raged virtually out of con-trol. The "surge," as it was called, yielded mixed results in its early phase. General David Petraeus, the new commander in Iraq, rebilleted army troops out of their fortified bases into Iraqi neighborhoods and let the people know they were there to protect them. He also launched heavy strikes against al Qaeda-in-Iraq strongholds. He returned to Washington in late April to report a significant reduction of ethnic violence in Baghdad despite several spectacular suicide bombings that included the penetration of the parliament building in the supposedly secure Green Zone. In September, Petraeus was back in Washington to report better news: U.S. casualties were down and some tribal leaders in Anbar were cooperating with American forces.

The Iraqi Sunnis had grown disenchanted with their foreign Islamist allies who enforced strict sharia law in areas they came to dominate, including the execution of tribal leaders and family members for alleged violations of the Islamist code. The Sunnis then took stock of their unexpected plight and approached the Ameri-cans about switching sides. Initially, they were rebuffed, but the Americans came to realize that the Sunni offer was in their own best interests. So insurgents who had been fighting and killing U.S. troops became willing recipients of American training and arms. In 2007, when America sent reinforcements to Iraq to implement the "surge," the Sunni fighters teamed with U.S. troops to attack Islamists strongholds in Baghdad and other areas of Iraq. The U.S. military reported that it dealt devastat-ing blows to al Qaeda in Iraq, which resulted in a 50 percent decline in suicide bombings. The success of these initiatives led neoconservatives and other war sup-porters in Washington to claim victory, but the generals on the ground in Iraq remained cautious about writing epitaphs for the Islamists.

Even though momentum may have shifted in favor of the Americans, the occupa-tion of Iraq remained a losing enterprise. Despite all the energy, good and bad, that America has put into the effort, the new Shia-dominated government in Baghdad had so far failed to put together a viable coalition government with shared power and equitable distribution of the oil wealth. Violence was down in Baghdad partly because the Shia militia had for all practical purposes achieved the ethnic cleansing it sought of driving Sunnis out of mixed neighborhoods. Yet, bombs were still going off and people were getting killed. The insurgents, after all, had not lost, and in Kissinger's phrase, if they do not lose, they win.

—

Michael Berg, the father of Nick Berg who was beheaded in Iraq, advised President Bush in a remembrance published in the *Guardian* to "stop speaking to the people we labeled our enemies and start listening to them. Stop giving preconditions to our peaceful coexistence on this small planet, and start honoring and respecting every human's need to live free and autonomously, to truly respect the sovereignty of every state. [S]top making up rules by which others must live and then [following] separate rules for ourselves."[53]

Paul E. Schroeder, the father of one of fourteen Marines killed by an IED explosion on August 3, 2005 near Haditha, mourned the loss of his son, Edward, with an op-ed article in the *Washington Post*. He expressed outrage at a situation "that makes our troops sitting ducks," and questioned the president's "twisted logic" of promising to honor the fallen by finishing the job. Did he mean, Schroeder asked, "honor [them] by killing another 2,000 troops in a broken policy?"[54]

Grieving parents who suffer the worst of outrageous fortune, the death of an offspring, can sometimes see through the pain with perfect clarity. These two see that the Bush Administration has embarked on a dangerous adventure that leads to unintended dire consequences. With profound sympathies for the bereaved, this book seeks to make a very practical point, that the Iraq invasion was a risky, even reckless endeavor against a foe that posed no imminent threat to the United States. When you clear away the false claims about WMD and connections to al Qaeda and 9/11, and the rationalizations boil down to regime change and the illusionary spread of democracy, you have to measure the cost of war against the purpose for which it was undertaken, because from the start, the historical odds have been heavily against an American victory.

Afterword: The Limits of Power

We must face the fact that the United States is neither omnipotent nor omniscient—that we are only six percent of the world's population; that we cannot impose our will upon the other ninety-four percent of mankind; that we cannot right every wrong or reverse each adversity; and therefore there cannot be an American solution to every world problem.

—John F. Kennedy (1961)

The problem in Iraq started with a preemptive war based on a blind faith in America's might that led the Bush Administration to adopt a simplistic military solution to a frustrating political problem. America was dazzled by its own grandeur—by the "can do" attitude that the greatest nation on earth can accomplish any mission it sets its mind to do. But it was not the first prominent power in recent history to run roughshod over a Middle Eastern Muslim nation and pay a heavy price.

Israel showed us the way with its 1982 invasion of Lebanon. Starting in the mid-1970s, the Lebanese Christian right wanted Israel to join them in their civil war against superior Muslim forces. Israel's Labor government, beset with artillery bombardments and cross-border terrorist attacks from the PLO lodged in southern Lebanon, saw the Christians as a useful ally, but remained wary about being drawn into the Lebanese conflict. Prime Minister Yitzhak Rabin stated his government's guiding principle to a Lebanese Christian emissary: "[W]e are prepared to help you help yourselves."[1] In other words, the Israelis would send arms, not troops.

But the Israeli election of 1977 brought the conservative Likud to power, and the new Prime Minister, Menachem Begin, the Zionist insurgency leader of Mandate days, gradually threw caution to the wind and warmed to his ideological brothers on the Lebanese right. In his second term beginning in 1981, he appointed Ariel Sharon defense minister. Sharon, whose daring leadership had turned the tide of battle in the 1973 Yom Kippur War, trumpeted a hard line on military policy. His mind swirled with thoughts of changing the politics of the Middle East in Israel's favor. Using a combination of bullying and subterfuge to keep his plans from spilling into the public arena, he prepared for an all-out invasion of Lebanon, with a view to driving the PLO out of the country, elbowing out Syrian influence, and installing a Christian right-wing government friendly to Israel.[2] In June 1982, he struck. The error of his judgment was not immediately apparent. The IDF advanced rapidly to Beirut and up the Bekaa Valley, bloodied the Syrian army, expelled the PLO, and then stayed behind for eighteen years in a gradually shrinking and ultimately disastrous occupation of southern Lebanon.

The American adventure in Iraq has shown striking similarities to the Israeli experience: first, hawkish policymakers spoiling for a fight; second, the preconceived ideas offered by neoconservatives about using America's military superiority to impose political change; third, the secrecy and deception that stood out in the manipulation of intelligence to fit policy; fourth, false allegations about an Iraqi role in 9/11, parallel to Begin's canard that Yasser Arafat could be blamed for trying to assassinate Ambassador Shlomo Argov in London, which triggered the Lebanon invasion (ironically, Baghdad was more complicit in the Argov affair, staged by the Iraqi-sponsored, bitter-Arafat-rival Abu Nidal group, than in 9/11); fifth, the success of the initial thrust to Baghdad, and finally, the lengthy occupation and insurgency, which at this writing was four-and-a-half years old. The U.S. superpower had many years to go to match the length of Israel's folly—but had already exceeded its depth.

President Bush has acknowledged that losing in Iraq will have negative consequences for America. That admission came three-and-a-half years late in defense of his illusory goal of winning. If he had thought of it before he started the war, he might have avoided the ugly quagmire that will define his place in history. We cannot yet know all the damage Bush has done in Iraq because the end game is still being played out as of early 2008. But he has done more than enough already. Beyond exceeding the limits of American power, he has set the stage for a killing field of sectarian violence, just as the U.S. invasion of Cambodia in 1970 touched off a killing field of class violence, both resulting in the wholesale slaughter of innocents. He has created a venue for jihadists to practice their deadly skills and train for future terrorist operations. If the terrorist onslaught keeps spreading it could lead to more and worse 9/11s—and lest we forget, Bush took the pressure off al Qaeda in 2002 to prepare for war in Iraq. Bush policies, including the Iraq war, have weakened the dollar and turned a budget surplus into a crippling deficit. The cost of crude oil tripled from March 2003 when America invaded to the end of 2007. "The soaring cost of oil is clearly related to the Iraq war," said Nobel laureate Joseph Stiglitz.[3]

The American intervention has also changed the geopolitics of the Middle East: Already Iran has gained influence in Iraq and the wider region that it never had before the invasion.[4]

It should be obvious that leaving Saddam Hussein contained, rogue that he was, amounted to the lesser of two evils in 2003 (the greater evil being what actually happened: invasion, occupation, and insurgency). Irrational fear of militant Islam after 9/11 led us into an irrational war against Iraq. Punishing Saddam for the crimes of Osama bin Laden compares to prosecuting a man with a bad rap sheet for a murder he did not commit. Having invaded Iraq, however, America faced no good options. The less bad option would be a negotiated withdrawal that would free us to focus more on the real enemy, militant Islam.

What seemed a glimmer of hope arose in Anbar Province when Sunni tribal chiefs, disenchanted with the foreign Islamists who imposed strict sharia law to the extent of executing alleged tribal violators, made overtures to forge an alliance with the American military command. The Americans were slow to respond, but eventually accommodated them, and the odd couple of American Marines and tribal fighters joined together in the war against al Qaeda. After sending reinforcements to Iraq in what has been called the "surge," the Bush administration took credit for this strange turn in Anbar as a success for its new strategy to win. It was certainly good news, but attributable more to the cruelty of the Islamists than any strategy cooked up in the White House.

On the downside were a lack of political consensus in Baghdad and the danger of greater ethnic warfare. In reality, America was arming the insurgents it had been fighting in the first three years of the occupation, and these new Sunni allies had no commitment to the central government. Arming the Sunnis only added to the problem. America had already been arming and training a national security force made up of individuals with loyalties to Shia militias, not the central government. The Center for American Progress, a liberal think tank, warned in June 2007 that to continue the national security training program risked "making Iraq's civil war bloodier and more vicious" and increased the danger that the weapons will be turned on U.S. forces standing between the warring factions.[5] How much bloodier would it be with the United States arming both sides?

Beware the danger, too, that the gains of the "surge" will mean a longer stay in Iraq so that U.S. troops can insure "victory." That, in turn, will mean that the troops will sustain more deaths and devastating injuries, if at a lower rate. As that scenario plays out, the policymakers had better pay attention to the morale of the men and women they put in harm's way.

This is where the initial decision to invade in 2003 looms so importantly in the end game. Having made that error, Bush and his inner circle are loath to admit it because they dread the political consequences of acknowledging failure. As the White House continues to talk tough and the neocons bask in the glow of the surge, the chances of a breakthrough during the Bush tenure seem slim. In Iraq, the administration has been building the largest U.S. embassy in the world, plus what

are called "enduring" bases that can either accommodate a long-term U.S. occupation or be turned over to a supposedly friendly Iraqi military when America departs.[6]
Bush has bet all his marbles on "winning," and says he will not withdraw before the
job is done. On that point, he is consistent with the history of the recent past, which
shows that it takes bold new leadership to clean up the mess by quitting an unwinna-
ble insurgent war.

President Bush seems to lump all Islamists in one basket. He has carried on the
counterinsurgency in Iraq as if it was all about fighting the so-called war on terror,
even though perhaps 90 percent of the insurgents were considered from the beginning to be non-Islamist Sunni Muslims. Four years on, Shia militias engaged in the
ethnic cleansing of Sunni neighborhoods, fought intrasectarian battles against other
Shia militias, and challenged the American occupation troops, sometimes with support from Iranian sources, thus creating a de facto civil war that compromises the
American role. (In 2007, the powerful Shia militia leader Muktada al-Sadr called a
temporary halt to fighting, and as this was written the moratorium was still in effect.)
Bush has admitted that Iraq took no part in the 9/11 atrocity, yet at every opportunity he justifies America's presence in Iraq by citing 9/11. He claims that America is
in Iraq to fight al Qaeda and other Islamists, but the Islamists came only after
America invaded.

By now it should be clear, whether fighting Islamists or Iraqi insurgents, that a
full-throttle military deployment is no way to go about it. Chalmers Johnson, the
distinguished emeritus professor at the University of California, San Diego who sees
9/11 as "blowback" for American imperial aggression, notes that military attacks in
Afghanistan and Iraq have only increased the threat of al Qaeda. In dismissing the
military option to fight terrorists, he refers to the pointed eloquence of British historian Correlli Barnett. "Rather than kicking down the front doors and barging into
ancient and complex societies with simple nostrums of 'freedom and democracy,'"
said Barnett, "we need tactics of cunning and subtlety, based on a profound understanding of the people and cultures we are dealing with—an understanding up till
now entirely lacking in the top-level policy makers in Washington, especially in the
Pentagon."[7]

The United States needs to find battlefields more suitable to its capabilities and to
fit its capabilities more precisely to the nature of the enemy. For nongovernment
entities like al Qaeda, Iraq is the wrong battlefield and full-scale military power the
wrong instrument of policy. While the American military and its coalition partners
have floundered in Iraq, international police and U.S. Special Forces have racked
up notable successes. The Pakistani police, working in cooperation with American
agencies, have caught important Islamists, such as 9/11 plotter Khalid Sheikh
Mohammed, his accomplice Ramsi Binalshibh, top bin Laden aide Abu Zubaydah,
and the killers of *Wall Street Journal* reporter Daniel Pearl. Spanish police, operating

in the wake of a horrendous terrorist event in Madrid, moved efficiently to bring the perpetrators to justice. In a joint operation with Thai police in August 2003, the CIA captured the Indonesian terrorist, Riduan bin Isomoddin, better known as Hambali, as he and his followers prepared explosive cocktails for an economic summit conference later that year in Bangkok of Asian Pacific leaders that included President Bush. Hambali is thought to be the mastermind of the notorious Bali nightclub bombings in 2002 and 2005. Some militants have been dispatched with missiles fired from remotely controlled drones, including a top bin Laden lieutenant, Abu Laith al-Libi, who was killed in northwest Pakistan.[8] To be sure, police and special military operations can have their ugly sides, but these achievements have been cost-effective with minimal bloodshed and relatively low financial investment, in stark contrast to the heavy-handed military occupation of Iraq.

Militant Islam should have been challenge enough for the greatest power in history without begging for more trouble. Great powers survive longer by not squandering their power. Yet, we should recognize that most Muslims bear no animosity toward America—at least they did not prior to our invasion of Iraq. The need is to isolate the extreme ideologues from the multitudes, and for that we must be careful about identifying our enemy.

Islamism is not necessarily violent. Hassan al-Banna, the Egyptian founder of the Muslim Brotherhood, did not declare jihad in the sense of holy war, but saw it rather as a struggle against inner devils. He was a teacher who inspired the Arab victims of colonialism. He propagated Islam as a total way of life that he believed would bring the Muslim people to a realization of their own destiny. Before his death in 1949, probably at the hands of government assassins, he ran for legislative office in Egypt, and today many of his adherents, including those in our NATO ally Turkey, follow his example of participating nonviolently in democratic politics. Islamism as preached by Banna is no more a threat to world peace than the Christian Coalition in America, which compares to the Banna-oriented Muslim Brotherhood in its political orientation and moral rigidity. They worship the same God with different sacred books and, together with the Jews, trace their ancestry to the same founding father, Abraham. It was Sayyid Qutb writing bitter passages from his prison cell that turned heads in the Muslim Brotherhood and reshaped parts of the movement into a specter that haunts the world. Even some violent Islamist organizations like Hamas, Palestinian Islamic Jihad, and Hezbollah are more narrowly focused on Israel, and do not threaten U.S. security interests as long as America does not threaten theirs. Israel has proved over and over that it can take care of itself without the need for America to fight its battles. On the other hand, we cannot ignore the hard edge to bin Laden's brand of Islamism. It is violent, Manichaean, well financed, a magnet for young Muslim idealists, and if allowed to get out of hand, a threat to American security.

By adhering to a goal of military victory, Bush not only deceives himself, he defies the odds of history, which are unfavorable for occupiers. Lieutenant General William Odom (Ret.), the former national security advisor to President Reagan turned academician, dismisses warnings of dire consequences arising from an American withdrawal because the chaos predicted already exists, brought on by the American presence. He argues for a complete pullout within six months. "It is beyond U.S. power," he writes, "to prevent bloody sectarian violence in Iraq, the growing influence of Iran throughout the region, the probable spread of Sunni–Shiite strife to neighboring Arab states, the eventual rise to power of the anti-American cleric Muqtada [al-]Sadr or some other anti-American leader in Baghdad, and the spread of instability beyond Iraq. All of these things and more became unavoidable the day that U.S. forces invaded."[9] Odom's clarity puts Washington's foggy debate in a readily understandable context. It frames a timeless question asked of Britain by the wise old khan of Kalat in nineteenth-century Afghanistan: having entered and violated a small sovereign nation, how does the intruder get out?

There is no good way. Withdrawal will likely have bad consequences, but could they possibly be worse than the mess that now exists? For the next president, in the words of noncandidate Al Gore, "taking charge of the war policy and extricating [all] our troops as quickly as possible without making a horrible situation even worse is a little like grabbing a steering wheel in the middle of a skid."[10] America got out of Vietnam after training the South Vietnamese army to take over the fighting. In Afghanistan, the Soviet evacuation left behind a communist government and a trained, well equipped army. In each case, the defenders collapsed within a few years. History is repeating itself in Iraq where America is training an army to defend the American-made Iraqi government. When America leaves, how long will the Iraqi security forces hold up?

While the 9/11 attacks justified our invasion of Afghanistan, we and our NATO allies should be wary about lingering there too long, lest we trap ourselves in a long, un-winnable asymmetric war comparable to the Soviet experience in the 1980s. We had opportunities to kill or capture Osama bin Laden in the late 1990s, and again after the invasion of 2001. Had we been able to carry off any of the early ones on the Bill Clinton watch, it might have headed off the 9/11 attacks, while success in the later time period would have satisfied the principle of vendetta that the tribal cultures of that region understand and we could have pulled our troops out (if we had the wits to do so). Since then, al Qaeda has found sanctuary in the semi-autonomous mountain provinces of western Pakistan, restored its strength, and resumed its global jihad. Our goal must be to eliminate the sanctuary and liquidate the threat of terrorism by negotiation and political pressure with the help of Pakistan and its neighbors—not an easy task. Then we must let Afghanistan determine its own fate and withdraw our troops, better sooner than later.

Bush has made enemies of people who once respected America. By unleashing on Iraq the "shock and awe" of America's military might under the pretense of spreading democracy, he has violated the tenets of the democracy he seeks to spread. Democracy gains its legitimacy from the inside, i.e., from the will of the people, not from outside invaders. He has failed to live by, or even recognize the principle of national self-determination, which the United States championed in 1945. It is too late to save ourselves from Bush's strategic error. The insurgents need only hold on to win. The occupation weakens America. Withdrawal is inevitable; the argument is over when and under what conditions. Then, together with our allies, we can focus on the threat of global terrorism, and hope that future American leaders will pay more attention to the lessons of history.

NOTES

Introduction

1. CNN.com, from *Associated Press* (November 21, 2006).

2. CNN.com, "Late Edition with Wolf Blitzer" (February 18, 2007).

3. "Today," *NBC News* (December 6, 2006).

4. "Meet the Press," *NBC News* (December 3, 2006).

5. Lt. Gen. William Odom (Ret.), "Retreating in Good Order," *National Interest,* no. 76 (Summer 2004), online at www.nationalinterest.org.

6. Gen. Anthony Zinni (Ret.), Comments...during a speech before the Florida Economic Club (August 23, 2007), online at www.npr.org/programs/morning/zinni.html.

7. Patrick J. Buchanan, *Where the Right Went Wrong: How Neoconservatives subverted the Reagan Revolution and Hijacked the Bush Presidency* (New York: Thomas Dunne Books, 2004), 3.

8. Jeffrey Record, "Bounding the Global War on Terrorism," *Strategic Studies Institute* (Carlisle, PA: U.S. Army War College, December 2003), online at http://www.strategicstudiesinstitute.army.mil/pubs/display.cfm?publD=207.

9. Jeffrey Goldberg, "Breaking Ranks: What turned Brent Scowcroft against the Bush Administration?" *New Yorker* (October 31, 2005): 54–65.

10. Henry Kissinger, *Foreign Affairs* (January 1969).

11. See the discussion in Robert M. Cassidy, "Russia in Afghanistan and Chechnya: Military Strategic Culture and the Paradoxes of Asymmetric Conflict," *Strategic Studies Institute* (Carlisle, PA: U.S. Army War College, February, 2003), 1–12.

12. "Fox News Sunday," Fox network (June 26, 2005).

13. "Fox News Sunday" (June 17, 2007).

14. Charter of the United Nations, chap. 1, art. 1 (2).

15. "Meet the Press," *NBC News* (February 13, 2005).

16. Record, "Bounding the Global War on Terrorism."

17. *Oxford English Dictionary,* second edition, vol. vii (Oxford: Clarenden Press, 1989).

18. *The American Heritage College Dictionary,* third edition (New York: Houghton Mifflin, 1997).

19. *Webster's Third New International Dictionary,* unabridged (Springfield, MA: Merriam-Webster, Inc., 1986).

20. Buchanan, *Where the Right Went Wrong,* 89.

21. Flavius Josephus, *The Wars of the Jews,* Book V, chap. xi, sect. 1.

22. Amin Maalouf, *The Crusades Through Arab Eyes,* translated by Jon Rothschild (New York: Schocken Books, 1984), 26.

23. Martin Ewans, *Afghanistan: A Short History of Its People and Politics* (New York: HarperCollins, 2002), 17.

24. See "Country Reports on Terrorism," U.S. Department of State, chap. 7, "definition of terrorism" (April 30, 2008), online at http://www.state.gov/s/ct/rls/crt/2007/103715.htm.

Chapter 1

1. Barbara W. Tuchman, *The March of Folly: From Troy to Vietnam* (New York: Ballantine Books, 1984), 4.

2. Dick Cheney, Soref Symposium speech (April 29, 1991), quoted in *Middle East Web Log,* "Was winning in Iraq an afterthought?" (January 2, 2004), online at http://www.mideastweb.org/log/archives/00000149.htm.

3. Brent Scowcroft, "Don't Attack Saddam," *Opinion Journal from The Wall Street Journal Editorial Page* (August 15, 2002), online at WSJ.com.

4. "Armey: Unprovoked War Would Be Illegal," *Chicago Tribune* (August 9, 2002).

5. Bob Woodward, *Plan of Attack* (New York: Simon and Schuster, 2004), 150.

6. Thomas E. Ricks, *Fiasco: The American Military Adventure in Iraq* (New York: The Penguin Press, 2006), 67.

7. Ibid., 51.

8. Douglas Jehl, and David Sanger, "Prewar Assessment on Iraq Saw Chance of Strong Divisions," *New York Times* (September 28, 2004): Al, A9.

9. William Kristol, and Robert Kagan, "Toward a Neo-Reganite Foreign Policy," *Foreign Affairs* (July /August, 1996), reprinted online at http://www.ceip.org/people/kagfaff.htm, Council on Foreign Relations, Inc.

10. "Statement of Principles," Project for the New American Century.

11. James Risen, *State Of War: The Secret History of the CIA and the Bush Administration* (New York: Free Press, 2006), 62–63, 68–69.

12. James Mann, *Rise of the Vulcans: The History of Bush's War Cabinet* (New York: Viking, 2004), 210.

13. Patrick E. Tyler, "Lone Superpower Plan," *New York Times* (March 10, 1992): A1.

14. Mann, *Rise of the Vulcans,* 212.

15. *Rebuilding America's Defenses: Strategy, Forces and Resources for a New Century,* a report of the Project for the New American Century (September 2000).

16. Zalmy Khalilzad, and Paul Wolfowitz, "Overthrow Him," *Weekly Standard* (December 1, 1997): 14.

17. Borzou Daragahi, "Envoy to Iraq Sees Threat of Wider War," *Los Angeles Times* (March 7, 2006): A1.

18. Kathleen Christison, and Bill Christison, "A Rose By Another Name: The Bush Administration's Dual Loyalties," *CounterPunch* (December 13, 2002), online at http://www .counterpunch.org/christison1213.html.

19. Richard Perle, James Colbert, Charles Fairbanks, Jr., Douglas Feith, Robert Loewenberg, Jonathan Torop, David Wurmser, and Meyrav Wurmser, "Study Group on a New Israeli Strategy Toward 2000," The Institute for Advanced Strategic and Political Studies (1996).

20. Marc Perelman, "Cheney Taps Syria Hawk as Advisor on the Mideast," *Forward* (October 31, 2003).

21. Ricks, *Fiasco,* 77.

22. General Tommy Franks, with Malcolm McConnell, *American Soldier* (New York: HarperCollins, 2004), 330, 362.

23. George Packer, *The Assassins' Gate: America in Iraq* (New York: Farrar, Straus and Giroux, 2005), 128.

24. Ricks, *Fiasco,* 77.

25. Libby was indicted in the second Bush term for obstruction of justice and lying to a grand jury in the outing of CIA agent Valerie Plame.

26. Laurie Mylroie, *Study of Revenge: The First World Trade Center Attack and Saddam Hussein's War against America* (Washington, DC: The AEI Press, 2001), 251.

27. Leslie Stahl, "60 Minutes," *CBS News* (March 22, 2004). See also Ronald Suskind, *The Price of Loyalty: George W. Bush, the White House, and the Education of Paul O'Neill* (New York: Simon and Schuster, 2004), 72–76.

28. Richard A. Clarke, *Against All Enemies: Inside America's War on Terror* (New York: Free Press, 2004), 30–31.

29. Ibid., 32–33.

30. Warren P. Strobel, "Former CIA Director Looks for Evidence that Iraq Had Role in Attacks," *Knight Ridder Newspapers* (October 11, 2001).

31. Woodward, *Plan of Attack,* 2.

32. Packer, *The Assassins' Gate,* 107.

33. John B. Judis, and Spencer Ackerman, "The Selling of the Iraq War: The First Casualty," *New Republic* (June 30, 2003), online at http://www.tnr.com/doc.mhtml?i =20030630&s=ackermanjudis063003.

34. Richard A. Oppel Jr., "U.S. to Halt Payments to Iraqi Group Headed by Onetime Pentagon Favorite," *New York Times* (May 18, 2004), online at http://www.nytimes.com/ 2004/05/18/politics/18CHAL.html?.

35. Inspector General, U.S. Department of Defense, "Review of the Pre-Iraq War Activities of the Office of the Under Secretary of Defense for Policy" (February 9, 2007). The review was requested by Democratic Senator Carl Levin of Michigan, who became chairman of the Senate Armed Services Committee after the Democrats took control of Congress in 2007.

36. R. Jeffrey Smith, "Hussein's Prewar Ties to Al-Qaeda Discounted," *Washington Post* (April 6, 2007): A01, online at http://www.washingtonpost.com/wp-dyn/content/article/ 2007/04/05/AR2007040502263.html.

37. The 9/11 Commission Report, 228–9. See also Epstein, Edward Jay, "Atta in Prague? An Iraqi prisoner holds the answer to this 9/11 mystery," *Opinion Journal, from The Wall Street Journal Editorial Page* (November 22, 2005). WSJ.com.

38. "Levin Says Newly Declassified Information Indicates Bush Administration's Use of Pre-War Intelligence Was Misleading," Press Release, Office of Carl Levin (D-Michigan).

39. *Iraq on the Record: The Bush Administration's Public Statements on Iraq,* House Committee on Government Reform—Minority Staff, *Special Investigation Division* (March 16, 2004): 18, online at http://www.reform.house.gov/min/.

40. *Report on the U.S. Intelligence Community's Prewar Intelligence Assessment on Iraq,* Senate Select Committee on Intelligence (Roberts Committee), 108th Congress (July 7, 2004), 36–55.

41. Risen, *State Of War,* 85–107.

42. Jonathan S. Landay, and Drew Brown, "INC supplied defectors who were sources of questionable pre-war information, officials say," *Knight Ridder Newspapers* (April 3, 2004), online at http://www.mcclatchydc.com/reports/intelligence/story/10225.html.

43. Walter Pincus, "British Intelligence Warned of Iraq War," *Washington Post* (May 13, 2005): A18, online edition.

44. Michael R. Gordon, and Judith Miller, "U.S. Says Hussein Intensifies Quest for A-Bomb Parts," *New York Times* (September 8, 2002): 1, 25.

45. *Meet the Press, NBC News* (September 8, 2002).

46. *Late Edition with Wolf Blitzer, CNN* (September 8, 2002).

47. *Fox News Sunday, Fox TV* (September 8, 2002).

48. Robert Dreyfuss, and Jason West, "The Lie Factory," *Mother Jones* (January/February, 2004).

49. Walter Pincus, and Karen DeYoung, "Senators Debate Significance of Pentagon Report on Intelligence," *Washington Post* (February 10, 2007): A01.

50. Administration officials have denied any manipulation of prewar Iraq intelligence. The account here was based on published reports.

51. Walter Pincus, and Dana Priest, "Some Analysts Felt Pressure from Cheney Visits," *Washington Post* (June 5, 2003): A01.

52. Dreyfuss and West, *Mother Jones* (January/February, 2004).

53. Pincus and Priest, "Some Analysts Felt Pressure," *Washington Post.*

54. Bob Graham, "What I Knew Before the Invasion," *Washington Post* (November 20, 2005): B07.

55. Dana Priest, "Report Says CIA Distorted Iraq Data," *Washington Post* (July 12, 2004): A01.

56. *Iraq on the Record,* 4.

57. Ibid., 12.

58. *President's Remarks at the United Nations General Assembly,* New York, NY, White House, Office of the Press Secretary (September 12, 2002).

59. *Iraq on the Record,* 16.

60. Ibid., 26.

61. *President Bush Outlines Iraqi Threat: Remarks by the President on Iraq,* White House Release, Cincinnati, Ohio (October 7, 2002).

62. Priest, "Report Says," *Washington Post.*

63. *Iraq on the Record,* 4.

64. *President Delivers* "State of the Union," White House Release (January 28, 2003).

65. Woodward, *Plan of Attack,* 271.

66. Greg Miller, "Flaws Cited in Powell's Speech on Iraq," *Los Angeles Times* (July 15, 2004), online at http://www.commondreams.org/cgi-bin/print.cgi?file=/headlines04/07 15-05.htm.

67. *U.S. Secretary of State Colin Powell Addresses the U.N. Security Council,* White House Release (February 5, 2003).

68. Ricks, *Fiasco,* 19.

69. James Gannon, *Stealing Secrets, Telling Lies: How Spies and Codebreakers Helped Shape the Twentieth Century* (Dulles, VA: Brassey's, Inc., 2001), 118–29.

Chapter 2

1. *Holy Bible,* New Revised Standard Version (Iowa Falls: World Bible Publishers, 1989), 200–201.

2. Nathan Birnbaum first coined the term "Zionism" in 1893 in his brochure, "The National Rebirth of the Jewish People in the Homeland as a Means of Solving the Jewish Problem." Theodore Herzl wrote his famous tract, "The Jewish State," in 1896. From the Jewish Virtual Library.

3. Conor Cruise O'Brien, *The Siege: The Saga of Israel and Zionism* (New York: Simon and Schuster, 1986), 27.

4. David Ben Gurion, *Memoirs* (Cleveland: World Publishing Company, 1970), 26. Ben Gurion's comment bespeaks a clash of cultures. Part of the Jewish claim to the land he based on the Arab failure to develop it and create wealth—a typically Western disrespect of other cultures.

5. Benny Morris, *Righteous Victims: A History of the Zionist–Arab Conflict* (New York: Alfred A. Knopf, 1999), 49.

6. Morris, *Righteous Victims,* 76.

7. J. Bowyer Bell, *Terror out of Zion: Irgun Zvai Leumi, LEHI, and the Palestine Underground, 1929–1949* (New York: St. Martin's Press, 1977), 3–7.

8. Amos Elon, *The Israelis, Founders and Sons* (New York: Penguin Books, 1983), 158.

9. Bell, *Terror out of Zion,* 14–21.

10. Ibid.

11. Simha Flapan, *The Brith of Israel: Myths and Realities* (New York: Pantheon Books, 1987), 22.

12. Morris, *Righteous Victims,* 147.

13. Bell, *Terror out of Zion,* 42.

14. Rashid Khalidi, *Resurrecting Empire: Western Footprints and America's Perilous Path in the Middle East* (Boston: Beacon Press, 2004), 28.

15. Shmuel Katz, *Lone Wolf: A Biography of Vladimir (Ze'ev) Jabotinsky* (New York: Barricade Books, 1983), 1667.

16. Bell, *Terror out of Zion,* 64–65.

17. Ibid., 71.

18. Ibid., 72, n. 101. Morton claimed later that Stern broke toward the window and that he (Morton) feared Stern would set off a bomb. Bell's account, repeated here, was given years later by Sergeant Daniel Day on behalf of the unnamed policeman who was an eyewitness to the killing.

19. Ibid., 99–100.

20. Katz, *Lone Wolf,* 1626–29.

21. Bell, *Terror out of Zion,* 112.

22. Ned Temko, *To Win or To Die: A Personal Portrait of Menachem Begin* (New York: William Morrow and Company, 1987), 73.

23. That principle applied to open civil war. In the course of their underground work or to settle "internal accounts," Irgun and LHI operatives killed at least forty Jews, according to Haganah archives. The Haganah also punished Jewish informers. See Noam Chomsky, *Fateful Triangle: The United States, Israel, and the Palestinians* (Cambridge, MA: South End Press, 1999), 164–n5.

24. Morris, *Righteous Victims,* 174–76.

25. Bell, *Terror out of Zion,* 169–73.

26. Temko, *To Win or To Die,* 93.

27. A. J. Sherman, *Mandate Days: British Lives in Palestine, 1918–1948* (New York: Thames and Hudson, 1997) 183.

28. Nicholas Bethel, *The Palestine Triangle: The Struggle for the Holy Land, 1935–84* (London, 1979), 323. Quoted in Sherman, 187.

29. Sherman, *Mandate Days,* 190–1.

30. Bell, *Terror out of Zion,* 201–2.

31. Ibid., 235–8.

32. Quoted in Sherman, *Mandate Days,* 208.

33. Bell, *Terror out of Zion,* 245.

34. Quoted in "British Reaction on Palestine Plan," *New York Times* (September 2, 1947): 3, 8.

35. Flapan, *The Brith of Israel,* 31–32.

36. Sherman, *Mandate Days,* 232.

Chapter 3

1. Alistair Horne, *A Savage War of Peace: Algeria, 1954–1962* (New York: Viking Press, 1977), 28–30.

2. John Talbot, *The War Without a Name: France in Algeria, 1954–1962* (New York: Alfred A. Knopf, 1980), 12–13.

3. Horne, *A Savage War of Peace,* 23–6.

4. Arslan Humbaraci, *Algeria: A Revolution that Failed. A Political History Since 1954* (New York: Frederick A. Praeger, 1966), 45.

5. Horne, *A Savage War of Peace,* 28.

6. Humbaraci, *Algeria,* 46–49.

7. General Paul Aussaresses, *The Battle of the Casbah, Terrorism and Counter-Terrorism in Algeria, 1955–1957,* translated by Robert L. Miller (New York: Enigma Books, 2002), 2, originally published as *Services Speciaux Algerie, 1955–1957* (Paris: Perrin, 2001).

8. Horne, *A Savage War of Peace,* 98.

9. Ibid., 112. From the glossary of French black humor, another smile, *le grand sourire* (the big smile), was the slit throat, at which the FLN was very adept.

10. Horne, *A Savage War of Peace,* 119.

11. Aussaresses, *The Battle of the Casbah,* 44–54.

12. Horne, *A Savage War of Peace,* 122.

13. Gillo Pontecorvo, "The Battle of Algiers" (New York: Axon Video, 1993).

14. Horne, *A Savage War of Peace,* 183–4.

15. Ibid., 188.

16. Aussaresses, *The Battle of the Casbah,* 77.

17. Ibid., 126.

18. Ibid., 128.

19. Ibid., 118–21.

20. Ibid., 140.

21. Ibid., 142–7.

22. Horne, *A Savage War of Peace,* 211.

23. Aussaresses, *The Battle of the Casbah,* 151.

24. Horne, *A Savage War of Peace,* 208–9.

25. Ibid., 210.

26. Ibid., 203.

27. Aussaresses, *The Battle of the Casbah,* 118.

28. C.L. Sulzberger, *The Test: de Gaulle and Algeria* (New York: Harcourt, Brace and World, Inc., 1962), 32, 33.

29. Jean Lacouture, *De Gaulle, the Ruler, 1945–1970,* translated from the French by Alan Sheridan (New York: W.W. Norton and Company, 1992), 167.

30. Horne, *A Savage War of Peace,* 345; see also the discussion in Lacoutre, *De Gaulle, the Ruler,* 243–50.

31. Ibid., 301

32. Paul Henissart, *Wolves in the City: The Death of French Algeria* (New York: Simon and Schuster, 1970), 530–4.

Chapter 4

1. Phillip Deery, "Malaya, 1948: Britain's Asian 'Cold War?'" *International Center for Advanced Studies, New York University, The Cold War as Global Conflict, Working Paper #3* (April 2002): 11.

2. K.G. Tregonning, *A History of Modern Malaya* (New York: David McKay Company, 1964), 287–302; James Corum, "Training Indigenous Forces in Counterinsurgency: A Tale of Two Insurgencies," *Strategic Studies Institute* (March 2006): 1–24, online at http://www .StrategicStudiesInstitute.army.mil/.

3. Caroline Elkins, *Imperial Reckoning: The Untold Story of Britain's Gulag in Kenya* (New York: Henry Holt and Company, 2005), 27.

4. Elkins, *Imperial Reckoning,* 39–44.

5. David Anderson, *Histories of the Hanged: The dirty War in Kenya and the End of Empire* (New York: W.W. Norton and Company, 2005), 125–30.

6. Anderson, *Histories of the Hanged,* 261, 268.

7. Anderson, *Histories of the Hanged,* 200–4.

8. Elkins, *Imperial Reckoning,* 153.

9. Elkins, *Imperial Reckoning,* 346–7.

10. Anderson, *Histories of the Hanged,* 4.

11. Elkins, *Imperial Reckoning,* 366.

Chapter 5

1. Neil Sheehan, *A Bright Shining Lie: John Paul Vann and America in Vietnam* (New York: Vintage Books, 1988), 134.

2. Truong Nhu Tang, with David Chanoff and Doan Van Toai, *A Viet Cong Memoir: An Inside Account of the Vietnam War and Its Aftermath* (New York: Harcourt Brace Jovanovich, 1985), 40; Sheehan, 137–41.

3. Douglas Valentine, *The Phoenix Program* (New York: William Morrow and Company, Inc., 1990), 29–30.

4. Truong Nhu Tang, *A Viet Cong Memoir,* 68.

5. Ibid., 70–72.

6. Valentine, *The Phoenix Program,* 38.

7. Douglas Pike, *War, Peace, and the Viet Cong* (Cambridge: The MIT Press, 1969), 7–8.

8. Pike, *Viet Cong: The Organization and Techniques of the National Liberation Front of South Vietnam* (Cambridge, MA: The MIT Press, 1966), 234–6.

9. Valentine, *The Phoenix Program,* 43.

10. Pike, *Viet Cong,* 247.

11. Ibid., 243.

12. Pike, *War, Peace,* 63; *Viet Cong,* 248.

13. Douglas Pike, "The Vietcong Secret War," *War in the Shadows, The Vietnam Experience,* edited by Samuel Lipsman (Boston: Boston Publishing Company, 1988), 11.

14. Valentine, *The Phoenix Program,* 21.

15. Pike, *Viet Cong,* 241.

16. Ibid., 247.

17. Ibid.

18. Pike, *Viet Cong,* 241.

19. David Chanoff and Doan Van Toai, *Portrait of the Enemy: The Other Side of the War in Vietnam, Told Through Interviews with North Vietnamese, former Viet Cong and Southern Opposition Leaders* (New York: Random House, 1986), 105.

20. Ibid., 104–6.

21. Ibid., 168.

22. Ibid., 169–71.

23. Pike, *Viet Cong,* 244.

24. Ibid., 244–52.

25. Pike, *War in the Shadows,* 11.

26. From the Associated Press, *New York Times* (March 30, 1965): 1, 14.

27. Pike, *War in the Shadows,* 16.

28. John Prados, *The Hidden History of the Vietnam War* (Chicago: Ivan R. Dee, 1995), 154–5; Don Oberdorfer, *Tet!* (New York: Doubleday & Company, Inc., 1971), 210–16.

29. Oberdorfer, *Tet!* 214–6

30. Prados, *The Hidden History of the Vietnam War,* 154.

31. Oberdorfer, *Tet!* 211–4.

32. James Adams, *Secret Armies: Inside the American, Soviet and European Special Forces* (New York: Atlantic Monthly Press, 1987), 49–50.

33. Valentine, *The Phoenix Program,* 60–63.

34. Peer DeSilva, *Sub Rosa* (New York: New York Times Books, 1978) 249, cited in Valentine, *The Phoenix Program,* 59.

35. Valentine, *The Phoenix Program,* 85.

36. Truong Nhu Tang, *A Viet Cong Memoir,* 110.

37. Truong Nhu Tang, *A Viet Cong Memoir,* 108–16.

38. Kevin Dockery, *Navy SEALs: A History, Part II* (New York: Berkley Books, 2002), 210.

39. First Class Radioman Jack Rowell, U.S.N. (Ret.), *The Teams, An Oral History of the U.S. Navy SEALs,* edited by Kevin Dockery and Bill Fawcett (New York: William Morrow and Company, Inc., 1998), 195–6.

40. Valentine, *The Phoenix Program,* 284–5.

41. James William Gibson, "Operation Phoenix," Pike, *War in the Shadows,* 67–68.

42. Ibid., 70–71.

43. Ibid.

44. Ibid.

45. Seymour Hersh, *My Lai 4, A Report on the Massacre and Its Aftermath* (New York: Random House, 1970). Michael D. Sallah, and Mitch Weiss, "Experts: Earlier Tiger Force Probe Could Have Averted My Lai Carnage," *Toledo Blade* (October 22, 2003), online at toledoblade.com. This was one of several articles about Tiger Force, 101st Airborne Division, for which the Toledo Blade was awarded the Pulitzer Prize in 2004.

46. Valentine, *The Phoenix Program,* 346.

Chapter 6

1. Augustus Richard Norton, "Lebanon: Internal Conflict and the Iranian Revolution," in *The Iranian Revolution: Its Global Impact,* edited by John L. Esposito (Miami: Florida International University Press, 1990), 119.

2. To call the Phalange "Christian" is to put it charitably. Or as Thomas L. Friedman wrote, "They were Christians like the Godfather was a Christian." They were "a corrupt, wealthy, venal collection of mafia-like dons, who favored gold chains, strong cologne, and Mercedes with armor plating." See Thomas L. Friedman, *From Beirut to Jerusalem* (New York: Farrar, Straus, and Giroux, 1989), 137.

3. Jimmy Carter, *Palestine Peace Not Apartheid* (New York: Simon and Schuster, 2006), 44–5.

4. Federation of American Scientists, Military Analysis Network, "Lebanon," May 24, 2000, online at http://www.fas.org/man/dod-101/ops/war/lebanon.htm. (Hereafter FAS.)

5. Robin Wright, *Sacred Rage: The Wrath of Militant Islam* (New York: Linden Press/ Simon and Schuster, 1985), 233–4.

6. Avner Yaniv, *Dilemmas of Security: Politics, Strategy, and the Israeli Experience in Lebanon* (New York: Oxford University Press, 1987), 109–10.

7. Friedman, *Beirut to Jerusalem,* 130–1.

8. "The Phalangists were always ready to fight to the last Israeli," Friedman, *Beirut to Jerusalem,* 140.

9. A full and not-too-friendly account of Sharon's management of the war is found in, Schiff, Ze'ev, and Ehud Ya'ari, *Israel's Lebanon War* (New York: Simon and Schuster, 1984).

10. Carter, *Palestine Peace Not Apartheid,* 95.

11. Jacobo Timerman, *The Longest War, Israel in Lebanon,* translated from the Spanish by Miguel Acoca (New York: Alfred A. Knopf, 1982), 11; for a similar perspective see, Amos Oz, *The Slopes of Lebanon,* translated from the Hebrew by Maurie Goldberg-Bartura (New York: Harcourt Brace Jovanovich, 1989).

12. Friedman, *Beirut to Jerusalem,* 163.

13. Noam Chomsky, *Fateful Triangle: The United States, Israel, and the Palestinians* (Cambridge, MA: South End Press, 1999), 370.

14. Hala Jaber, *Hezbollah: Born With a Vengeance* (New York: Columbia University Press, 1997), 77–78.

15. Yitzhak Kahan, chairman, Aharon Barak, and Yona Efrat, "Report of the Commission of Inquiry into the Events at the Refugee Camps in Beirut, 8 February 1983."

16. Jaber, *Hezbollah: Born With a Vengeance,* 107–9.

17. Ibid., 75–76; FAS, Military Analysis Network. That Ms. Jaber identifies the suicide bomber and cites eyewitness accounts of the "white Mercedes" approaching IDF headquarters just prior to the explosion give credibility to her reporting. But it is at variance with the Israeli version of what happened. An official military investigation reported ten days afterward that the blast was accidental, caused by leaking bottled gas that caught fire, and the Israeli Cabinet accepted the finding. See "Israel Calls Tyre Blast Accidental," *New York Times* (November 22, 1982): A13. Subsequent studies either accept the Israeli account or do not mention this major terrorist incident.

18. Jaber, *Hezbollah: Born With a Vengeance,* 76.

19. Wright, *Sacred Rage,* 37.

20. Friedman, *Beirut to Jerusalem,* 192.

21. Ibid., 191–5.

22. David C. Martin, and John Walcott, *Best Laid Plans: The Inside Story of America's War Against Terrorism* (New York: Harper and Row, 1988), 96.

23. Friedman, *Beirut to Jerusalem,* 197.

24. Jaber, *Hezbollah: Born With a Vengeance,* 81–82.

25. Wright, *Sacred Rage,* 78.

26. Jaber, *Hezbollah: Born With a Vengeance,* 83.

27. Martin and Walcott, *Best Laid Plans,* 147.

28. Ibid., 151–2

29. Quoted in Wright, *Sacred Rage,* 107.

30. Norton, *Iranian Revolution,* 128.

31. Jaber, *Hezbollah: Born With a Vengeance,* 48.

32. Ibid., 52–3.

33. Friedman, *Beirut to Jerusalem,* 225.

34. Quoted in Jaber, *Hezbollah: Born With a Vengeance,* 54–55.

35. Ibid., 59.

36. Ibid., 60.

37. That, at least, is what numerous sources have reported, including Wright, *Sacred Rage,* 220. Noam Chomsky, for one, is dubious about such reports, noting the difference between external gestures and the look in the eyes of conquered people. See Chomsky, *Fateful Triangle,* 304–9. If there was a "honeymoon," however, it did not last long.

38. Yaniv, *Dilemmas of Security,* 232.

39. Ibid., 241.

40. Wright, *Sacred Rage,* 222.

41. Thomas L. Friedman, "Israel's Dilemma: Living With a Dirty War," ProQuest Historical Newspapers, *New York Times* (January 20, 1985): SA 32.

42. Ibid.

43. Friedman, *Beirut to Jerusalem,* 181; Wright, *Sacred Rage,* 224.

44. Wright, *Sacred Rage,* 223–4.

45. Ibid., 224.

46. Ibid., 225.

47. Ibid., 216.
48. Avraham Burg, quoted in Friedman, "Israel's Dilemma."
49. Yaniv, *Dilemmas of Security,* 255.
50. Wright, *Sacred Rage,* 218.
51. Yaniv, *Dilemmas of Security,* 245.
52. Quoted in Friedman, "Israel's Dilemma."
53. Jaber, *Hezbollah: Born With a Vengeance,* 25.
54. Augustus Richard Norton, "Hizballah and the Israeli Withdrawal from Southern Lebanon," *Journal of Palestine Studies,* no. 117 (Autumn 2000): 28.
55. Ibid., 26.
56. Ibid., 30.
57. Ibid., 27.
58. Jaber, *Hezbollah: Born With a Vengeance,* 173.
59. Ibid., 1–6.
60. Ibid., 178.
61. Ibid., 198–9.
62. FAS, Military Analysis Network.
63. Norton, "Hizballah and the Israeli Withdrawal," 30.

Chapter 7

1. Jeffrey Goldberg, "Among the Settlers: Will They Destroy Israel?" *New Yorker* (May 31, 2004): 50.
2. Goldberg, "Among the Settlers," 49–50.
3. Ibid., 63.
4. "Israel and the Occupied Territories and the Palestinian Authority: Without Distinction—Attacks on Civilians by Palestinian Armed Groups," *Amnesty International* (July 11, 2002), online.
5. Benny Morris, *Righteous Victims: A History of the Zionist–Arab Conflict* (New York: Alfred A. Knopf, 1999), 332.
6. Ehud Sprinzak, *Brother Against Brother: Violence and Extremism in Israeli Politics from Altalena to the Rabin Assassination* (New York: The Free Press, 1999), 150–1.
7. F. Robert Hunter, *The Palestinian Uprising: A War by Other Means* (Berkeley: University of California Press, 1991), 48–49.
8. Anita Miller, Jordan Miller, and Sigalit Zetouni, *Sharon: Israel's Warrior–Politician* (Chicago: Academy Chicago Publishers & Olive Publishing, 2002), 184.
9. *The Mitchell Report, Report of the Sharm el-Sheikh Fact-Finding Committee,* (May 20, 2001).
10. Hunter, *The Palestinian Uprising,* 55; Michael L. Gross, "Just and Jewish Warfare—Israeli soldiers seem to disregard rules of war," *Tikkun* (September, 2001), online. In 1987, the Landau Commission documented the Israeli abuse of Palestinian prisoners over the preceding 16 years. The commission gave a green light to certain techniques, never made public, that it characterized as degradation but not torture. Since then, as terrorism escalated in the occupied territories, Shin Bet, the Israeli General Security Service, has reportedly resorted to beatings and other forms of physical torture. The Israeli High Court outlawed these practices in 1999, but Amnesty International reported in 2002 that it continued to

receive complaints of Israeli torture of Palestinian prisoners. "Israel: Briefing for the Committee Against Torture," *Amnesty International* (May 2002), online.

11. Wendy Pearlman, *Occupied Voices: Stories of Everyday Life From the Second Intifada*
(New York: Thunder's Mouth Press/Nation Books, 2003), 9–10.

12. Molly Moore, "Checkpoints Take Toll on Palestinians, Israeli Army," *Washington Post*
(November 29, 2004): A01, online.

13. Ze'ev Schiff, and Ehud Ya'ari, *Intifada: The Palestinian Uprising—Israel's Third Front*
(New York: Touchstone, Simon and Schuster, 1989), 97.

14. Sprinzak, *Brother Against Brother,* 157–72.

15. Ibid., 210–11.

16. F. Robert Hunter, *Palestinian Uprising,* 98–101.

17. Ziad Abu-Amr, *Islamic Fundamentalism in the West Bank and Gaza* (Bloomington:
Indiana University Press, 1994), 98–101.

18. Ze'ev Schiff, and Ehud Ya'ari, *Intifada: The Inside Story of the Palestinian Uprising
That Changed the Middle East Equation* (New York: Simon and Schuster (Touchstone),
1991), 17–21.

19. Hunter, *The Palestinian Uprising,* 59–61.

20. Schiff and Ya'ari, *Intifada: Inside Story,* 23–25.

21. Ibid., 45–49.

22. Benny Morris, *Righteous Victims,* 577.

23. Ibid., 575–6.

24. Nicholas Guyatt, *The Absence of Peace: Understanding the Israeli–Palestinian Conflict*
(London: Zed Books, 1998), 31–32, 81–82.

25. The Fourth Geneva Convention prohibits an occupying power from establishing
settlements in occupied territory. See *The Mitchell Report, Report of the Sharm el-Sheikh
Fact-Finding Committee* (May 20, 2001).

26. *The Mitchell Report* quotes James Baker, Secretary of State during the administration of
President George H.W. Bush, who said, "Every time I have gone to Israel in connection with
the peace process, on each of my four trips, I have been met with the announcement of new
settlement activity. This does violate United States policy." The report also notes that on
two committee visits to Israel during its inquiry, the government also announced settlement
expansion. In every case, the Palestinians raised the settlement issue as its first item of business.

27. Miller, Miller, and Zetouni, *Sharon,* 472.

28. Edward Said, "Palestinians under Siege." In *The New Intifada: Resisting Israel's Apartheid* (New York: Verso, 2001), 40.

29. Guyatt, *The Absence of Peace,* 82. From an interview with Ari Shavit, *Ha'aretz* (July 19,
1996).

30. Ibid., 32–34.

31. Sprinzak, *Brother Against Brother,* 1–4.

32. "Major Palestinian Terror Attacks Since Oslo," *Jewish Virtual Library* (October 27,
2004), online.

33. *Mitchell Report,* n.3; from Jane Perlez, "U.S. Envoy Recalls the Day Pandora's Box
Wouldn't Shut," *New York Times* (January 29, 2001).

34. "Elusive Peace—Israel and the Arabs," *BBC: Brook Lapping Productions,* Norma Percy,
series producer, broadcast on PBS (October 18–19, 2005).

35. See James Fallows, "Who Shot Mohammed al Dura?" *Atlantic Monthly* (June, 2003):
49.

36. *Mitchell Report.*

37. "Israel and the Occupied Territories and the Palestinian Authority: Without Distinction Attacks on Civilians by Palestinian Armed Groups," *Amnesty International* (July 11, 2002), online.

38. Ron Suskind, *The Price of Loyalty: George W. Bush, the White House, and the Education of Paul O'Neill* (New York: Simon & Schuster, 2004), 71–72.

39. Miller, Miller, and Zetouni, *Sharon,* 365.

40. Ibid., 477–9.

41. "Mystery of suspected Israeli traitors: Officials try to determine motives behind ammo sale to Palestinians," *WorldNetDaily* (July 23, 2002), online edition.

42. Miller, *Sharon,* 548.

43. "Elusive Peace."

44. Penny Young, "Bethlehem 2002," *History Today* (January 2003), online.

45. Matt Rees, "The Battle of Jenin," *Time* (May 13, 2002), online.

46. "Israel and the Occupied Territories," *Amnesty International* (Report 2003), online.

47. "Amnesty International Reports Child Casualties," *Associated Press* (October 5, 2002), online.

48. "Elusive Peace."

49. Arnon Regular, "Road map is a life saver for us, PM Abbas tells Hamas," *Ha'aretz* (October 23, 2005), online.

50. "Elusive Peace."

51. "Israel and the Occupied Territories and the Palestinian Authority: Without Distinction—Attacks on Civilians by Palestinian Armed Groups," *Amnesty International* (July 11, 2002), online.

52. "Major Palestinian Terror Attacks Since Oslo," *Jewish Virtual Library* (October 27, 2004), online.

53. "Abbas Says Intifada Ruined 'Everything We Built'," *Associated Press dispatch, Diplomat Recorder* (November 30, 2002), online.

54. "UN Report Slams Israeli Wall as Illegal Annexation of Palestinian Land," *Agence France Presse* (September 30, 2003), online.

55. "Israel Seizes Palestinian Land in Jerusalem Cut Off by Barrier," *Washington Post,* from the *Associated Press* (January 24, 2005): A16.

Chapter 8

1. Martin Ewans, *Afghanistan: A Short History of Its People and Politics* (New York: Harper-Collins, 2002), 45.

2. Raja Anwar, *The Tragedy of Afghanistan: A First-Hand Account* (London: Verso, 1988), 11, citing Qasim Rishtia, *Afghanistan dar Qaran-I-Nauzdham,* publisher and date unknown.

3. Ewans, *Afghanistan,* 49–50.

4. Ewans, *Afghanistan,* 1–9; Ralph H. Magnus, and Eden Naby, *Afghanistan: Mullah, Marx, and Mujahid* (Boulder, CO: Westview Press, 1998), 11–17; Anwar, *The Tragedy of Afghanistan,* 1–8.

5. Ewans, *Afghanistan,* 64.

6. Ibid., 142.

7. Anthony H. Cordesman, and Abraham R. Wagner, *The Lessons of Modern War, Volume III: The Afghan and Falklands Conflicts* (Boulder, CO: Westview Press, 1990), 35.

8. Svetlana Savranskaya, "Afghanistan: Lessons from the Last War," *National Security Archives* (October 9, 2001).

9. Christian Friedrich Osterman, "New Evidence on the War in Afghanistan: Introduction," *Bulletin: Cold War International History Project,* Woodrow International Center for Scholars (Winter 2003–2004): 139–40.

10. Major General Oleg Sarin, and Colonel Lev Dvoretsky, *The Afghan Syndrome: The Soviet Union's Vietnam* (Novato, California: Presidio Press, 1993), 165.

11. Cordesman and Wagner, *The Lessons of Modern War,* 10.

12. Ibid.

13. Robert M. Cassidy, *Russia in Afghanistan and Chechnya: Military Strategic Culture and the Paradoxes of Asymmetric Conflict* (Carlisle, PA: Strategic Studies Institute, U.S. Army War College, February 2003).

14. Ali Ahmad Jalali, and Lester W. Grau, *The Other Side of the Mountain: Mujahideen Tactics in the Soviet-Afghan War* (Quantico, VA: U.S. Marine Corps Studies and Analysis Division, 1995), 22.

15. Jalali and Grau, *The Other Side of the Mountain,* 401.

16. Cordesman and Wagner, *The Lessons of Modern War,* 35.

17. Abdul Baqi Balots, "Battle for Kama," in Jalali and Grau, *The Other Side of the Mountain,* 253.

18. Haji Sayed Mohammad Hanif, "Ambush South of the Tangi Waghjan Gorge," in Jalali and Grau, *The Other Side of the Mountain,* 13–16.

19. Cordesman and Wagner, *The Lessons of Modern War,* 44, 145–6.

20. Steve Coll, *Ghost Wars: The Secret History of the CIA, Afghanistan, and Bin Laden, from the Soviet Invasion to September 10, 2001* (New York: Penguin Group, 2004), 117–9.

21. Cordesman and Wagner, *The Lessons of Modern War,* 10.

22. Ibid.

23. Coll, "Anatomy of a Victory: CIA's Covert Afghan Victory," *Washington Post* (July 19, 1992); Cordesman and Wagner, *The Lessons of Modern War,* 172–7.

24. George Crile, *Charlie Wilson's War: The Extraordinary Story of the Largest Covert Operation in History* (New York: Atlantic Monthly Press, 2003), 8–20, 30–32, 64–88, 77–78, 97–114, 138–53, 238, 256–60, 408–13.

25. Coll, *Anatomy of a Victory;* Cordesman and Wagner, *The Lessons of Modern War,* 44.

26. Cordesman and Wagner, *The Lessons of Modern War,* 84.

27. Anonymous, *Through Our Enemies' Eyes* (Washington, DC: Brassey's, Inc., 2002), 100. At the time of publication, the author, Michael Scheuer, was the CIA's leading expert on Osama bin Laden, and the agency would not allow him to use his name.

Chapter 9

1. Susan Page, "Confronting Iraq," *USA Today* (April 1, 2003), online at http://www.usatoday.com/educate/war28article.htm; *Newsweek* (February 17, 2003), previewed in PRNewswire, "Post-war Iraq Hope Would be to Withdraw Troops in 30–90 Days" (February 9, 2003), http://www.prnewswire.com/cgi-bin/stories.pl?ACCT=105&STORY=/www/story/02-09-2003/0001887606.

2. Iraq Coalition Casualty Count, Statistics—Casualty Trends Since Fall of Baghdad, online at http://icasualties.org/oif_a/CasualtyTrends.htm.

3. "Iraq Casualties," *Washington Post* (December 25, 2005): A28. The Pentagon does not tally Iraqi civilian casualties. For that, the Post cited a private British web site, www.iraqibody
count.net, and mentioned the largest figure from a study by the Johns Hopkins Bloomberg School of Public Health. David Brown, "Study Claims Iraq's 'excess' Death Toll Has Reached 655,000," *Washington Post* (October 11, 2006): A12.

4. Lawrence K. Altman, and Richard A. Oppel, Jr., "W.H.O. Says Iraq Civilian Death Toll Higher Than Cited," *New York Times* (January 10, 2008): A14.

5. Congressional Research Service, "The Cost of Iraq, Afghanistan, and other Global War on Terror Operations Since 9/11" (updated March 14, 2007), online at http://www.fas.org/sgp/crs/natsec/RL33110.pdf.

6. White, Josh, "Hidden Costs' Double Price of Two Wars, Democrats Say," *Washington Post* (November 13, 2007): A14, online at http://www.washingtonpost.com/wp-dyn/content/article/2007/11/12/AR2007111202008_p...

7. Lori Montgomery, "The Cost of War, Unnoticed," *Washington Post* (May 8, 2007): D01.

8. Susan B. Glasser, "U.S. Figures Show Sharp Global Rise in Terrorism," *Washington Post* (April 27, 2005): A01.

9. National Counter Terrorism Center, "NCTC Fact Sheet and Observations Related to 2005 Terrorist Incidents (as of March 21, 2007).

10. George Packer, "The Assassin's Gate: America in Iraq" (New York: Farrar, Straus and Giroux, 2005), 299.

11. Thomas E. Ricks, *Fiasco: The American Military Adventure in Iraq* (New York: The Penguin Press, 2006), 191.

12. Lional Behner, "Iraq: Status of Iraq's insurgency," *Council on Foreign Relations* (September 13, 2005), online at http://www.cfr.org/publications/8853/iraq.html?breadcrumb=default.

13. Ellen Knickmeyer, and Jonathan Finer, "In Iraq, 425 Foreigners Estimated Kidnapped Since 2003," *Washington Post* (December 25, 2005): A28.

14. Sean Laughlin, "Bush warns militants who attack U.S. troops in Iraq," *CNN.com/Inside Politics* (July 3, 2003), online at http://www.cnn.com/2003/ALLPOLITICS/07/02/sprj.nitop.bush/; "CBS Evening News with Katie Couric," *CBS News* (September 7, 2006).

15. "Iraq Index: Tracking Variables of Reconstruction and Security in Post-Saddam Iraq," *The Brookings Institution* (November 21, 2005): 5, online at http://www.brookings.edu/fp/saban/iraq/index20051121.pdf.

16. Michael Knights, "US responds to Iraq IED threat," *Jane's Intelligence Review* (October 7, 2005), online at http://www.janes.com/defence/land_forces/news/jir/jir051007_1_n.shtml.

17. Tony Capaccio, "More U.S. Troops Die in Iraq Bombings Even as Armoring Improves," *Bloomberg.com* (October 13, 2005), online at http://www.bloomberg.com/apps/news?pid=10000103=aftH7bcepI8I=us.

18. Fourteen Marines, civilian killed in bombing," CNN.com (August 4, 2005), online at http://cnn.worldnews.printthis.clickability.com/pt/cpt?action=cpt&title=CNN.com+-+Fou.

19. Capaccio, "More U.S. Troops Die in Iraq Bombing," *bloomberg.com*.

20. *Bloomberg.com*, "More U.S. Troops Die in Iraq Bombings."

21. Michael Moss, "Pentagon Study Links Fatalities to Body Armor," *New York Times* (January 7, 2006), online at http://www.nytimes.com/2006/01/07/politics/07armor.html?; Ann Scott Tyson, "More Body Armor Is On the Way for U.S. Troops," *Washington Post* (January 12, 2006): A14.

22. Dana Priest, and Anne Hull, "Soldiers Face Neglect, Frustration at Army's Top Medical Facility," *Washington Post* (February 18, 2007): A01; "The Hotel Aftermath," *Washington Post* (February 19, 2007): A01.

23. Dexter Filkens, and Richard A. Oppel, Jr., "Huge Suicide Blast Demolishes U.N. Headquarters in Baghdad," *New York Times* (August 20, 2003): A1, A8.

24. Mohamad Bazzi, "Zarqawi kin reportedly bombed shrine in Iraq," *Newsday.com* (February 7, 2005).

25. Bennis and Leaver, "The Iraq Quagmire," *Institute for Policy and Foreign Policy in Focus.*

26. Karl Vick, Khalid Saffar, and Bassam Sebti, "Dozens of Children Killed in Iraq Attack," *Washington Post* (October 1, 2004).

27. Peter Grier, and Faye Bowers, "Iraq's bin Laden? Zarqawi's rise," *Christian Science Monitor* (May 14, 2004), online at http://www.csmonitor.com/2004/0514/p03s01-usfp.htm; "'Zarqawi' beheaded US man in Iraq," *BBC News* (May 13, 2004), online at http://news.bbc.co.uk/go/pr/fr/-/2/hi/middle_east/3712421.stm; "Arrests in abduction of American worker," *MSNBC* (May 21, 2004), online at http://www.msnbc.msn.com/id/4953015/.

28. Jackie Spinner, and Anthony Faiola, "S. Korean Is Beheaded in Iraq," *Washington Post* (June 23, 2004): A01, online at http://www.washingtonpost.com/ac2/wp-dyn/A620 68-2004Jun22?language=printer.

29. Cesar G. Soriano, and Larry Copeland, "Zarqawi group says it has killed 2nd American," *USA Today* (September 21, 2004), online at http://www.usatoday.com/news/world/ 2004-09-21-second-hostage_x.htm.

30. Nelson Hernandez, and Salih Saif Aldin, "In Brazen Roundup, 56 Vanish from Baghdad," *Washington Post* (June 6, 2006): A01.

31. Jeffrey Gettleman, "Four From U.S. Killed in Ambush in Iraq; Mob Drags Bodies," *New York Times* (April 1, 2004): 1, 12.

32. Rajiv Chandrasekaran, "Key General Criticizes April Attack in Fallujah," *Washington Post* (September 13, 2004): A17, online at http://www.washingtonpost.com/ac2/wp-dyn/ A16309-2004Sep12?language=printer.

33. Gregg Zoroya, "If Ramadi falls 'province goes to hell'," *USA Today* (July 11, 2004), online at http://www.usatoday.com/news/world/iraq/2004-07-11-ramadi-usat_x.htm.

34. "Militants massacre 21 Iraq police," *BBC News* (November 7, 2004), online at http://news.bbc.co.uk/2/hi/middle_east/3989671.stm.

35. Jonathan F. Keiler, "Who Won the Battle of Fallujah?" *The Naval Institute: Proceedings* (January 2005), online at http://www.military.com/NewContent/0,13190,NI_0105_Fallu jah-P2,00.html.

36. "Spy chief says 200,000 fighters in Iraq," News Arab World, *ALJAZEERA.NET* (January 3, 2005), online at http://english.aljazeera.net/NR/exeres/8F661038-B3AD-4E B2-B5A0-739FEDA1F597.htm.

37. Scott Wilson, "Twin Attacks in Iraq Kill at Least 30," *Washington Post* (December 3, 2004), online at http://www.washingtonpost.com/ac2/wp-dyn/A30498-2004Dec3?language =printer.

38. Karl Vick, "Military Updates Mosul Attack Casualty Toll," *Washington Post* (December 22, 2004), online at http://www.washingtonpost.com/ac2/wp-dyn/A18847-2004Dec22?language=printer.

39. "Multiple Iraq blasts kill many police," News Arab World, *ALJAZEERA.NET* (December 28, 2004), online at http://english.aljazeera.net/NR/exers/58C7FDB0-4587-4E9D-9F7C-B7F4C8B7591C.htm.

40. Dexter Filkins, "Defying Threats, Millions of Iraqis Flock to Polls," *New York Times* (January 31, 2005): 1, 10.

41. Richard A. Oppel, Jr., and Robert F. Worth, "Wave of Attacks in Iraq Kill 40 and Wound 100," *New York Times* (April 30, 2005): A1, A7.

42. "U.S. launches 'Operation Lightning'," *USA Today* from Associated Press (May 29, 2005), online at http://usatoday.printthis.clickability.com/pt/cpt?action=cpt&title=USA TODAY.com+-+U; Robert F. Worth, "Iraq's Assembly accepts Cabinet Despite Tension," *New York Times* (April 29, 2005): A1, A13.

43. "Iraq insurgency in 'last throes,' Cheney says," CNN.com (May 31, 2005), online at http://edition.cnn.com/2005/US/05/30/cheney.iraq/.

44. Extrapolated from http://icasualties.org/oif/. Nonhostile deaths are factored out.

45. Sheryl Gay Stolberg, "After Iraq Visit, An Upbeat Bush Urges Patience," *New York Times* (June 15, 2006): A1, A13.

46. "NewsHour," *PBS* (January 30, 2006).

47. Ann Scott Tyson, "U.S. Sets Plans to Aid Iraq in Civil War," *Washington Post* (March 10, 2006): A01.

48. "Memo from Khalilzad to SecState," in "Outlook: A Grim Report from Iraq's Embassy," *Washington Post* (June 18, 2006): B01.

49. Lourdes Navarro, "Iraqi security forces 'worked against' U.S.," *Associated Press/ Washington Times* (April 23, 2004), online at http://www.washtimes.com/world/200404 22-114403-9180r.htm.

50. Mohamad Bazzi, "Mosul attack highlights problems facing U.S.," *Newsday* (December 22, 2004), online at http://www.newsday.com/news/nationworld/world/ny-womosu1223 ,0,5608781.story; Rory McCarthy and Michael Howard, "New insurgency confronts US forces," *Guardian Unlimited* (November 12, 2004), online at http://www.guardian.co.uk/ Iraq/Story/0,2763,1349505,00.html; Mohammed Tawfeeq, Cal Perry, Kevin Flower, and David Albritton, "Insurgents target governor in Mosul," CNN.com (November 18, 2004), online at http://cnn.worldnews.printthis.clickability.com/pt/cpt?action=cpt&title=CNN.com +-+Insur.

51. Paul Reynolds, "Iraq security forces face onslaught," *BBC News* (December 3, 2004), online at http://news.bbc.co.uk/1/hi/world/middle_east/3950791.stm.

52. Nelson Hernandez, "Mosul Gains Against the Chaos," *Washington Post* (February 2, 2006): A14, online at http://www.washingtonpost.com/wp-dyn/content/article/2006/02/01/ AR2006020102235_pf.html.

53. Michael Berg, "George Bush never looked into Nick's eyes," *Guardian* (May 21, 2004), online at http://www.guardian.co.uk/Iraq/Story/0,2763,1221644,00.html.

54. Paul E. Schroeder, "A Life, Wasted," *Washington Post* (January 3, 2006): A17.

Afterword

1. Ze'ev Schiff, and Ehud Ya'ari, *Israel's Lebanon War* (New York, Simon and Schuster, 1984), 18.

2. Schiff and Ya'ari, *Israel's Lebanon War,* 23–44.

3. Joseph E. Stiglitz, "The Economic Consequences of Mr. Bush," *Vanity Fair* (December 2007), online at http://www.vanityfair.com/politics/features/2007/12/bush200712?current-Page=1.

4. See Anthony Shadid, "With Iran Ascendant, U.S. Is Seen at Fault," *Washington Post* (January 30, 2007): A01.

5. Brian Katulis, Lawrence J. Korb, and Peter Juul, "Strategic Reset: Reclaiming Control of U.S. Security in the Middle East," *Center for American Progress* (June 25, 2007).

6. David R. Francis, "US bases in Iraq: sticky politics, hard math," *Christian Science Monitor* (September 30, 2004), online at http://www.csmonitor.com/2004/0930/p17s 02-cogn.html; Joseph Gerson, "'Enduring' U.S. Bases in Iraq: Monopolizing the Middle East Prize," *Fellowship of Reconciliation* (Winter 2007), online at http://www.forusa.org/fellowship/winter07/josephgerson.html; Bradley Graham, "Commanders Plan Eventual Consolidation of U.S. Bases in Iraq," *Washington Post* (May 22, 2005): A27.

7. Chalmers Johnson, and Tom Englehardt, "Empire V. Democracy: Why Nemesis Is at Our Door," online at anti-war.com.

8. Eric Schmitt, "Senior Qaeda Commander Is Killed by U.S. Missile Strike in Pakistani Tribal Areas," *New York Times* (February 2, 2008): 14.

9. William Odom, "How to Cut and Run," *Los Angeles Times* (October 31, 2006), online at http://www.latimes.com/news/opinion/la-oe-odom31oct31,0,6123563,story?coll =la-opinion-rightrail.

10. Bob Herbert, "The Passion of Al Gore," *New York Times* (June 5, 2007): A23

BIBLIOGRAPHY

Books

Abu-Amr, Ziad. *Islamic Fundamentalism in the West Bank and Gaza.* Bloomington: Indiana University Press, 1994.

Aburish, Said K. *Arafat: From Defender to Dictator.* London: Bloomsbury Publishing, 1998.

Anderson, David. *Histories of the Hanged: The Dirty War in Kenya and the End of Empire.* New York, London: W.W. Norton and Company, Ltd., 2005.

Andrews, Gowers, and Tony Walker. *Behind the Myth: Yasser Arafat and the Palestinian Revolution.* New York: Olive Branch Press, 1992.

Anonymous (Michael Scheuer). *Imperial Hubris: Why the West Is Losing the War on Terror.* Washington, DC: Brassey's Inc., 2004.

———. *Through Our Enemies' Eyes.* Washington, DC: Brassey's, Inc., 2002.

Anwar, Raja. *The Tragedy of Afghanistan: A First-Hand Account.* London: Verso, 1988.

Armstrong, Karen. *Muhammad: A Biography of the Prophet.* San Francisco: Harper, 1992.

———. *Holy War: The Crusades and Their Impact on Today's World.* New York: Anchor Books, 2001.

Aussaresses, General Paul. *The Battle of the Casbah: Terrorism and Counter-Terrorism in Algeria, 1955–1957.* translated by Robert L. Miller. New York: Enigma Books, 2002.

Bell, J. Bowyer. *Terror out of Zion: Irgun Zvai Leumi, LEHI, and the Palestine Underground, 1929–1949.* New York: St. Martin's Press, 1977.

Ben Gurion, David. *Memoirs.* Cleveland: World Publishing Company, 1970.

Benjamin, Daniel, and Steven Simon. *The Age of Sacred Terror.* New York: Random House, 2002.

Bergen, Peter L. *Holy War, Inc.: Inside the Secret World of Osama bin Laden.* New York: The Free Press, 2001.

Bethel, Nicholas. *The Palestine Triangle: The Struggle for the Holy Land, 1935–84.* London: Putnam, 1979.

Buchanan, Patrick J. *Where the Right Went Wrong: How Neoconservatives Subverted the Reagan Revolution and Hijacked the Bush Presidency.* New York: Thomas Dunne Books, 2004.

Burke, Jason. *Al-Qaeda: Casting a Shadow of Terror.* London: I.B. Tauris and Co., 2003.

Chanoff, David, and Doan Van Toai. *Portrait of the Enemy: The Other Side of the War in Vietnam, Told Through Interviews with North Vietnamese, former Viet Cong and Southern Opposition Leaders.* New York: Random House, 1986.

Chomsky, Noam. *Fateful Triangle: The United States, Israel, and the Palestinians.* Cambridge, MA: South End Press, 1999.

Clarke, Richard A. *Against All Enemies: Inside America's War on Terror.* New York: Free Press, 2004.

Coll, Steve. *Ghost Wars: The Secret History of the CIA, Afghanistan, and Bin Laden, from the Soviet Invasion to September 10, 2001.* New York: Penguin Group, 2004.

Cordesman, Anthony H., and Abraham R. Wagner. *The Lessons of Modern War, Volume III: The Afghan and Falklands Conflicts.* Boulder, CO: Westview Press, 1990.

Crile, George. *Charlie Wilson's War: The Extraordinary Story of the Largest Covert Operation in History.* New York: Atlantic Monthly Press, 2003.

Dockery, Kevin. *Navy SEALs: A History, Part II.* New York: Berkley Books, 2002.

Elkins, Caroline. *Imperial Reckoning: The Untold Story of Britain's Gulag in Kenya.* New York: Henry Holt and Company, 2005.

Elon, Amos. *The Israelis: Founders and Sons.* New York: Penguin Books, 1983.

Esposito, John L. "The Iranian Revolution: A Ten-Year Perspective." In *The Iranian Revolution, Its Global Impact,* edited by John L. Esposito. Miami: Florida International University Press, 1990.

———. *Islam and Politics.* 3rd ed. Syracuse, New York: Syracuse University Press, 1991.

Ewans, Martin. *Afghanistan: A Short History of Its People and Politics.* New York: HarperCollins, 2002.

Fanon, Franz. *The Wretched of the Earth: The Handbook for the Black Revolution That Is Changing the Shape of the World.* New York: Grove Press, Inc., 1963.

Flapan, Simha. *The Brith of Israel, Myths and Realities.* New York: Pantheon Books, 1987.

Franks, General Tommy, with Malcolm McConnell. *American Soldier.* New York: HarperCollins, 2004.

Friedman, Thomas L. *From Beirut to Jerusalem.* New York: Farrar, Straus, and Giroux, 1989.

Gannon, James. *Stealing Secrets, Telling Lies: How Spies and Codebreakers Helped Shape the Twentieth Century.* Dulles, VA: Brassey's, Inc., 2001.

Gold, Dore. *Hatred's Kingdom: How Saudi Arabia Supports the New Global Terrorism.* Washington, DC: Regnery, 2003.

Guyatt, Nicholas. *The Absence of Peace: Understanding the Israeli–Palestinian Conflict.* London: Zed Books, 1998.

Henissart, Paul. *Wolves in the City: The Death of French Algeria.* New York: Simon and Schuster, 1970.

Hersh, Seymour. *My Lai 4: A Report on the Massacre and Its Aftermath.* New York: Random House, 1970.

Hiro, Dilip. *Iran Under the Ayatollahs.* London: Routledge and Kegan Paul, 1985.

Holden, David, and Richard Johns. *The House of Saud: The Rise and Rule of the Most Powerful Dynasty in the Arab World.* New York: Holt, Rinehart and Winston, 1981.

Horne, Alistair. *A Savage War of Peace: Algeria, 1954–1962.* New York: Viking Press, 1977.

Humbaraci, Arslan. *Algeria: a Revolution that Failed, a Political History Since 1954.* New York: Frederick A. Praeger, 1966.

Hunter, F. Robert. *The Palestinian Uprising: A War by Other Means.* Berkeley: University of California Press, 1991.

Jaber, Hala. *Hezbollah: Born With a Vengeance.* New York: Columbia University Press, 1997.

Jalali, Ali Ahmad, and Lester W. Grau. *The Other Side of the Mountain: Mujahideen Tactics in the Soviet–Afghan War.* Quantico, VA: U.S. Marine Corps Studies and Analysis Division, 1995.

Josephus, Flavius. *The Wars of the Jews.* Book V.

Katz, Shmuel. *Lone Wolf: A Biography of Vladimir (Ze'ev) Jabotinsky.* Vol. 2. New York: Barricade Books, 1996.

Khalidi, Rashid. *Resurrecting Empire: Western Footprints and America's Perilous Path in the Middle East,* Boston: Beacon Press, 2004.

Lacey, Robert. *The Kingdom.* New York and London: Harcourt Brace Jovanovich, 1981.

Lacouture, Jean. *De Gaulle: The Ruler, 1945–1970.* Translated from the French by Alan Sheridan, New York: W.W. Norton and Company, 1992.

Maalouf, Amin. *The Crusades Through Arab Eyes.* Translated by Jon Rothschild. New York: Schocken Books, 1984.

Magnus, Ralph H., and Eden Naby. *Afghanistan: Mullah, Marx, and Mujahid.* Boulder, CO: Westview Press, 1998.

Mann, James. *Rise of the Vulcans: The History of Bush's War Cabinet.* New York: Viking, 2004.

Martin, David C., and John Walcott. *Best Laid Plans, The Inside Story of America's War Against Terrorism.* New York: Harper and Row, 1988.

Melman, Yossi. *The Master Terrorist: The True Story of Abu-Nidal.* New York: Adama Books, 1986.

Miller, Anita, Jordan Miller, and Sigalit Zetouni. *Sharon: Israel's Warrior–Politician.* Chicago: Academy Chicago Publishers and Olive Publishing, 2002.

Morris, Benny. *Righteous Victims: A History of the Zionist–Arab Conflict.* New York: Alfred A. Knopf, 1999.

Mylroie, Laurie. *Study of Revenge: The First World Trade Center Attack and Saddam Hussein's War against America.* Washington, DC: The AEI Press, 2000.

Nassar, Jamal R. *The Palestine Liberation Organization: From Armed Struggle to the Declaration of Independence.* New York: Praeger, 1991.

Naylor, Sean. *Not a Good Day to Die: The Untold Story of Operation Anaconda.* New York: The Berkeley Publishing Group, 2005.

Oberdorfer, Don. *Tet!* New York: Doubleday and Company, Inc., 1971.

O'Brien, Conor Cruise. *The Siege: The Saga of Israel and Zionism.* New York: Simon and Shuster, 1986.

Oz, Amos. *The Slopes of Lebanon.* Translated from the Hebrew by Maurie Goldberg-Bartura. New York: Harcourt Brace Jovanovich, 1989

Packer, George. *The Assassins' Gate: America in Iraq.* New York: Farrar, Straus and Giroux, 2005.

Pearlman, Wendy. *Occupied Voices: Stories of Everyday Life From the Second Intifada.* New York: Thunder's Mouth Press/Nation Books, 2003.

Pike, Douglas. *Viet Cong: The Organization and Techniques of the National Liberation Front of South Vietnam.* Cambridge, MA: The M.I.T. Press, 1966.

———. *War, Peace, and the Viet Cong.* Cambridge, MA: The M.I.T. Press, 1969.

————. "The Vietcong Secret War." In *War in the Shadows: The Vietnam Experience,* edited by Samuel Lipsman. Boston: Boston Publishing Company, 1988.

Prados, John. *The Hidden History of the Vietnam War.* Chicago: Ivan R. Dee, 1995.

Rashid, Ahmed. *Taliban: Militant Islam, Oil and Fundamentalism in Central Asia,* New Haven: Yale Nota Bene, 2000.

Ricks, Thomas E. *Fiasco: The American Military Adventure in Iraq.* New York: The Penguin Press, 2006.

Risen, James. *State Of War: The Secret History of the CIA and the Bush Administration.* New York: Free Press, 2006.

Rowell, First Class Radioman Jack, U.S.N. (Ret.). *The Teams, an Oral History of the U.S. Navy SEALs,* edited by Kevin Dockery and Bill Fawcett. New York: William Morrow and Company, Inc., 1998.

Said, Edward. "Palestinians under Siege." In *The New Intifada: Resisting Israel's Apartheid.* New York: Verso, 2001.

Sarin, Major General Oleg, and Colonel Lev Dvoretsky. *The Afghan Syndrome: The Soviet Union's Vietnam.* Novato, CA: Presidio Press, 1993.

Schiff, Ze'ev, and Ehud Ya'ari. *Israel's Lebanon War.* New York: Simon and Schuster, 1984.

————. *Intifada: The Palestinian Uprising—Israel's Third Front.* New York: Touchstone, Simon and Schuster, 1989.

Schwartz, Steven. *The Two Faces of Islam: The House of Saud From Tradition to Terror.* New York: Doubleday, 2002.

Sheehan, Neil. *A Bright Shining Lie: John Paul Vann and America in Vietnam.* New York: Vintage Books, 1988.

Sherman, A.J. *Mandate Days: British Lives in Palestine 1918–1948.* New York: Thames and Hudson, 1997.

Smucker, Phillip. *Al Qaeda's Great Escape: The Military and the Media on Terror's Trail.* Washington, DC: Brassey's, 2004.

Sprinzak, Ehud. *Brother Against Brother: Violence and Extremism in Israeli Politics from Altalena to the Rabin Assassination.* New York: The Free Press, 1999.

Sulzberger, C.L. *The Test: de Gaulle and Algeria.* New York: Harcourt, Brace and World, Inc., 1962.

Suskind, Ronald. *The Price of Loyalty: George W. Bush, the White House, and the Education of Paul O'Neill.* New York: Simon and Schuster, 2004.

Talbot, John. *The War Without a Name: France in Algeria, 1954–1962.* New York: Alfred A. Knopf, 1980.

Temko, Ned. *To Win or To Die: A Personal Portrait of Menachem Begin.* New York: William Morrow and Company, 1987.

Teveth, Shabtai. *Ben Gurion: The Burning Ground, 1886–1948.* Boston: Houghton Mifflin, 1987.

Thomas, Gordon. *Gideon's Spies: The Secret History of the Mossad.* New York: St. Martin's Press, 1999.

Timerman, Jacobo. *The Longest War: Israel in Lebanon,* translated from the Spanish by Miguel Acoca. New York: Alfred A. Knopf, 1982.

Tregonning, K.G. *A History of Modern Malaya.* New York: David McKay Company, 1964.

Truong Nhu Tang, with David Chanoff and Doan Van Toai. *A Viet Cong Memoir: An Inside Account of the Vietnam War and Its Aftermath.* New York: Harcourt Brace Jovanovich, 1985.

Tuchman, Barbara W. *The March of Folly: From Troy to Vietnam.* New York: Ballantine Books, 1984.

Valentine, Douglas. *The Phoenix Program.* New York: William Morrow and Company, Inc., 1990.

Williams, Charles. *The Last Great Frenchman: A Life of General de Gaulle.* New York: John Wiley, 1993.

Woodward, Bob. *Plan of Attack.* New York: Simon and Schuster, 2004.

Wright, Robin. *Sacred Rage: The Wrath of Militant Islam.* New York: Linden Press, 1985.

———. *In the Name of God: The Khomeini Decade.* New York: Simon and Schuster, 1989.

Yaniv, Avner. *Dilemmas of Security: Politics, Strategy, and the Israeli Experience in Lebanon.* New York: Oxford University Press, 1987.

Newspapers, Magazines, Journals

Agence France Presse. "UN Report Slams Israeli Wall as Illegal Annexation of Palestinian Land" (September 30, 2003).

Associated Press. "U.S. launches 'Operation Lightning'. *USA TODAY* (May 29, 2005), online at http://usatoday.printthis.clickability.com/pt/cpt?action=cpt=USATODAY.com+-+U...

———. "Amnesty International Reports Child Casualties" (October 5, 2002).

———. "Abbas Says Intifada Ruined 'Everything We Built'," *Diplomat Recorder* (November 30, 2002).

———. "Israel Seizes Palestinian Land in Jerusalem Cut Off by Barrier," *Washington Post* (January 24, 2005): A16.

Bazzi, Mohamad. "Mosul attack highlights problems facing U.S.." *Newsday* (December 22, 2004), online at http://www.newsday.com/news/nationworld/world/ny-womosu 1223,0,5608781.story.

———. "Zarqawi kin reportedly bombed shrine in Iraq," *Newsday.com* (February 7, 2005), online at http://.newsday.com/news/nationworld/world/ny-wozarq0208,0,7506060, print.story?c...

Berg, Michael. "George Bush never looked into Nick's eyes," *Guardian* (May 21, 2004), online at http://www.guardian.co.uk/Iraq/Story/0,2763,1221644,00.html.

Burke, Jason. "How the Perfect Terrorist Plotted the Ultimate Crime," *Observer* (April 7, 2002), online at http://observer.gurdian.co.uk/waronterrorism/story/0,1373,6803 20,00.html.

———. "Margaret Hassan," *Guardian Unlimited* (November 17, 2004), online at http:// www/guardian.co.uk/obituaries/story/0,,1352892,00.html.

Cassidy, Robert M. "Russia in Afghanistan and Chechnya: Military Strategic Culture and the Paradoxes of Asymmetric Conflict," *Strategic Studies Institute.* Carlisle, PA: U.S. Army War College (February, 2003): 1–12.

Chandrasekaran, Rajiv. "Violence in Iraq Belies Claims of Calm, Data Show," *Washington Post* (September 26, 2004): A01.

———. "Key General Criticizes April Attack in Fallujah," *Washington Post* (September 13, 2004): A17, online at http://www.washingtonpost.com/ac2/wp-dyn/A16309-2004Sep12 ?language=printer.

Chicago Tribune: "Armey: Unprovoked War Would Be Illegal" (August 9, 2002).

Christison, Kathleen and Bill. "A Rose By Another Name: The Bush Administration's Dual Loyalties," *CounterPunch* (December 13, 2002), online at http://www.counterpunch.org/christison1213.html.

Coll, Steve. "Anatomy of a Victory: CIA's Covert Afghan Victory," *Washington Post* (July 19, 1992).

Daragahi, Borzou. "Envoy to Iraq Sees Threat of Wider War," *Los Angeles Times* (March 7, 2006), online at http://www.latimes.com/news/nationworld/world/la-fg-envoy7mar07,0,6674768,print.story? . . .

Deery, Phillip. "Malaya, 1948: Britain's 'Asian Cold War?'" International Center for Advanced Studies, New York University, *The Cold War as Global Conflict, Working Paper #3* (April 2002): 11.

Dreyfuss, Robert, and Jason West. "The Lie Factory," *Mother Jones* (January/February 2004).

Dyer, Timothy, and Jerry Markon. "Flight Instructor Recalls Unease with Moussaoui," *Washington Post* (March 10, 2006): A02, online at http://www.washingtonpost.com/wp-dyn/content/article/2006/03/09/AR2006030901143_p . . .

Eckholm, Erik. "Pakistanis Arrest Qaeda Figure Seen as Planner of 9/11," *New York Times* (March 2, 2003): 1.

Epstein, Edward Jay. "Atta in Prague? An Iraqi prisoner holds the answer to this 9/11 mystery," *Opinion Journal, from The Wall Street Journal Editorial Page* (November 22, 2005), WSJ.com.

Fainaru, Steve. "Handoff to Iraqi Forces Being Tested in Mosul," *Washington Post* (April 7, 2005).

Fallows, James. "Who Shot Mohammed al Dura?" *Atlantic Monthly* (June, 2003).

Filkens, Dexter, and Richard A. Oppel, Jr. "Huge Suicide Blast Demolishes U.N. Headquarters in Baghdad," *New York Times* (August 20, 2003): A1, A8.

———. "Defying Threats, Millions of Iraqis Flock to Polls," *New York Times* (January 31, 2005): 1, 10.

Friedman, Thomas L. "Israel's Dilemma: Living with a Dirty War," ProQuest Historical Newspapers *New York Times* (January 20, 1985): SA 32.

Gellman, Barton, and Thomas E. Ricks. "U.S. Concludes Bin Laden Escaped at Tora Bora Fight," *Washington Post* (April 17, 2002): A01, online at http://www.washingtonpost.com/ac2/wp-dyn/A62618-2002Apr16?language=printer.

Gellman, Barton, and Dafna Linzer. "Afghanistan, Iraq: Two Wars Collide," *Washington Post* (October 22, 2004): A01, online at http://www.washingtonpost.com/ac2/wp-dyn/A52673-2004Oct21?language=printer.

Gettleman, Jeffrey. "Four from U.S. Killed in Ambush in Iraq; Mob Drags Bodies," *New York Times* (April 1, 2004): 1, 12.

Goldberg, Jeffrey. "Among the Settlers: Will They Destroy Israel?" *New Yorker* (May 31, 2004): 50.

———. "Breaking Ranks: What turned Brent Scowcroft against the Bush Administration?" *New Yorker* (October 31, 2005): 54–65.

Gordon, Michael R., and Judith Miller. "U.S. Says Hussein Intensifies Quest for A-Bomb Parts," *New York Times* (September 8, 2002): 1, 25.

Graham, Bob. "What I Knew Before the Invasion," *Washington Post* (November 20, 2005): B07.

Grier, Peter, and Faye Bowers. "Iraq's bin Laden? Zarqawi's rise," *Christian Science Monitor* (May 14, 2004), online at http://www.csmonitor.com/2004/0514/p03s01-usfp.htm.

Gross, Michael L. "Just and Jewish Warfare—Israeli soldiers seem to disregard rules of war," *Tikkun* (September, 2001).

Hernandez, Nelson. "Mosul Gains Against the Chaos," *Washington Post* (February 2, 2006): A14, online at http://www.washingtonpost.com/wp-dyn/content/article/2006/02/01/AR2006020102235_pf...

"Iraq Casualties," *Washington Post* (December 25, 2005): A28.

"Israel Calls Tyre Blast Accidental," *New York Times* (November 22, 1982): A13.

Jehl, Douglas, and David Sanger. "Prewar Assessment on Iraq Saw Chance of Strong Divisions," *New York Times* (September 28, 2004): Al, A9.

Judis, John B., and Spencer Ackerman. "The Selling of the Iraq War: The First Casualty," *New Republic* (June 30, 2003), online at http://www.tnr.com/doc.mhtml?i=20030630&s=ackermanjudis063003.

Keiler, Jonathan F. "Who Won the Battle of Fallujah?" The Naval Institute: *Proceedings* (January 2005), online at http://www.military.com/NewContent/0,13190,NI_0105_Fallujah-P2,00.html.

Khalilzad, Zalmy, and Paul Wolfowitz. "Overthrow Him," *Weekly Standard* (December 1, 1997).

Knickmeyer, Ellen, and Jonathan Finer. "In Iraq, 425 Foreigners Estimated Kidnapped Since 2003," *Washington Post* (December 25, 2005): A28.

Knights, Michael. "US responds to Iraq IED threat," *Jane's Intelligence Review* (October 7, 2005), online at http://www.janes.com/defence/land_forces/news/jir/jir051007_1_n.shtml.

Kristol, William, and Robert Kagan. "Toward a Neo-Reaganite Foreign Policy," *Foreign Affairs* (July/August, 1996).

Landay, Jonathan S., and Drew Brown. "INC supplied defectors who were sources of questionable pre-war information, officials say," *Knight Ridder Newspapers* (April 3, 2004), online at krwashington.com.

McCarthy, Rory, and Michael Howard. "New insurgency confronts US forces," *Guardian Unlimited* (November 12, 2004), online at http://www.guardian.co.uk/Iraq/Story/0,2763,1349505,00.html.

Miller, Greg. "Flaws Cited in Powell's Speech on Iraq," *Los Angeles Times* (July 15, 2004), online at http://www.commondreams.org/cgi-bin/print.cgi?file=/headlines04/0715-05.htm.

Moore, Molly. "Checkpoints Take Toll on Palestinians, Israeli Army," *Washington Post* (November 29, 2004): A01.

Navarro, Lourdes. "Iraqi security forces 'worked against' U.S.," *Associated Press/Washington Times* (April 23, 2004), online at http://www.washtimes.com/world/20040422-114403-9180r.htm.

Norton, Augustus Richard. "Hizballah and the Israeli Withdrawal from Southern Lebanon," *Journal of Palestine Studies* no. 117 (Autumn 2000): 28.

Oppel, Richard A. Jr. "U.S. to Halt Payments to Iraqi Group Headed by Onetime Pentagon Favorite," *New York Times* (May 18, 2004), online at http://www.nytimes.com/2004/05/18CHAL.html?ex=1400299200&en=aebed...

Oppel, Richard A., Jr., and Robert F. Worth. "Wave of Attacks in Iraq Kill 40 and Wound 100," *New York Times* (April 30, 2005): A1, A7.

Osterman, Christian Friedrich. "New Evidence on the War in Afghanistan: Introduction," *Bulletin: Cold War International History Project, Woodrow Wilson International Center for Scholars,* no. 14/15 (Winter 2003–Spring 2004).

Perelman, Marc. "Cheney Taps Syria Hawk as Advisor on the Mideast," *Forward* (October 31, 2003), online at http://www.forward.com/issues/2003/03.10.31/news2.wurmser.html.

Perlez, Jane. "U.S. Envoy Recalls the Day Pandora's Box Wouldn't Shut," *New York Times* (January 29, 2001).

Pincus, Walter. "British Intelligence Warned of Iraq War," *Washington Post* (May 13, 2005): A18.

————. and Dana Priest. "Some Analysts Felt Pressure from Cheney Visits," *Washington Post* (June 5, 2003): A01.

Priest, Dana. "Report Says CIA Distorted Iraq Data," *Washington Post* (July 12, 2004): A01.

————. "Iraq New Terror Breeding Ground, War Created Haven, CIA Advisers Report," *Washington Post* (January 14, 2005): A01.

Record, Jeffrey. "Bounding the Global War on Terrorism," *Strategic Studies Institute,* Carlisle, Pennsylvania: U.S. Army War College, (December 2003), online at 'http://www.strategic studiesinstitute.army.mil/pubs'display.cfm?publD=207.

Rees, Matt. "The Battle of Jenin," *Time* (May 13, 2002).

Regular, Arnon. "Road map is a life saver for us, PM Abbas tells Hamas," *Ha'aretz* (October 23, 2005).

Reynolds, Paul. "Iraq security forces face onslaught," *BBC News* (December 3, 2004).

Sallah, Michael D., and Mitch Weiss. "Experts: Earlier Tiger Force Probe Could Have Averted My Lai Carnage," *Toledo Blade* (October 22, 2003), online at toledoblade.com.

Savranskaya, Svetlana. "Afghanistan: Lessons from the Last War," *National Security Archives* (October 9, 2001).

Schroeder, Paul E. "A Life, Wasted," *Washington Post* (January 3, 2006): A17.

Scowcroft, Brent. "Don't Attack Saddam," *Opinion Journal from The Wall Street Journal Editorial Page* (August 15, 2002), online at WSJ.com.

Shahzad, Syed Saleem. "A Chilling Inheritance of Terror," *Asia Times* (October 30, 2002).

Smucker, Philip. "How Bin Laden Got Away," *Christian Science Monitor* (March 4, 2002).

Soriano, Cesar G., and Larry Copeland. "Zarqawi group says it has killed 2nd American," *USA TODAY* (September 21, 2004), online at http://www.usatoday.com/news/world/2004-09-21-second-hostage_x.htm.

Spinner, Jackie, and Anthony Faiola. "S. Korean Is Beheaded in Iraq," *Washington Post* (June 23, 2004): A01, online at http://www.washingtonpost.com/ac2/wp-dyn/A62068-2004Jun22?language=printer.

Strobel, Warren P. "Former CIA Director Looks for Evidence that Iraq Had Role in Attacks," *Knight Ridder Newspapers* (October 11, 2001).

Tawfeeq, Mohammed, Cal Perry, Kevin Flower, and David Albritton. "Insurgents target governor in Mosul," CNN.com (November 18, 2004), online at http://cnn.worldnews.printthis.clickability.com/pt/cpt?action=cpt&title=CNN.com+-+Insur...

Tyler, Patrick E. "Lone Superpower Plan," *New York Times* (March 10, 1992): A1.

Tyson, Ann Scott. "More Body Armor Is on the Way for U.S. Troops," *Washington Post* (January 12, 2006): A14, online at http://washingtonpost.com/wp-dyn/content/article/2006/01/11/AR2006011102235_p...

————. "U.S. Sets Plans to Aid Iraq in Civil War," *Washington Post* (March 10, 2006): A01, online at http://www.washingtonpost.com/wp-dyn/content/article/2006/03/09/AR2006030900280_p...

Vick, Karl, Khalid Saffar, and Bassam Sebti. "Dozens of Children Killed in Iraq Attack," *Washington Post* (October 1, 2004).

————. "Military Updates Mosul Attack Casualty Toll," *Washington Post* (December 22, 2004), online at http://www.washingtonpost.com/wp-dyn/articles/A18847-2004 Dec22.html.

Whitlock, Craig, and Walter Pincus. "Bin Laden: Attacks on U.S. Being Prepared," *Washington Post* (January 19, 2006): A01, online at http://www.washingtonpost.com/wp-dyn/content/article/2006/01/19/AR2006011901465_p…

Williams, Daniel. "Egyptian Police Kill Suspect in Red Sea Attacks," *Washington Post* (May 10, 2006): A20.

Wilson, Scott. "Twin Attacks in Iraq Kill at Least 30," *Washington Post* (December 3, 2004), online at http://www.washingtonpost.com/ac2/wp-dyn/A30498-2004Dec3?language =printer.

Wolff, Alexander. "The Mastermind," *Sports Illustrated* (August 20, 2002), online at CNNSI.com—SI Online—The Mastermind—Tuesday August 20, 2002 02:35 p.m.

Young, Penny. "Bethlehem 2002," *History Today* (January 2003).

Zoroya, Gregg. "If Ramadi falls 'province goes to hell'," *USA TODAY* (July 11, 2004), online at http://www.usatoday.com/news/world/iraq/2004-07-11-ramadi-usat_x.htm.

Documents, Studies, Speeches, Press Releases

Amnesty International. "Israel and the Occupied Territories and the Palestinian Authority: Without Distinction—Attacks on Civilians by Palestinian Armed Groups" (July 11, 2002).

————. "Israel: Briefing for the Committee against Torture," (May 2002).

Behner, Lional. "Iraq: Status of Iraq's insurgency" *Council on Foreign Relations* (September 13, 2005), online at http://www.cfr.org/publications/8853/iraq.html?breadcrumb=default.

Bennis, Phyllis, and Erik Leaver, "The Iraq Quagmire: The Mounting Costs of War and the Case for Bringing Home the Troops," *Institute for Policy* and *Foreign Policy in Focus* (August 31, 2005).

Bin Laden, Osama. "Ladenese Epistle: Declaration of War," Parts II and III.

Birnbaum, Nathan. "The National Rebirth of the Jewish People in the Homeland as a Means of Solving the Jewish Problem," 1893.

Charter of the United Nations

Cheney, Dick. Soref Symposium speech (April 29, 1991), quoted in *Middle East Web Log,* "Was winning in Iraq an afterthought?" (January 2, 2004), online at http://www.mideast web.org/log/archives/00000149.htm.

Federation of American Scientists. Military Analysis Network, "Lebanon," (May 24, 2000), online at http://www.fas.org/man/dod-101/ops/war/lebanon.htm.

Holy Bible, New Revised Standard Version. Iowa Falls: World Bible Publishers, 1989.

Intelligence Review, Military Intelligence Service (February 14, 1946), online at http://www.fas.org/irp/agency/army/intelreview/pdf.

"Iraq Index: Tracking Variables of Reconstruction and Security in Post–Saddam Iraq," *The Brookings Institution* (November 21, 2005): 5, online at http://www.brookings.edu/fp/saban/iraq/index20051121.pdf.

Iraq on the Record: The Bush Administration's Public Statements on Iraq, House Committee on Government Reform—Minority Staff, Special Investigation Division (March 16, 2004), online at www.reform.house.gov/min.

Jewish Virtual Library. "Major Palestinian Terror Attacks Since Oslo" (October 27, 2004).

Kahan, Yitzhak, chairman, Aharon Barak, and Yona Efrat. "Report of the Commission of Inquiry into the Events at the Refugee Camps in Beirut, 8 February 1983."

Levin, Sen. Carl (D-Michigan). "Levin Says Newly Declassified Information Indicates Bush Administration's Use of Pre-War Intelligence Was Misleading," Press Release.

Metz, Helen Chapin, ed., "Wahhabi Theology," *Country Studies, Saudi Arabia.* Washington, DC: Library of Congress, 1992.

The Mitchell Report, Report of the Sharm el-Sheikh Fact-Finding Committee, (May 20, 2001).

The 9/11 Commission Report: Final Report of the National Commission on Terrorist Attacks upon the United States, Authorized Edition, New York, London: W.W. Norton and Co.

Perle, Richard, James Colbert, Charles Fairbanks, Jr., Douglas Feith, Robert Loewenberg, Jonathan Torop, David Wurmser, and Meyrav Wurmser, "Study Group on a New Israeli Strategy Toward 2000," The Institute for Advanced Strategic and Political Studies (1996).

Powell, U.S. Secretary of State Colin, *Address to the U.N. Security Council,* White House Release (February 5, 2003).

President's Remarks at the United Nations General Assembly. New York, NY: White House, Office of the Press Secretary (September 12, 2002).

President Bush Outlines Iraqi Threat: Remarks by the President on Iraq, White House Release, Cincinnati, Ohio (October 7, 2002).

President Delivers "State of the Union," White House Release (January 28, 2003).

Project for the New American Century, Statement of Principles (June 3, 1997).

————. *Rebuilding America's Defenses: Strategy, Forces and Resources for a New Century,* Project for the New American Century (September 2000).

Report on the U.S. Intelligence Community's Prewar Intelligence Assessment on Iraq, Senate Select Committee on Intelligence (Roberts Committee), 108th Congress (July 7, 2004).

"Saudi Arabia," *The World Factbook,* Central Intelligence Agency, online at http://www.cia.gov /cia/publications/factbook/geos/sa.html.

"Text of Bush's Wednesday comments," *USA Today* (July 2, 2003), online at http:// www.usatoday.com/news/washington/2003-07-02-bush-speech-text_x.html.

Transcript, *New York Times* (September 21, 2001): B4.

United Nations General Assembly, Resolution 2649, (November 30, 1970).

"United States Humanitarian Mine Action in the Middle East: A Six-Year Progress Report," U.S. Department of State, Bureau of Political-Military Affairs (December 6, 2002), online at http://www.csmonitor.com/2003/0214/p07s01-WOME.html.

Television, Radio, Videos, Internet, Blogs

Al-Ahram Weekly Online. "Politics in God's Name," Cairo, Egypt, no. 247, November 16–22, 1995.

ALJAZEERA.NET. "Spy chief says 200,000 fighters in Iraq," News Arab World (January 3, 2005), online at http://english.aljazeera.net/NR/exeres/8F661038-B3AD-4EB2-B5A0-739FEDA1F597.htm.

————. "Multiple Iraq blasts kill many police," *News Arab World* (December 28, 2004), online at http://english.aljazeera.net/NR/exers/58C7FDB0-4587-4E9D-9F7 C-B7F4C8B7591C.htm.

BBC."Elusive Peace—Israel and the Arabs," *Brook Lapping Productions,* Norma Percy, series producer, broadcast on PBS (October 18–19, 2005).

BBC News, "Six al-Qaeda Killed at Hospital Siege" (January 28,2002), online at http://news
.bbc.co.uk/1/hi/world/south_asia/1786011.stm.

———. "'Zarqawi' beheaded US man in Iraq" (May 13, 2004), online at http://news
.bbc.co.uk/go/pr/fr/-/2/hi/middle_east/3712421.stm.

———. "Militants massacre 21 Iraq police" (November 7, 2004), online at http://news
.bbc.co.uk/2/hi/middle_east/3989671.stm

Bloomberg.com. "Seven U.S. Marines Killed in Action West of Baghdad" (August 2,
2005): http://www.bloomberg.com/apps/news?pid=10000087&sid=abfA0HVFgJQw
&refer=top_. . .

Bloomberg.com. "More U.S. Troops Die in Iraq Bombings Even as Armoring Improves"
(October 13, 2005), online at http://www.bloomberg.com/apps/news?pid=71000001
&refer=us&sid=aftH7bcepI8I.

CNN.com. "Family heartbreak over Hassan fate" (November 17, 2004), online at www.cnn
.com/2004/11/16/iraq/hassan/.

———. "Iraq insurgency in 'last throes,' Cheney says" (May 31, 2005), online at http://www/
cnn.com/2005/US/05/30/cheney.iraq.

———. "Fourteen Marines, civilian killed in bombing" (August 4, 2005), online at http://
cnn.worldnews.printthis.clickability.com/pt/cpt?action=cpt&title=CNN.com+-+Fou. . .

"Fox News Sunday." Fox TV (September 8, 2002).

———. (June 26, 2005).

Iraq Coalition Casualty Count, Statistics—Casualties Trends Since Fall of Baghdad, online at
http://icasualties.org/oif_a/CasualtyTrends.htm.

Jewish Virtual Library. online at http://www.us-israel.org/jsource/zion/html.

"Late Edition with Wolf Blitzer." *CNN* (September 8, 2002).

"Meet the Press." *NBC News* (September 8, 2002).

———. (February 13, 2005).

Miller, John. Interview with Osama bin Laden, "World News Tonight," *ABC News* (May 28,
1998).

MSNBC: "Arrests in abduction of American worker" (May 21, 2004), online at http://
www.msnbc.msn.com/id/4953015/.

NewsHour. *PBS* (January 30, 2006).

Pontecorvo, Gillo. "The Battle of Algiers," New York: Axon Video, 1993.

Soldiers for the Truth/DefenseWatch: "Interceptor OTV Body Armor Cost Lives, An Internal
USMC Report Shows (January 11, 2006), online at http://www.sftt.org/main.cfm?
actionId=globalShowStaticContent&screenkey=cmpDefens. . .

Stahl, Leslie. "60 Minutes," *CBS News* (March 22, 2004).

Wikipedia. "Douglas Feith," online at http://en.wikipedia.org/wiki/Douglas_Feith.

WorldNetDaily. "Mystery of suspected Israeli traitors: Officials try to determine motives
behind ammo sale to Palestinians" (July 23, 2002).

Yacoub, Sameer N. "130 Dead in Series of Attacks in Iraq," *ABC News,* from *Associated Press,*
(January 11, 2006), online at http://abcnews.go.com/International/print?id=1474224.

INDEX

About the Author

JAMES GANNON is a journalist who spent twenty years as a writer, producer, and director at NBC News. He produced documentaries in the early 1980s that won several awards. In retirement, he wrote *Stealing Secrets, Telling Lies* (2001).